Rejection

McMaster New Testament Studies

Patterns of Discipleship in the New Testament (1996)

The Road from Damascus: The Impact of Paul's Conversion on His Life, Thought and Ministry (1997)

Life in the Face of Death: The Resurrection Message of the New Testament (1998)

The Challenge of Jesus' Parables (2000)

Into God's Presence: Prayer in the New Testament (2001)

Reading the Gospels Today (2004)

Contours of Christology in the New Testament (2005)

Hearing the Old Testament in the New Testament (2006)

The Messiah in the Old and New Testaments (2007)

Translating the New Testament: Text, Translation, Theology (2009)

Christian Mission: Old Testament Foundations and New Testament Developments (2010)

Empire in the New Testament (2011)

The Church, Then and Now (2012)

Rejection
God's Refugees in Biblical and Contemporary Perspective

edited by
STANLEY E. PORTER

PICKWICK *Publications* · Eugene, Oregon

REJECTION
God's Refugees in Biblical and Contemporary Perspective

Copyright © 2015 Wipf and Stock Publishers. All rights reserved. Except for brief quotations in critical publications or reviews, no part of this book may be reproduced in any manner without prior written permission from the publisher. Write: Permissions. Wipf and Stock Publishers, 199 W. 8th Ave., Suite 3, Eugene, OR 97401.

Pickwick Publications   McMaster Divinity College Press
An Imprint of Wipf and Stock Publishers   1280 Main Street West
199 W. 8th Ave., Suite 3   Hamilton, Ontario, Canada
Eugene, OR 97401   L8S 4K1

www.wipfandstock.com

ISBN 13: 978-1-4982-0772-0

Manufactured in the U.S.A.   04/24/2015

Scripture marked ESV® is from the Holy Bible, English Standard Version®, copyright© 2001 by Crossway, a publishing ministry of Good News Publishers. All rights reserved.

Table of Contents

Preface / vii

List of Contributors / ix

Abbreviations / xi

Introduction: What Does It Mean to Be Rejected and Alienated?
—Stanley E. Porter / xv

1. Identity in Diaspora: Reading Daniel, Ezra-Nehemiah, and Esther as Diasporic Narratives
   —Mark J. Boda / 1

2. Who Says "You Can't Go Home"? Reconsidering the Models of Exile and Diaspora as Metaphors for the Church Today in Light of Recent Exilic Research
   —Paul S. Evans / 27

3. Identity and Identification in Israel's Diaspora—Socio-Cultural and Biblical Perspectives: A Response to Mark J. Boda and Paul S. Evans
   —Gordon K. Oeste / 48

4. Coping with Alienating Experience: Four Strategies from the Second Temple Period
   —Loren T. Stuckenbruck / 57

5. Cities of Refuge: The Role of the Jewish Christian Communities in the Spread of Christianity
   —Cynthia Long Westfall / 84

6. Jewish and Gentile Refugees in the Second Temple Period: A Response to Loren T. Stuckenbruck and Cynthia Long Westfall
   —Benjamin E. Reynolds / 113

Table of Contents

7   From Diaspora to Diaspora: Paul Writes to Fellow Refugees
    —*Stanley E. Porter* / 125

8   Persecution in the Early Christian Mission
    according to the Book of Acts
    —*Eckhard J. Schnabel* / 141

9   Paul and the Alienation of the Jews: A Response
    to Stanley E. Porter and Eckhard J. Schnabel
    —*Christopher D. Land* / 181

10 "Diaspora Missions": Contemporary Missiological
    Significance of People on the Move
    —*Narry F. Santos* / 191

Modern Authors Index / 209

Ancient Sources Index / 213

Preface

THE 2013 H. H. Bingham Colloquium in the New Testament at McMaster Divinity College in Hamilton, Ontario, Canada was entitled "Rejection: God's Refugees." The Colloquium was the seventeenth in a continuing series held here at the College. This conference continued to develop the format that we use for such conferences. Rather than having a singular respondent, as we have on previous occasions, we had a formal response prepared in advance to each set of two papers. This means that there are three responses that formally react to the sets of papers in Old Testament, Second Temple literature, and the New Testament. We also included a paper on the theme of the conference by a pastor/scholar who has long worked with diasporic Christians. Dr. Narry Santos has a PhD in New Testament and teaches in this area (as well as having a doctorate in Philippine studies). He has also been a church planter and pastor among refugees, especially of the Filipino community here in Canada. In fact, since the conference, Narry has returned to the Philippines to plant a church in the Manila area. We asked Narry to draw on his years of experience in various refugee and diasporic communities and to address the issue of God's refugees from a contemporary theological and biblical standpoint. Besides Narry, we had four other participants from outside of McMaster Divinity College. From nearby institutions, we welcomed Dr. Gordon K. Oeste in Old Testament and Dr. Benjamin Reynolds in New Testament. From Gordon-Conwell Theological Seminary, we welcomed the participation of Dr. Eckhard Schnabel, and from Munich University we welcomed Dr. Loren Stuckenbruck. We thoroughly enjoyed the wide ranging conversation and participation of all of those involved.

The Bingham Colloquium is named after Dr. Herbert Henry Bingham, who was a noted Baptist leader in Ontario, Canada. His leadership abilities were recognized by Baptists across Canada and around the world. His qualities included his genuine friendship, dedicated leadership, unswerving Christian faith, tireless devotion to duty, insightful service as a preacher and pastor, and visionary direction for congregation and denomination alike. These qualities endeared him both to his own church members and to believers in other denominations. The Colloquium has been endowed by his daughter as an act of appreciation for her father. We are pleased to be able to continue this tradition.

The volumes in this series are published by McMaster Divinity College Press, in conjunction with Wipf & Stock Publishers of Eugene, Oregon. We appreciate this active publishing relationship that continues to grow and develop. Previous Colloquia published (or to be published) in this series include the following: *Patterns of Discipleship in the New Testament* (1996), *The Road from Damascus: The Impact of Paul's Conversion on His Life, Thought and Ministry* (1997), *Life in the Face of Death: The Resurrection Message of the New Testament* (1998), *The Challenge of Jesus' Parables* (2000), *Into God's Presence: Prayer in the New Testament* (2001), *Reading the Gospels Today* (2004), *Contours of Christology in the New Testament* (2005), *Hearing the Old Testament in the New Testament* (2006), *The Messiah in the Old and New Testaments* (2007), *Translating the New Testament: Text, Translation, Theology* (2009), *Christian Mission: Old Testament Foundations and New Testament Developments* (2010), *Empire in the New Testament* (2011), *The Church, Then and Now* (2012), *Rediscovering Worship: Past, Present and Future* (forthcoming 2015), *The Bible and Social Justice* (forthcoming 2015). As I write this preface, we are about to convene the eighteenth Bingham Colloquium on the book of Romans, and we anticipate publishing this volume in due course as well.

Finally, we would like to thank the individual contributors for accepting the assignments, for all their efforts in the preparation and presentation of papers that make a significant contribution of benefit to New Testament scholars, students of the Bible, and believers concerned about the perceived rejection of God's people, and the refuge that can sometimes only be had in him. We would also like to thank the staff and student helpers and volunteers at McMaster Divinity College, all of whom were integral in creating a pleasant environment and a supportive atmosphere. Thanks go to my graduate assistant, Bryan Fletcher, for his work on the manuscript.

—Stanley E. Porter

List of Contributors

MARK J. BODA, Professor of Old Testament, McMaster Divinity College, Hamilton, Ontario

PAUL S. EVANS, Assistant Professor of Old Testament, McMaster Divinity College, Hamilton, Ontario

CHRISTOPHER D. LAND, Assistant Professor of New Testament and Linguistics, McMaster Divinity College, Hamilton, Ontario

GORDON K. OESTE, Professor of Old Testament, Heritage College and Seminary, Cambridge, Ontario

STANLEY E. PORTER, President, Dean, and Professor of New Testament, McMaster Divinity College, Hamilton, Ontario

BENJAMIN E. REYNOLDS, Associate Professor of New Testament, Tyndale University College and Seminary, Toronto, Ontario

NARRY F. SANTOS, formerly Senior Pastor, Greenhills Christian Fellowship, Toronto, Canada, now Pastor, Saddleback Manila, South Manila, Philippines

ECKHARD J. SCHNABEL, Professor of New Testament Studies, Gordon-Conwell Theological Seminary, South Hamilton, Massachusetts

LOREN T. STUCKENBRUCK, Professor of New Testament, Ludwig-Maximilians-Universität München, Munich, Germany

CYNTHIA LONG WESTFALL, Assistant Professor of New Testament, McMaster Divinity College, Hamilton, Ontario

Abbreviations

AB Anchor Bible

ABD *Anchor Bible Dictionary.* Edited by D. N. Freedman. 6 vols. New York: Doubleday, 1992.

BDAG Walter Bauer, Frederick W. Danker, W. F. Arndt, and F. W. Gingrich. *Greek-English Lexicon of the New Testament and Other Early Christian Literature.* 3rd ed. Chicago: University of Chicago Press, 2000.

BDB Francis Brown, S. R. Driver, and Charles A. Briggs. *Hebrew and English Lexicon of the Old Testament.* Oxford: Clarendon, 1907.

BNP Brill's New Pauly: Encyclopaedia of the Ancient World

BZAW Beihefte zur Zeitschrift für die alttestamentliche Wissenschaft

BZNW Beihefte zur Zeitschrift für die neutestamentliche Wissenschaft

EDNT *Exegetical Dictionary of the New Testament.* Edited by H. Balz, G. Schneider. ET. Grand Rapids, 1990–93.

ESV English Standard Version

FRLANT Forschungen zur Religion und Literatur des Alten und Neuen Testaments

ICC International Critical Commentary

JAJSup Journal of Ancient Judaism Supplements

JBL *Journal of Biblical Literature*

Abbreviations

JGRChJ	*Journal of Greco-Roman Christianity and Judaism*
JNTSup	Journal for the Study of the New Testament Supplement Series
JSJSup	Journal for the Study of Judaism Supplements
JSNT	*Journal for the Study of the New Testament*
JSOTSup	Journal for the Study of the Old Testament Supplement Series
JSP	*Journal for the Study of the Pseudepigrapha*
JSPSup	Journal for the Study of the Pseudepigrapha Supplement Series
KJV	King James Version (Authorized Version) of the Holy Bible
LCL	Loeb Classical Library
LSJ	Liddell, H. G., R. Scott, H. S. Jones. *A Greek-English Lexicon*. 9th ed. with revised supplement. Oxford, 1996.
MNTS	McMaster New Testament Studies
MT	Masoretic Text
NASB	New American Standard Bible
NET	New English Translation
NICNT	New International Commentary on the New Testament
NIDB	*New International Dictionary of the Bible*. Edited by J. D. Douglas and M. C. Tenney. Grand Rapids, 1987.
NIGTC	New International Greek Testament Commentary
NIV	New International Version
NLT	New Living Translation
NovTSup	Supplements to Novum Testamentum
NRSV	New Revised Standard Version

Abbreviations

NTS	*New Testament Studies*
RSV	Revised Standard Version
SBL	Society of Biblical Literature
SBLSymS	Society of Biblical Literature Symposium Series
SNTSMS	Society for New Testament Studies Monograph Series
TDNT	*Theological Dictionary of the New Testament.* Edited by G. Kittel and G. Friedrich. Translated by G. W. Bromily. 10 vols. Grand Rapids: Eerdmans, 1964–76.
TDOT	*Theological Dictionary of the Old Testament.* Edited by G. J. Botterweck and H. Ringgren. Translated by J. T. Willis, G. W. Bromily, and D. E. Green. 8 vols. Grand Rapids: Eerdmans, 1974–
TNTC	Tyndale New Testament Commentaries
TSAJ	Texte und Studien zum antiken Judentum
TynBul	*Tyndale Bulletin*
VT	*Vetus Testamentum*
VTSup	Supplements to Vetus Testamentum
WBC	Word Biblical Commentary
WUNT	Wissenschaftliche Untersuchungen zum Neuen Testament
ZNW	*Zeitschrift für die neutestamentliche Wissenschaft und die Kunde der älteren Kirche*

Introduction

What Does It Mean to Be Rejected and Alienated?

Stanley E. Porter

REJECTION IS A PHENOMENON that can be discussed in a wide variety of ways. There are simple acts of rejection that we hardly think about. By choosing one thing—such as a cup of coffee over a cup of tea—we in effect reject another. We are involved in simple acts like these every day and we think nothing of them. Their consequences are in most cases minimal. Rejection, however, can also function at many much more important levels. Some of these choices have consequences that we might not envision at the time, but that may have long-lasting effects. We may reject an opportunity for employment, not realizing that an offer such as this may not be given to us again. We reject a person for whatever reason, perhaps even for a very inconsequential reason, and we find that we have rejected a friend and ruined a friendship. I am sure that we have all had occasion to experience, and perhaps even to think more deeply about, such acts of acceptance and rejection and their consequences.

What if the rejection is based upon fundamental beliefs and results in entire people groups being affected? Even if this sounds rather extreme, we do not need to think very hard before we realize that human history is filled with various groups of people being rejected simply for who they are or what they believe. These kinds of rejections—all too frequently repeated and often for very poor reasons—can result in, and in fact have resulted in, cataclysmic consequences. In the most extreme cases, efforts have been made not just to reject but even to eliminate an entire group of people—perhaps for no other reason than who they are as people, or for no other cause than that they believe something other than what is believed by those who exercise the draconian power to reject others. Some are fortunate simply to be forced to leave their homes and travel sometimes great distances

Introduction

to live as strangers in a strange land. Others lose their lives. A topic such as this could easily merit many conferences, where we might consider what it is about human beings that makes them turn upon each other in such dreadful ways simply because of perceived difference.

The purpose of the conference that led to the papers presented in this volume was, in some respects at least, much more modest in scope than treating the human proclivity for self-annihilation. The papers in this volume are all focused upon the idea of God's people and some of the various ways in which they have been rejected and exiled throughout history, so as to become a diasporic people. The papers also treat the ways God's scattered people have had to deal and cope with the resulting alienation as they have sought after God in their embattled situation.

The first set of papers focuses upon the Old Testament. In the first essay, Mark Boda does an excellent job of introducing this volume by surveying some of the major theories from Diaspora studies. These studies have focused upon the notion of what it means to be a diasporic people, including issues of self- and group-identity, the nature of their dispersal, the longing for return to a real or imagined homeland, their relationships to those around them, and the like. Boda applies these contemporary studies of Diaspora to the biblical books of Daniel, Ezra-Nehemiah, and Esther. He treats all of these diasporic narratives first in their general orientation to Diaspora and then in comparison and contrast with each other. We might expect such books to have a large number of similarities. Even though they are all Diaspora oriented, in fact their differences are significant. Some are more religiously oriented and some more culturally. Some focus more upon God while others do not. Some are more culturally accommodating while others are less so. Finally, some are more oriented toward return to the homeland, and in fact achieve that goal, while others are not. The Diaspora literature of the Old Testament is rich in its exploration of the Diaspora tradition, and with it the kinds of decisions and responses that those of the Diaspora must make. There are also clear implications for contemporary Christians who may themselves be living in their own Diaspora.

Whereas Boda focuses upon a select number of later Diaspora writings, Paul Evans addresses the notions of exile and Diaspora throughout the Old Testament. In fact, Evans sees the notion of exile as present from the start of the Bible, beginning with the expulsion of Adam and Eve from the garden, but continuing into the exiles to Assyria and to Babylon. Some have even suggested that the Babylonian exile was still perceived to be in force

Introduction

during the time of Jesus. Evans explores whether the notion of exile may be used as a metaphor for Christian experience as well as for the experience of ancient Israel—although this requires admittedly difficult definition and precision. What we find is that biblical notions of exile vary considerably, so it is not surprising that modern conceptions will vary as well—and have more or less relationship to historical factors of various exiles. Evans, however, shows the problematic nature of the concept of exile, to the point where he makes a distinction between exile and Diaspora. One of the most telling difficulties is knowing when exile is over, especially since it seems to imply a scattering. He instead contends that the notion of Diaspora is probably a better way for Christians to explain their own contemporary existence. This is because it implies a situated but not assimilated culture that looks forward to a new home.

In the first of the three focused responses, the paper by Gordon K. Oeste addresses both of these papers, noting that, even though their scope appears to be different, they use models of exile and Diaspora that reinforce each other, especially in their focus upon Diaspora as the best way to characterize contemporary Christian experience. However, Oeste also makes clear that he wishes to retain the concept of exile, and he makes a case for the retention of the notion of exile, as well as Diaspora. He notes that the idea of exile and return was prevalent and continued throughout the Old Testament, and still may have useful application to Christian experience.

The second set of papers focuses upon Second Temple Judaism and Jewish Christianity. These naturally go together, as Jewish Christianity, along with its affirmation of Jesus as Messiah, remained closely centered upon its Second Temple theological and literary orientation. In the first paper of this set, Loren Stuckenbruck accepts that the Second Temple period literature was written within a context of alienation. In fact, the major focus of the writers of this literature is upon addressing how their contemporaries living in the Diaspora are to confront the alienation of their existence. Instead of treating all of this literature simply as crisis literature most closely related to apocalyptic writings, Stuckenbruck instead focuses upon examples from it that attempt to come to terms with the writers' belief in God and their diasporic experience of being outside of their homeland and subjected to others. Some of this literature attempts to reinforce the religious norms, against the threat of outside influence. Other writings are more accommodating and pragmatic in their approach. Others hold out

Introduction

hope of God's ultimate judgment. Finally, there are those who simply grieve their loss of the presence of God and lament their situation.

In the next essay, Cynthia Westfall brings Jewish Christianity into dialogue with Second Temple Judaism and Paul. Westfall is concerned that Jewish Christianity has been neglected both in its contribution to the development of early Christianity and within New Testament scholarship as a whole. As a result, she wishes to examine how Jewish Christianity embraced Jesus as Messiah but did so within the religio-cultural milieu of Second Temple Judaism. She finds that Jewish Christianity, though itself living in the Diaspora, evangelized the Gentile world and then brought the converted within the fold of Second Temple Jewish belief and practice. The result of such efforts was a second missionary front to Christianity, apart from that of Paul, one that is often neglected and overlooked. There were Diaspora Jewish Christian communities—cities of refuge, Westfall calls them—throughout the Mediterranean world that brought Gentiles within their ambit. As is typical of Diaspora communities, however, the Jewish Christian communities experienced rejection similar to what other such groups underwent, specifically pressures from Rome, from fellow Jews, and even, eventually, from Gentile Christianity.

In his response to the two related yet diverse papers of Stuckenbruck and Westfall, Benjamin Reynolds appreciates the range of issues raised by each of the contributors within the parameters of their varied assignments. Nevertheless, he also wishes to challenge some of the fundamental matters raised by each of them. Reynolds wishes to draw Stuckenbruck's attention to the significance of an apocalyptic orientation in interpreting the works represented. He also wishes to make much more problematic the notion of alienation and how to respond to it. Finally, he suggests that the strategies for coping with alienation may be greater than the four that Stuckenbruck suggests. In response to Westfall, Reynolds finds problematic the notion of "cities of refuge," because the notion that Westfall defines appears to be at odds with how the Old Testament cities of refuge functioned. Without necessarily defining his view of Paul, Reynolds also finds more common ground between Paul and Jewish Christianity than does Westfall, who tends to oppose them. Reynolds raises a number of questions that suggest further consideration of the notion of Diaspora in Second Temple Judaism.

The third set of papers includes two further New Testament papers, one focusing on Paul's letters and the other on the book of Acts. As a result, there is some inevitable overlap. The first paper, by Stanley Porter, focuses

Introduction

upon Paul's letters but with some reference to Acts. In this paper, Porter defines Christian alienation as a spiritual rather than a physical condition. For Paul, this condition begins in Paul's own life as a diasporic Jew born and reared in Tarsus. We do not know Paul's motives for going to Jerusalem to study with Gamaliel, but there may have been a sense of wishing to undo this diasporic alienation. However, for Paul, there was a double diaspora in this. His initial diaspora then led to a second diaspora in which he was alienated from God—a situation remedied by his encounter on the Damascus road. This divine encounter transformed Paul from having a mistaken understanding to receiving a true understanding of what it means to be one of God's Diaspora people. Porter then defines two major tenets of Paul's diasporic theology. These include, first, his salvific progression from alienation to eternal habitation, best seen perhaps in the argument of Romans 1–8. The second is recognition of the Christian calling as a call to be an alien in an alien land, in which those following Christ should not be too comfortable in their cultural context. Paul here exemplifies a different type of double diaspora, including both physical and spiritual alienation, the latter of which can only be overcome through faith in Jesus Christ. Its culmination is reached in eschatological inclusion, when earthly alienation is overcome. In the meantime, the church serves as a bulwark against the world at large, in which we enjoy spiritual citizenship, until God's alienated Diaspora people (not creation itself) are redeemed.

In the second paper of this set, Eckhard Schnabel offers an analysis of persecution within the early Christian mission on the basis of the book of Acts. Since there is no sustained study of this topic, Schnabel offers a thumbnail sketch of persecution within Acts, beginning with the persecution of Peter and John in Acts 4 and ending with the persecution of Paul in Acts 24–25. This persecution involves a variety of initiators or perpetrators (including Paul himself), arranged in three clusters of events and encompassing a wide variety of geographical locations. The targets of Christian persecution are first, Jesus, then any number of his followers, and the account contains a variety of types of persecutorial acts. The question that all of these actions raise is: why? The reasons are numerous, from the theological to the practical. The result was that Christians needed to respond to such persecution, and they did so in different ways—although most of these ways involved continuing positive affirmation of the message of Jesus in various contexts. In other words, despite the wide range of persecution brought against all quarters of the early Christian movement,

Introduction

this persecution did not divert the church from its purpose of obeying and proclaiming God's word.

In the final response, Christopher Land examines the arguments of both Porter and Schnabel. Although he is fundamentally in agreement with both papers, he raises some interesting and provocative questions to prompt further thought and research. Concerning Paul and his letters, he questions whether there are other coherent accounts that can be offered of Paul's background and orientation before his Damascus road experience that at least as well, if not better, account for Paul's actions before his conversion. Like Porter, Land admits that the evidence we have is limited, and so such reconstructions are open to speculation. Concerning the book of Acts, Land is in fundamental agreement with Schnabel regarding the historicality of Acts, and hence he does not agree with those who see an unjustified apologetic agenda at work in the book. Against those who are overly sensitive to some of the persecutors in Acts, contending that depictions of them reveal some type of agenda, Land points out that if the book is historical in its nature, then one is not justified in positing undue and untoward apologetics. The issue is not whether Acts is anti-Jewish but that Paul and other Christians are persecuted because they proclaim the message that all are alienated from God.

The final paper in many ways could be the first paper of the volume, because in it Narry Santos defines a number of useful terms regarding the field of Diaspora studies and examines many of the reasons for migration of people groups and the trends associated with such movements. On the other hand, however, the paper also fits well as the conclusion, because it brings together in a contemporary context many of the strands of thought suggested throughout the volume. One factor becomes clear in this paper—and is well supported by the previous papers—and that is that the issue of migration of people groups for various reasons, whether compelled or voluntary, has a long history that shows no signs of abating in the contemporary world. In fact, we are increasingly a global community of people on the move for both compelling and attractive reasons. There are numerous missiological implications for this diasporic tendency. These include the simple fact that the time is right for missiological outreach, because the major people groups of the world are being brought by Diaspora right to our front doors. This has a direct effect on the way in which missions can be and should be done. Rather than missions being thought of in traditional ways—focusing upon geographical location and the need to send people

Introduction

into these foreign and often alien environments—contemporary missions does not know such geographical or socio-political boundaries. Canada has been particularly fortunate with regard to this new approach to missions, in which a number of new missionary efforts have been created right here in North America to reach out to people groups that otherwise might not have been reached.

We are always tempted to see the ancient world as distinctly different from the modern world. We often find it difficult to conceive of how the ancients did things when we compare how it is that we do similar things today. The issue of the alienation of God's people, whether they are conceived of as in exile or Diaspora (if these terms are to be distinguished), brings to the fore a number of perspectives on what it means to be an identifiable people group alienated from one's home, whether that home is physically or otherwise conceived. This was a situation that the ancient Israelites faced on repeated occasions as they longed to return to their land. However, even the ancient Israelites viewed Diaspora in different ways, depending upon how they conceived of themselves, their foreign context, and their relationship to God. This attitude became even more complex during the Second Temple Period, as alien influences grew larger and exerted more pressure. The New Testament in some ways both further problematizes the notion of Diaspora and embraces it as a template for mission. This is seen in both Jewish Christianity and Pauline Christianity, as well as being reflected in the book of Acts. The idea that spiritual alienation is a fundamental problem of human beings finds its contemporary resonance in the modern missions movement, which has once more turned the notion of alienation and Diaspora on its head as various refugee peoples now find themselves in the midst of the witnessing Christian community. As a result, many of the traditional barriers to missionary outreach are overcome, not just by proximity, but by the shared sense that we are all aliens in this world until we find our refuge in God through Christ.

1

Identity in Diaspora
Reading Daniel, Ezra-Nehemiah, and Esther as Diasporic Narratives[1]

MARK J. BODA

DIASPORA STUDIES

COHEN, IN HIS REVIEW of diasporic studies, speaks of four phases in modern research on this phenomenon.[2] It begins with the classical phase, which was focused on the Jewish and later Greek diasporic experience, and was extended in the 1960s and 70s to the Africans, Armenians, Irish, and Palestinians. In the 1980s there was a shift beyond ethnicity to categories of people including expats, expellees, political refugees, alien residents, and immigrants, besides the more common ethnic and racial minorities. By the mid-1990s there was a major push back from social constructionists who attacked two major foundations to diasporic definition: that of the homeland and diaspora. This has spawned a more recent consolidation phase that has resulted in a more careful definition of diaspora. Drawing on social-scientific tools that take into account the tension between emic and etic claims, as well as the temporal dimension of social formation, and allowing for identification of the most important features as well as delineation of ideal types,[3] Cohen has posited nine common

---

1. With thanks to my colleague Lee Beach (*Church in Exile*) for his own reflection on these key books, which enabled me to return to these texts with new eyes.

2. Cohen, *Global Diasporas*, 1–19. See also the helpful book by Dufoix, *Diasporas*.

3. See, however, Rose, *Last Resistance*, 41, who leverages Freudian psychoanalysis to explore the diasporic experience, picked up by Giri, "Diasporic Postcolonialism," 220–21, who notes: "The fact that diasporic displacements propel our uprooted bodies

Rejection

features and five ideal types of diaspora.[4] The nine common features include:

1. Dispersal from an original homeland, often traumatically, to two or more foreign regions

2. Alternatively or additionally, the expansion from a homeland in search of work, in pursuit of trade, or to further colonial ambitions

3. A collective memory and myth about the homeland, including its location, history, suffering, and achievements

4. An idealization of the real or imagined ancestral home and a collective commitment to its maintenance, restoration, safety, and prosperity, even to its creation

5. The frequent development of a return movement to the homeland that gains collective approbation even if many in the group are satisfied with only a vicarious relationship or intermittent visits to the homeland

6. A strong ethnic group consciousness sustained over a long time and based on a sense of distinctiveness, a common history, the transmission of a common cultural and religious heritage, and the belief in a common fate

7. A troubled relationship with host societies, suggesting a lack of acceptance or the possibility that another calamity might befall the group

8. A sense of empathy and co-responsibility with co-ethnic members in other countries of settlement even where home has become more vestigial

9. The possibility of a distinctive, creative, enriching life in host countries with a tolerance for pluralism

---

across the world's variously entrenched borders does not mean that our minds will follow suit. It is plausible to think that the diasporic mind constitutes its own unique place."

4. Cohen, *Global Diasporas*, 17, table 1.1. See Safran, "Diasporas in Modern Societies," 83–84, for six of these elements, to which Cohen adds three more. Clifford, "Diasporas," 305, identifies the following: "a history of dispersal, myths/memories of the homeland, alienation in the host (bad host?) country, desire for eventual return, ongoing support of the homeland, and a collective identity importantly defined by this relationship."

The ideal types include: Victim (Jews, Africans, Armenians, Irish, Palestinians, contemporary refugee groups), Labour (Indentured Indians, Chinese and Japanese, Turks, Italians, North Africans), Imperial (British, Russians, colonial powers), Trade (Lebanese, Chinese, Venetians, business and professional Indians, Japanese), and Deterritorialized (Caribbean peoples, Sindhis, Parsis, Roma, Muslims, religious diasporas) Diasporas.[5]

It appears to me that Cohen's nine categories can be broken down into four basic sections.[6] Features 1 and 2 appear to focus on *the basic originating incident(s)* that define diaspora as dispersal/expansion from an original homeland to hostland(s), for whatever reason (negative or positive). The remaining features (3–9) focus on the relationship of the *diasporic community to the homeland* (3–5), to *the diasporic community itself* (6, 8) or to the *hostland* (7, 9).[7] Dimensions of the *relationship to the homeland* include the collective idealized memory of the homeland (3–4a) as well as collective commitment to the homeland's prosperity (4b), and development of commitment to return to the homeland (5). Dimensions of *the relationship to the diasporic community itself* include development of a strong group consciousness with its own cultural and religious heritage (6) as well as connectivity to diasporic communities in other regions from the same homeland (8). Dimensions of *the relationship to the hostland* include both a collective sense of a troubled relationship to the hostland (7) as well as a collective sense of the possibilities of a creative, enriching life in the hostland (9).

The aspect of time has also taken on greater significance in contemporary research on diaspora. This was articulated nicely by Safran in the inaugural issue of the journal *Diaspora*:

---

5. Cohen, *Global Diasporas*, 18, table 1.2.

6. Brubaker, "The 'Diaspora' Diaspora," 5–7, refers to three basic elements: dispersion, homeland orientation, and boundary maintenance, with dispersion related to my basic originating incident(s), homeland orientation and relationship to homeland, and boundary maintenance as a combination of the relationship to the diasporic community to itself as well as to the hostland(s).

7. Safran, "Diasporas in Modern Societies," 92, speaks of the "triangular relationship" among the diaspora, the homeland, and the host society, noting Sheffer, *Modern Diasporas*, 1–15. Bottomley, "Culture," 313, speaks of "double or multiple consciousness," of "the habitus generated by a radical movement from one set of circumstances to another." It is important to realize that these relationships are negotiated simultaneously, thus there is multiple consciousness. Note Clifford, *Routes*, 254, who argues that diasporas "mediate, in a lived tension, the experiences of separation and entanglement, of living here and remembering/desiring another place."

How long does it take for diaspora consciousness to develop, and what are the necessary and sufficient conditions for its survival? Does such consciousness weaken with the passage of decades or centuries, as the relationship with the real homeland is lost, or, conversely, does the homeland focus become more deeply embedded in the collective consciousness of a minority as concrete experience is replaced by myth? What factors or conditions . . . are necessary or sufficient for the maintenance of a homeland myth?[8]

Since diasporic studies consistently admit that this area of research has emerged from the Jewish experience described in the biblical text,[9] it is not too difficult to leverage methodologies within this field of study for studying the Old Testament. The rich reflection on modern diasporas, however, needs to be treated with care, with a sensitivity to those elements of modern life that make today's diasporic experience distinct from that of ancient peoples like the Jewish community.[10]

What this field of study does provide, however, are frameworks and tools for discerning enduring sociological and even psychological dimensions of life for those who can be identified as diaspora. In the present article I will provide some general orientation to the books of Daniel, Ezra-Nehemiah, and Esther that will lay a foundation for reflection on the key motifs through which these books reflect the diasporic experience and showcase the variety of approaches to life within diaspora.[11] My focus is literary, that is, investigating the diasporic experience portrayed within

---

8. Safran, "Diasporas in Modern Societies," 95. See also Bottomley, "Culture," 313, who speaks of "spatial and temporal dimensions."

9. Tölölyan, "The Nation-State and Its Others," 4, in the inaugural issue of the journal *Diaspora*, notes that the term "diaspora," which "once described Jewish, Greek, and Armenian dispersion now shares meanings with a larger semantic domain that includes words like immigrant, expatriate, refugee, guest-worker, exile community, overseas community, ethnic community." Cf. Clifford, "Further Reflections," 306, who speaks of "the strong entailment of Jewish history on the language of diaspora," while discouraging us from "making that history a definitive model."

10. For instance the contemporary global village with its interconnectedness through transportation, technology, and media has changed the diasporic experience radically.

11. Giri, "Diasporic Postcolonialism," 223–24, provides a helpful critique of certain postcolonial approaches to literary and cultural theory that lump all diasporic culture/literature into a single category that stands in contrast to the colonial canons, especially because diasporas are comprised of members from various levels of society, concluding that diasporic culture's "worldiness has multiple and contradictory valences, which cannot be totalized under a singular bourgeois, liberal, nationalist, or collectivist logic" (p. 224).

the world of the text, which provides a window into certain perspectives on diaspora in the post-monarchial context.[12] In the conclusion I will provide some reflection on the significance of these books for Christian theology and ethics.

OLD TESTAMENT DIASPORIC NARRATIVES

Three Old Testament diasporic narrative complexes are set within the Achaemenid imperial context in the wake of the solidification of Persian power by the imperial founder Cyrus.[13] Cyrus formed the empire in the mid-sixth century, and later Darius created the structures that would sustain Persian dominance for the next two centuries. Darius's dynasty would rule until Alexander's arrival in the late fourth century. The books of Esther, Daniel, and Ezra-Nehemiah are set within this Achaemenid context.[14] Although Daniel begins in the Babylonian period, the narrator is careful to note Daniel's impact into the Persian period from the outset of the book, mentioning figures named Cyrus and Darius. Esther is placed within the reign of Darius's son Xerxes, with Nehemiah in the reign of Xerxes' son Artaxerxes. All these books share in common a focus on diasporic life, as Jews in the heartland of the Persian Empire negotiate life without their own national territory. Each story, however, has its own tone and emphasis, reflective of different responses to the diasporic experience. It is not surprising that all are found together in the *Kethubim* (Writings) of the Hebrew Bible, various books that appear to provide guidance for life in community in the post-

12. I am thus not concerned with identifying the dating or provenance of these books and with the historical reality that underlies them. Rather I will focus on the ideological expression within these books.

13. Much has been written on the genre designation of these narratives in Ezra-Nehemiah, Daniel, and Esther, with the closest connectivity seen between Daniel 1–6 and Esther, with Nehemiah 1–2 often seen as bearing some similarity. See further Berlin, *Esther*, xxxiv, who speaks of both "Diaspora story" and "Stories about Wise Courtiers"; Smith-Christopher, *Religion of the Landless*, 162, who refers to the "Diasporic Hero Tale"; Humphreys, "Life-Style for Diaspora"; Collins, *Daniel*, 38–52, and "Court-Tales." For intersections between Esther and Joseph, see Seow, *Daniel*, 9–11.

14. There has been considerable debate over the context in which these books were composed, with Ezra-Nehemiah usually placed within Yehud and Esther within the Mesopotamian Diaspora. Daniel is usually placed within Yehud due to connections to the Seleucid crisis, although some have argued that the Diaspora could have a perspective on the Seleucid crisis or that the diasporic narratives could represent an earlier diasporic collection that was incorporated into a Yehudite collection; cf. Lucas, "Daniel." Esther also has been linked recently to the Yehudite context, as a critique of the Diaspora; cf. Stern, "Esther and the Politics of Diaspora."

Rejection

monarchial situation. They include liturgical rhythms for the festal calendar (Megilloth) and communal/individual worship (Psalms), wise instructions for living (wisdom books), narrative representation of the history of Israel that ends with the invitation to return to the land (Chronicles), and narrative presentations of life within the new imperial realities (Daniel, Ezra-Nehemiah, Esther).[15]

Orientation to Old Testament Diasporic Narratives

Daniel

Of the three diasporic narratives, Daniel is set in the earliest phase of diasporic life, focused on the exile of four young Jewish men during the reign of Jehoiakim and their life within the Babylonian court, ending in the early Persian period in the reign of Cyrus and possibly also Darius. The book begins by tracing the movements of Daniel and his three friends Hananiah, Mishael, and Azariah as Jewish elites chosen by the Babylonians for service within the Babylonian court. While the opening chapter is clear that they were to be trained in "the literature and language of the Chaldeans" (1:4) for three years (1:5) and were given new names from their host country (1:6–7), it is also clear that they are depicted as resisting certain elements of their new host country, especially those related to dietary practices that threaten to defile them according to the Jewish law of their homeland (1:8).[16] God grants Daniel and his friends favor within the host country (1:9) as they are allowed to keep their dietary practices and are ultimately proven wisest among the emerging royal courtiers (1:19–20). The stories that follow highlight the task introduced by the opening chapter: Jews embedded within a new hostland seek to remain faithful to customs from their homeland. They are consistently depicted in scenes of power and influence, interacting with royal figures in their hostland. However, these scenes consistently highlight the hostile nature of life in the hostland as their lives are challenged in nearly every story, with God rescuing them in each case miraculously.[17]

15. See further Seow, *Daniel*, 2; Sweeney, "Tanak"; Dempster, "An 'Extraordinary Fact'"; Scobie, *Ways of Our God*, 68, although I do see an eschatological dimension to the *Kethubim*; cf. Boda, *Severe Mercy*, 513 n. 7.

16. There is some debate over the precise reason for the concern over dietary practices, with some seeing this related to some priestly food laws (cf. Porteous, *Daniel*, 28–32; Barton, "Theological Ethics," 661–62), while others see here a concern that the source of health not be reliant entirely upon the emperor (cf. Towner, *Daniel*, 14–16; Davies, *Daniel*, 89–90; Seow, *Daniel*, 25–26). See fully in Collins, *Daniel*, 141–43.

17. These negative aspects remind us not to idealize Daniel 1–6 as somehow depicting

These deliverances result in ever-increasing praise of their God by royal figures (2:47; 3:26, 28–29; 4:1–37; 6:25–27). Throughout the stories, Daniel and his three friends are depicted as faithful to their homeland traditions, not only in terms of dietary customs as in the opening chapter, but especially in relation to worship practices. They resist hostland practices (3:12; 6:12–13) that would compromise their homeland religious practices, and are depicted following their own religious practices of prayer and worship (2:19–23; 6:10–11; 9:1–21) even as God provides revelation through them for the hostland royal court. The focus within the book of Daniel is on the experience of diasporic figures within the hostland. While the book begins in the homeland and reference is made to the homeland implicitly through certain religious practices and explicitly through reference to the vessels that had been taken from the temple in Jerusalem (5:2, 3) and intercession on behalf of Jerusalem (6:10; ch. 9),[18] there is no expectation that the community will return to the land. Even in Daniel's prayer in ch. 9 that God will bring an end to Jeremiah's 70 years, the focus is on bringing an end to "the desolations of Jerusalem," with no reference to a return of the diaspora to the homeland.

Ezra-Nehemiah

Historically, Ezra-Nehemiah picks up largely where the book of Daniel ends, tracing diasporic figures beginning in the Cyrus-Darius phase of the early Persian period (Ezra 1–6)[19] before shifting to the later phase during the reign of Artaxerxes I in the mid-fifth century (Ezra 7–Nehemiah 13). While reference is made to the origins of the diasporic experience in the opening chapters of Ezra (ch. 1) and Nehemiah (ch. 1), these references follow the initial focus on the present reality of diasporic life in the hostland. This focus on diasporic life, however, in every case in Ezra-Nehemiah is shortlived, as all figures are depicted as in transition from hostland to homeland.[20] The identity of each of the figures, whether Sheshbazzar, Zerubbabel, Joshua, Ezra, or Nehemiah, is initially defined in each by their

---

an embracing of the imperial hegemony; cf. Smith-Christopher, "Book of Daniel"; Valeta, "Court or Jester Tales," 311.

18. Also note Dan 6:13 where Daniel is identified as "one of the exiles from Judah."

19. Reference is made in passing to a letter written during the period of Xerxes in 4:6, but no details are provided. The use of material related to Artaxerxes also appears in Ezra 1–6 in 4:7–23, see further Boda, "Flashforward."

20. For another reading of the diasporic dimension of Ezra-Nehemiah, see the superb article by Bedford, "Diaspora."

Rejection

experience among the diasporic community in Mesopotamia. In the case of Sheshbazzar, Ezra, and Nehemiah each of these figures functions in close proximity to the hostland royal court, empowered by the hostland to lead a group to the homeland or for renewal within the homeland. The consistent depiction of return to the homeland from the hostland is matched by the regular emphasis on the separation between the Jewish community and the surrounding culture, beginning with Zerubbabel's rejection of overtures from northerners desiring to participate in temple reconstruction (Ezra 4:1–5) and continuing through Ezra's rejection of intermarriage with foreigners (Ezra 9–10) and Nehemiah's creation of a holy city demarcated by his wall (Nehemiah 1–13). Religious activities are central to the book, not only as the characters take up residency again within the homeland, but even as they operate within the sphere of the hostland (Ezra 7:27–28; 8:21–23; Neh 1:4–11; 2:4).

Esther

The book of Esther fits historically into the period following that found in Daniel and between Ezra 1–6 and Ezra 7 to Nehemiah 13, that is, during the reign of Xerxes I of Persia. Unlike the other diasporic books, the book of Esther begins without any reference to the origins of diaspora, relating instead a scene within the Persian court in which no Jews participate. The reader must wait until 2:5–7 before Jewish characters are introduced, along with the only reference to the origin of the diaspora (2:6). Two Jewish characters are depicted at the outset. First is Mordecai, who is explicitly called a Jew with a three generation (son of Jair, son of Shimei, son of Kish) and tribal (Benjaminite) pedigree (2:5).[21] It is he who is identified with the experience of exile from Jerusalem (2:6). Contrasting him, however, is his relative's daughter, whom he has taken into his family. While she is given the Jewish name Hadassah at the outset of 2:7, she is immediately qualified as Esther, the Mesopotamian name that is used exclusively throughout the book. She is mentioned at the outset without pedigree, lacking a name for her father[22] and lacking living parents. These various factors set the tone for the book of Esther as a book where the hostland dominates.[23] The diasporic

---

21. His Jewishness is emphasized throughout with "the Jew" qualifying him eight times in the book (Fox, *Character and Ideology*, 185–86).

22. The name is given later in 2:15 as Abihail, but not at the outset, thus contrasting Mordecai.

23. It is this that is accentuated by Stern, "Esther and the Politics of Diaspora," 26, who sees Esther as "critical of strategies of Diaspora living that are not oriented toward

community represented by Esther is one distanced from their heritage in the homeland, cut off, so to speak, from their parents and adopting identity (a name) from the hostland. At the same time, the presence of Mordecai highlights an enduring link to the homeland. These two figures, Esther and Mordecai, vie for the status of hero in the book,[24] both ascending to high levels of power and influence within the imperial court. Interestingly, it is Mordecai whose legacy is trumpeted at the conclusion to the book, possibly suggestive that his model is placed above that of Esther. Esther enters into the royal court as consort to the king; one cannot imagine a more intimate liaison. As seen in the first introduction of her into the story in 2:7, in the court she initially hides her Jewish identity and is fully accepted into the bedroom of the king.[25] This contrasts with Mordecai, who stands outside the sphere of the court, hovering so to speak. This proximity grants him the opportunity to gain favor from the elite of the hostland, but it also has its risks, as it lands him in deep trouble when he comes into conflict with Haman. Haman's role as contrastive character to Mordecai is clear from his first introduction to the reader in 3:1, as his identity is provided both in generational (son of Hammedatha) and gentilic (Agagite) pedigree. Jewish readers who encounter a descendant of Agag contrasting a descendant of Benjamin with a pedigree related to Kish, would immediately think of the encounter between Saul and Agag in 1 Samuel 15.[26] Mordecai, the Jewish figure whose identity is linked most explicitly to the homeland, gets entangled in the hostland in a dispute driven by politics from the homeland. Ultimately Mordecai must appeal to Esther, who at first is reluctant to expose her Jewish identity carefully hidden behind her name and beauty.

Jerusalem and grounded in particularist practice," and thus in line with the values of the books of Ezra-Nehemiah and Daniel (p. 30).

24. For the interconnectedness of Esther and Mordecai, see Humphreys, "Life-Style for Diaspora," 214. For Esther as model for Jews, see White, "Esther." For Mordecai, see Fox, *Character and Ideology*, 185. Fox has a strong case in light of the fact that Mordecai is introduced first in 2:5 and praised last in 10:2–3 (see also 204).

25. On Jewish identity and the book of Esther, see especially Bedford, "Diaspora."

26. See Laniak, *Shame and Honor in the Book of Esther*, 73–78; Berlin, *Esther*, xxxviii, 24–25; Stern, "Esther and the Politics of Diaspora," 40, 50. Berlin (xxxviii) also notes the allusion to the Saulide tradition in the story of Vashti's loss of queenship לרעותה הטובה ממנה ("to her colleague who is better than she," Esth 1:19); cf. לרעך התוב ממך ("to your colleague who is better than you," 1 Sam 15:28). While Stern, "Esther and the Politics of Diaspora," 47, sees this link as part of a negative characterization of Mordecai, the book of Esther appears to laud Mordecai's character in the end, suggesting that Mordecai is redeeming the Saulide line.

Rejection

Mordecai's final appeal is to the fact that she will not be able to escape from the edict, that somehow her Jewish identity will be revealed (4:13). The signal that she has embraced her mission and with it her Jewish identity is her commitment to and call for a fast (4:16), the closest the story comes to any religious activity. The defeat of Haman and elevation of Mordecai exonerates Mordecai's approach to the hostland, while Esther reveals the importance of openness for some who have close liaisons with the hostland. The story reminds the reader that homeland identity cannot be ignored, it is an enduring reality,[27] but careful maneuvering within the hostland is essential to survival. The establishment of the feast of Purim is also key to the presentation of diasporic life in the book of Esther. This feast is not one articulated within the homeland traditions of the Torah, but rather is one established by the authority of diasporic figures (Esther, Mordecai) using hostland powers. Completely absent from the book is any reference to God, suggestive of the challenge of living in diaspora.

Comparing and Contrasting Old Testament Diasporic Narratives

With this basic diasporic orientation to the books in mind, we turn now to compare and contrast the three narratives in terms of basic motifs.

Similarities

The books of Daniel, Ezra-Nehemiah, and Esther all showcase diasporic figures and communities living within the new imperial reality of the Achaemenid empire, even though the depiction of Daniel begins in the Babylonian imperial context.[28] All these books reveal Jews at the center of the empire in scenes taking place at one of the functioning capitals of the Persian Empire: Daniel, Sheshbazzar, Zerubbabel, Joshua, and Ezra (Ezra 1, 2, 7) at Babylon, and Nehemiah and Esther at Susa.[29] Each book focuses

---

27. As Berlin, *Esther*, xxxviii, notes the oxymoron of the Torah treatment of Amalek, which must be remembered forever and yet its name blotted out (Exod 17:14; Deut 25:17–19): "Through the story of Esther the Jews of Persia are, by implication, the heirs of the ancient and never ending battle with Amalek, and thereby assert their continuity with the history of Israel."

28. For similarities among these three corpora, see Berlin, *Esther*, xl, who finds the closest resonance between Esther and Daniel. Cf. Berg, *Book of Esther*, 181.

29. The Achaemenids circulated among four centers in the ancient Near East: Babylon (former capital of the Babylonian Empire), Ecbatana (former capital of the Median Empire), Susa (former capital of the Elamite kingdom), and Persepolis, the last built by Darius as a Persian showcase capital to replace Cyrus's original Pasagardae, which did

attention on key main characters who have the ability to influence power structures within the imperial center, although reference is made in passing (especially in Ezra-Nehemiah and Esther) in a few cases to a broader diasporic community. In every case these characters and communities face some risk around which the narrative revolves, and through heroic efforts they are able to overcome these risks. Ancient (and modern) readers are invited into the stories through these characters whose actions and attitudes are designed to shape the readers' identities and behavior.[30]

Differences

These narratives, however, are not mere echoes of one another, but reveal some differences.

Dispersion

Each of the books provides some orientation to the origins of the diaspora. Both major sections of Ezra-Nehemiah (Ezra 1–10; Nehemiah 1–13) begin with a subtle allusion to the exilic dispersion narrative. In Ezra 1:7 the phrase "which Nebuchadnezzar had carried away from Jerusalem and put in the house of his gods" appears near the end of a chapter that has focused attention on the new Persian initiative to call the people to return to the land. In Nehemiah 1 the allusion is much earlier, with implicit reference to the "captivity" and "the remnant . . . who survived the captivity" in 1:2–3, and the explicit reference to the dispersion in 1:8: "If you are unfaithful I will scatter you among the peoples." However, the focus is on Yahweh's gathering of the community from exile (1:9), something made possible by Nehemiah's construction of the wall (7:1–5).[31]

The book of Daniel begins with a clear articulation of the origins of the dispersion, providing the most explicit description among the books. The depiction focuses on a dispersion that occurred during the reign of Jehoiakim, which includes reference to the siege of Nebuchadnezzar against

---

not have infrastructure to support a large-scale capital. See how Ecbatana is referred to in Ezra 6:1 as the location of an archival document that could not be found in Babylon. Ecbatana was the summer capital, while those on the Mesopotamian plain were winter capitals. Persepolis was probably more of a showcase capital and lay within the traditional homeland of the Persians.

30. As Humphreys, "Life-Style for Diaspora," 211, notes concerning Esther and Daniel: "They suggest and illustrate a certain style of life for the Jew in his foreign environment."

31. Boda, "Prayer as Rhetoric," 275–77.

Jerusalem, and God's delivering of Jehoiakim to Nebuchadnezzar along with the temple vessels and royal and noble family members.

The book of Esther does provide a short reference to the origins of the dispersion, but does so much later in the book as part of the description of Mordecai: "who had been taken into exile from Jerusalem with the captives who had been exiled with Jeconiah king of Judah, whom Nebuchadnezzar the king of Babylon had exiled" (2:6). This provides more information than Ezra-Nehemiah, but is less explicit and much later than that provided in Daniel.

Religious Activities

Ezra-Nehemiah is probably the most focused on the religious life of the individuals, and especially communities, depicted. The focus from the outset of the book is on the restoration of the temple and its services (Ezra 1–6). Even before the temple is founded, the book depicts the restoration of the cult (Ezra 3:1–6), but once the temple is completed, the community is depicted as celebrating the festal calendar (6:19–22). As Ezra enters the scene in Ezra 7–10, he is empowered by the Persian emperor to promulgate the law, and he institutes key reforms in the area of foreign marriages. Ezra's prayer in Ezra 9 prompts covenant renewal within the community. Although Nehemiah is often interpreted as a more secular figure focused on rebuilding the wall of Jerusalem, he is depicted from the outset as a deeply religious figure who prays to Yahweh and interprets Torah (Nehemiah 1). This depiction can be discerned throughout the wall building phase of the book (with short prayers described and inserted), but especially in the second half of Nehemiah (Nehemiah 7–13) where Nehemiah is depicted in scenes of prayer, interpretation, and renewal.

This religious orientation is also prominent in the book of Daniel,[32] although it functions in the life of the main characters with little insight into the broader community. While no feasts are mentioned in the book of Daniel, focus is placed on the individual piety of the characters and their resistance to non-Jewish religious activities. Daniel and his three friends are depicted following ritual law (1:8), seeking God in prayer and praising him for revelation (2:18–23), rejecting Babylonian forms of worship (3:12–18), practicing thrice daily prayer (6:10), receiving revelation from God, and studying Jeremiah and seeking God in prayer for the end of the

---

32. Cf. Humphreys, "Life-Style for Diaspora," 220.

exile (ch. 9).[33] Interestingly, a significant amount of religious description is devoted to various imperial figures, not only in terms of non-Jewish religion, but more particularly in terms of imperial figures giving or legislating praise and honor to the God of the Jews. No feasts, however, are mentioned in the book of Daniel.

While Ezra-Nehemiah and Daniel are dominated by allusions to the religious life of the community, this dimension is nearly absent from the book of Esther.[34] The book of Esther never refers explicitly to the practice of prayer, although fasting rituals are key responses to the crisis created by Haman's plot against the Jews, and fasting elsewhere in the Old Testament is always a religious act, accompanied by prayer and Scripture reading. While religious activity in Ezra-Nehemiah is both individual and communal and in Daniel it is focused on the individual, in Esther the religious activity of fasting involves individuals (Esther, Mordecai) and the community as a whole (the Jews). Even in relation to law, while fixated with law, the book of Esther never refers to the traditional Jewish legal traditions, focusing instead entirely on the law of the Persians.[35] One of the key outcomes of the book of Esther is the establishment of the feast of Purim, but this is unlike the book of Ezra-Nehemiah where the feasts celebrated are those traditional celebrations found in the Torah.[36]

NAME OF GOD

God's name is found countless times in Ezra-Nehemiah where the covenant name of Yahweh is employed as well as the more generic term "God" (including God of heaven [and earth], God who is in Jerusalem, God of Israel, God of our/your fathers, great, mighty and awesome God, their God). God and gods are mentioned many times throughout the book of Daniel, with references to "Lord" (Dan 1:2; 9:8, 9, 15, 16, 17, 19), several to Yahweh (9:2, 4, 10, 13, 14, 20), and most times to either the Jewish God (God of heaven,

---

33. Goldingay, *Daniel*, 12–20.

34. Humphreys, "Life-Style for Diaspora," 216–17, speaks of "a lack of any 'specifically Jewish religiosity'"; cf. Berlin, *Esther*, xxxiv.

35. Stern, "Esther and the Politics of Diaspora," 34–36.

36. Cf. ibid., 49–50, for the contrast between Ezra-Nehemiah and Esther on feasts and Jewish law, the latter showing "a holiday that originates as spontaneous communal practice . . . then authorized by a human being of questionable lineage," and the former seeing Jewish law as "divine in origin." Laniak, "Esther's *Volkscentrism*," 82–85, speaks of the book of Esther reframing the "Torahcentrism" of the period. For connections between Moses/Passover and Esther/Purim see Gerleman, *Studien zu Esther*, 14–28.

God of my fathers, their own/your/his/my/our God, God of Daniel, the living God, God of gods) or non-Jewish gods.[37] Interestingly, the covenant name of Yahweh is restricted to the vocalized prayer of Dan 9 and is not used elsewhere in the book. Most striking is the complete absence of God's name in the book of Esther.[38]

Names of Jews

Ezra-Nehemiah is filled with many lists of names at key junctures in the narrative. At times these lists are used to bolster the conception of participation in the community, whether in the return to the land or in the reconstruction of its infrastructure. At other times these lists are used as evidence for the genealogical purity of the community and their connection to earlier generations (whether pre-exilic or earlier post-exilic generations). In the midst of a narrative filled with long lists reflecting the community as a whole, one finds key leaders moving the narrative action along whose names are Hebrew: Joshua, Ezra, Nehemiah. However, interestingly, the initial leader of the community mentioned in the book is Sheshbazzar, a shadowy figure bearing a Mesopotamian name, who somehow initiates the project of return to the land and reconstruction of the temple. The next leader's name is Zerubbabel, also Mesopotamian in origin, but he is coupled with the priestly Joshua (2:2; 3:2),[39] after which Hebrew names dominate the account. The use of names in Ezra-Nehemiah reveals weakening diasporic influence.

In the book of Daniel the identity of the Jewish characters is established initially by the inclusion of their Jewish names (1:6), but these are soon changed to Mesopotamian names (1:7). In what follows the Jewish name of Daniel dominates for the first phase in 1:8–2:48. With Daniel's request for an appointment for his three friends there is a shift from Jewish names to Mesopotamian names (2:49—3:30). Daniel, however, continues

---

37. With thanks to Meghan Musy. See Barton, "Theological Ethics," 665, for a review of the names of God in Daniel, and especially the limiting of the name Yahweh to ch. 9. Barton concludes that "Daniel treats non-Jewish rulers as subject to the authority of his own God." Goldingay, "Daniel in the Context of Old Testament Theology," 648, reminds us that while there is no doubt that God acts and speaks, according to the book of Daniel, the book portrays this acting and speaking in indirect ways, "via the testimony of people who have seen God act."

38. Laniak, "Esther's *Volkscentrism*," 88–89, speaks of the book of Esther as reframing the "Yahwehcentrism" of the period.

39. Possibly it is significant that while the order is Zerubbabel-Joshua in 2:2, it is Joshua-Zerubbabel in 3:2, representing the shift from Mesopotamian to Hebrew influence.

as a Jewish name within the court narratives before and after 2:49, even though his Mesopotamian name is used at times, nearly always in citations of the Babylonian emperor (in 2:26; 4:8, 9, 18, 19; 5:12). The use of names in Daniel reveals greater diasporic influence, beginning with Jewish names and shifting towards the Mesopotamian.

In the book of Esther, no Jewish character or name is mentioned until 2:5, when finally a Jew with lineage is introduced. Reference is made to his relatives' daughter first with a Jewish name Hadassah, but this woman is immediately qualified as Esther, which appears to be a Mesopotamian name. Unlike Daniel, where the main character's Jewish name dominates, Esther's Mesopotamian name is used exclusively in the narrative.[40] Mordecai's name appears to be Mesopotamian, although he is at least qualified as Jewish by lineage linked to the line of Jair/Shimei/Kish/Benjamin. In the narrative of Esther, Mordecai has to explain to the courtiers that he is a Jew, a fact that Stern sees as exemplar of the presentation of Jewish identity in Esther that "is not immediately apparent; it must be revealed in order to be known."[41] The use of names and Jewish identity in Esther reveals an even greater diasporic emphasis than Daniel.

COMPROMISE AND SOCIAL POSITION

There is some inconsistency in the amount of concern or lack of concern over Jewish figures' involvement in potentially compromising situations. Ezra-Nehemiah is the most conservative of the books, expressing considerable concern over any actions that would compromise the purity of the Judean community or involve them with non-Jewish figures, especially in relation to religious activities. Thus, in Ezra 4:1–3, Zerubbabel and the family heads reject the overtures of Northerners linked to the Assyrians to participate in the temple reconstruction project. Ezra and Nehemiah both are involved in reversing intermarriage with foreigners, and there is a consistent fear of and separation from surrounding peoples and political figures. This concern for separation from outside influences that may compromise the community is expressed figuratively in the construction of the wall by Nehemiah and his concern over access to the gates in Nehemiah 13. Nearly all key figures in the book are portrayed in positions at the center of political life in the empire, seen either in their appointment by emperors

---

40. Laniak, "Esther's *Volkscentrism*," 86, speaks of the book of Esther as reframing the dominant "natocentricism" of the period.

41. Stern, "Esther and the Politics of Diaspora," 42.

at the imperial center, such as Sheshbazzar (Ezra 1) and Ezra (Ezra 7–8), or their function within the imperial center that results in an appointment, such as Nehemiah (Nehemiah). All figures ultimately move from the center of the empire to its periphery.

The book of Daniel also expresses a strong concern over compromise, especially seen in Daniel's refusal to eat some of the emperor's food and his desire to continue his religious practice of prayer, as well as the refusal of Shadrach, Meshach, and Abednego to bow down to foreign entities.[42] At the same time, it should not be missed that Daniel and the three friends are also intimately involved in the Persian administrative system, coming in contact with foreigners and providing advice and most likely administrative support. As in Ezra-Nehemiah, Daniel and his friends rise to power at the center of the empire, even to the highest level of authority, but they do not move at all to the periphery of the empire. Daniel 1 is very clear that they have to learn the "language and literature of the Chaldeans" and that they function within the mantic wisdom tradition of the imperial court, although operating according to Yahweh's revelation.[43]

The book of Esther, however, stands clearly apart from Ezra-Nehemiah and Daniel, as it depicts Esther in a seriously compromising position: marrying a foreigner.[44] This appears to be justified in the account of Esther in the words of Mordecai who declares that possibly she has "attained royalty for such a time as this." We thus see in Esther "critical compromise," which may be seen as a form of wise living in the midst of challenging circumstances.[45] Both Esther and Mordecai rise to powerful positions at the center of the empire, and like Daniel and his friends, do not move to the periphery.

---

42. See Davies, *Daniel*, 55, who notes that in Daniel, the Jew is "defined by his religion and its outward appearance, not by language, personal name, or profession."

43. See Lucas, *Daniel*, 78, in relation to Daniel's reference to his God as revealer in 2:20–30.

44. Stern, "Esther and the Politics of Diaspora," 43: "there is little, if anything distinctive about the Jews. There is no mention of God, the heroine marries a non-Jew, and neither the hero or heroine engage in any distinctive Jewish practices." Interestingly the only mention of Jewish distinctiveness is by Haman (3:8). Furthermore, in Esther, people of the land become Jews (8:17) and Jews begin to act like Persians with decrees, banquets, and killing of others.

45. See Bechtel, *Esther*, 12, and further, 7–11; cf. Costas, "Subversiveness of Faith."

Interaction with Surrounding Culture(s)

Ezra-Nehemiah clearly shows the move from the center of the empire to its periphery. Nehemiah represents a case of a Jew integrated into the imperial court who then uses the imperial system to create a Jewish physical space of security and protection in a homeland now controlled by the empire. Through this the reader can see the necessity of interaction with surrounding culture, but justified by the ultimate end of separation from that culture through a return to a homeland space carefully circumscribed by a walled city. The surrounding culture in diaspora consistently appears sympathetic to those who are in diaspora, indicated by the initiative of Cyrus towards the diaspora Jewish community in Ezra 1, the commission of Artaxerxes to Ezra in Ezra 7, and the response of Artaxerxes to Nehemiah in Nehemiah 2. At times Ezra-Nehemiah depicts the surrounding culture as a threat. While usually this sense of threat is depicted in relation to those who have returned to the homeland, one should not overlook that Nehemiah expresses considerable fear in Neh 2:2.[46]

The characters in Daniel live in diaspora and are able to function successfully within the imperial political system, rising to its highest levels.[47] However, the Jewish figures still establish lines of demarcation, especially focusing on the distinction between imperial and Jewish culture and religion. At times the surrounding culture is a dangerous place, with the life of Daniel and his friends put at risk on several occasions,[48] usually due to Jewish practices or convictions. But in each case the forces of destruction within the surrounding culture are thwarted by some miraculous action by God, which prompts the praise of the God of the Jews and often elevation of the Jews by the emperor.

The characters in Esther live in diaspora but there is more interaction with the surrounding culture than in Daniel, especially seen in Esther becoming queen, but also in the openness to non-Jews becoming Jews and of even a Jewish takeover of imperial power at the center. The story, however, clearly depicts a threatening surrounding culture,[49] although, surprisingly,

---

46. See Smith-Christopher, *Biblical Theology of Exile*, 42.

47. So Davies, *Daniel*, 93: "the story promotes the monarch as their ally and defender, while stressing that in this role he is by no means omnipotent, for only God can in the end secure his people's well-being."

48. Fear of the king is expressed by Persian figures (e.g., Dan 1:10).

49. This is introduced from the opening chapter, as the vulnerability of Vashti is described.

coming mainly from a figure who also is a member of a diaspora (Haman). While this same surrounding culture ultimately does provide protection for the Jewish community, there is no guarantee that this will be the case in the story (as Esther is unsure that she can get an audience with the king). Interestingly, the Jews are not protected by the emperor, who only empowers them to defend themselves if attacked (8:11), although when the Jews carry this out (9:1–2), imperial figures assist the Jews (all the princes of the provinces, the satraps, the governors, those who were doing the king's business), not by command of the emperor but because of "the dread of Mordecai," possibly a reference to his newly granted powers in the imperial court.[50]

Return to Homeland

Ezra-Nehemiah is focused on constant movement from center to periphery as everyone in the book is depicted as returning to the homeland.[51] Little value is placed on those living in diaspora, except for their key role in enabling the return home and the reconstructing and prosperity of those in the homeland. This movement from center to periphery is made clear from the initial presentation of the words of Yahweh and Cyrus in Ezra 1, which focus on the return of the community to the land and reconstruction of the temple.

In Daniel, the initial movement is from the homeland to the hostland, but there is no concern for return to the homeland. The dominating presence of the prayer in Daniel 9 reveals an enduring concern for the homeland, as Daniel focuses on the restoration of Jerusalem. But this concern is expressed through prayer, at a distance, without any mention of a return to the land. Furthermore, the heavenly interpretation in Daniel 9 that expands the exilic period of Jeremiah from seventy to seventy times seven years (based on a priestly principle in Leviticus 25), only accentuates this focus on hostland over homeland by releasing the community from any

---

50. See also the "dread of the Jews" in Esth 8:17; 9:2. This may be a contrast to the "dread of God" in earlier Jewish tradition (1 Sam 11:7; 2 Chron 14:13; 17:10; 20:29), possibly part of the trend of the absence of God in Esther. Another option is that this is a subtle reference to God akin to Gen 31:42, 53, which calls God "the fear of Isaac." However, note references to the fear of Israelites falling upon foreigners, whether of David (1 Chron 14:17) or Israel (Deut 2:25; 11:25; Ps 105:38).

51. Even Nehemiah, who returns to the emperor in Neh 13:6–7, only admits this when he can immediately tell the readers that he asked for leave from the king and returned to Jerusalem.

immediate need to return to the land and defining the diasporic experience as an enduring reality.

The book of Esther only mentions the homeland at one place, identifying Jerusalem as the place from which Mordecai had been exiled by Nebuchadnezzar (2:6). There is no concern for the homeland, let alone a concern for the community to return to the homeland.[52] Life is viewed exclusively through the lens of diaspora, with this condition considered normative, even when the very life of the Jewish community is at stake.

EZRA-NEHEMIAH, DANIEL AND ESTHER AS DIASPORIC LITERATURE

Having reviewed key elements relevant to the diasporic experience in Ezra-Nehemiah, Daniel, and Esther, we now have an opportunity to return to Cohen's basic categories and consider how Ezra-Nehemiah, Daniel, and Esther reflect the various dimensions of diasporic life. One can discern differences among the approaches taken in these books and this may suggest temporal development in diasporic consciousnesses.

Basic Originating Incident

The *basic originating incident* is present in all three narratives and in each case this incident is viewed negatively, that is, in terms of a victim ideal type. However, this incident is most prominent in the book of Daniel, as it is placed at the outset, unlike in Ezra-Nehemiah and especially Esther, where the incident is introduced at a later point. Part of this has to do with the fact that the book of Daniel depicts diasporic experience in the first phase of Jewish exile during the Babylonian period and in terms of referential historical setting (that setting of the story itself); Ezra-Nehemiah would come next followed by Esther. If this referential historical setting is significant, it may indicate a weakening of emphasis on the basic originating incident within the diasporic community as time progresses. The fact that the basic originating incident emerges in each narrative, however, does suggest that crisis is important to the maintenance of the tradition of the basic originating incident. Diasporic communities find in this incident some form of identity.

---

52. The contrast between Daniel/Ezra-Nehemiah on the one side and Esther on the other is noted by Stern, "Esther and the Politics of Diaspora," 46. Laniak, "Esther's *Volkscentrism*," 78–80, speaks of Esther reframing the "Jebucentrism" of the period.

Rejection

Relationship of the Diasporic Community to the Homeland

Cohen's category of "relationship of the diasporic community to the homeland" is depicted most strongly in the book of Ezra-Nehemiah, with its stories of the return of the community to the land. The harsh realities of the homeland, however, restrict any temptation towards what Cohen called "idealized memory of the homeland," although Ezra-Nehemiah stresses Cohen's "collective commitment to the homeland's prosperity" and "return to the homeland." Daniel does establish a relationship to the homeland at the outset by relating the basic originating incident, but then largely ignores the homeland. In Daniel 9, however, one can discern a "collective commitment to the homeland's prosperity," as Daniel prays for the restoration of Jerusalem.[53] Nevertheless, this restoration is pushed off into the distant future in the angelic interpretation that follows the prayer. While on the one hand the book of Esther displays the weakest connection to the homeland, lacking an idealized memory and commitment to prosperity and return, on the other, it does reveal the enduring impact of the homeland on diasporic identity. The deadly scuffle between Haman and Mordecai, one defined by traditions from the homeland, reveals that the homeland continues to define the Jewish community in diaspora. While the book of Esther contains the least connectivity to the homeland, it may be that it was written to remind such a community that it is important to not lose that dimension of their identity exemplified by Mordecai as opposed to Esther. Tracking these three books chronologically (in terms of referential historical context), it is possible that Daniel reflects the early phase of diasporic experience in which the Diaspora seeks to live within their new hostland and yet has significant concern for the homeland, but not to return to the land. As time progresses, there are two options: return to the homeland (Ezra-Nehemiah) or remain in the hostland (Esther). Both options have their dangers, but those who remain in the hostland are reminded not to forget the homeland and its traditions.

Relationship to the Diasporic Community Itself

Cohen's "relationship to the diasporic community itself" can be discerned within this literature. All three books depict a strong group consciousness, although in different ways. In Daniel this group consciousness is developed

---

53. Blumenthal, "Book of Daniel," 78, may overstate this point when he speaks of "the strong and unbreakable bond with the homeland" as "vividly described in the book," while only citing Daniel 6 and 9.

only among the four diasporic individuals, displayed in their commitment to key religious activities and values. There is no sense, however, of the broader community. While Ezra-Nehemiah displays strong group consciousness, nourished through articulation of its religious heritage, this is only portrayed for those functioning in the homeland. The focus of the group consciousness in those scenes in the hostland is on the traditions of return to the land, thus undermining diasporic life. While Esther appears to showcase those attitudes that would undermine diasporic identity, this time (contrasting Ezra-Nehemiah) by assimilation into the surrounding culture, Mordecai encourages group consciousness through his establishment of fasts and feasts within the Jewish community. Chronologically, Daniel displays a nascent diasporic communal identity, focused on individuals and a small group banding together, but lacking broader cohesion as a Jewish community.[54] As time progresses, again two options appear: Ezra-Nehemiah rejects any group consciousness that would encourage an enduring diasporic group identity—emphasizing identity in the homeland, while Esther encourages diasporic group consciousness—but highlights the danger of losing identity that can only be drawn from traditions from the homeland.[55]

Relationship to the Hostland

Cohen's "relationship to the hostland" can also be discerned in these Old Testament books. The book of Daniel straddles the two common diasporic experiences of the hostland as a place of troubled relationship and as a place of creative, enriching life.[56] On the one hand, Daniel and his friends

---

54. As noted by Blumenthal, "Book of Daniel," 77: they are not "a sizeable, organized group who could take its religious orientation with it. They depended on their inner, personal faith and convictions . . . a faith of the individual . . . personal creed." Cf. Humphreys, "Life-Style for Diaspora," 220, who contrasts Daniel and Esther on this issue.

55. Contra Oded, "Exile—the Biblical Perspectives," 92, who argues against a "Diasporism," with its attendant view of "infinite exile," as ever the basis for Jewish identity. It appears that books like Daniel and certainly Esther envision an identity that is not defined by return to the land. Cf. Boyarin and Boyarin, "Diaspora."

56. Much appreciated is the work of Cohen, *Global Diasporas*, 23, who has highlighted in passing that while Babylonian diaspora did "evoke a sense of captivity, exile, alienation and isolation" for Jews, there is a need for a "revisionist view of Babylon" that highlights "the benefits of integration into a rich and diverse alien culture" exemplified by the reality that "a substantial number adopted Babylonian names and customs; the group as a whole used the Babylonian calendar and embraced the language of Aramaic." Hopefully the present paper contributes further to this "rereading" by pointing out

find new opportunities, advancement, and prosperity in diaspora.[57] On the other, it is a place of great danger that at times threatens their very lives. In one way, the book of Ezra-Nehemiah portrays the hostland in positive ways, as emperors enable the agenda of diasporic figures in Ezra 1, 7 and Nehemiah 1. In another way, the fact that these figures are all seeking to leave Mesopotamia suggests a troubled relationship with the hostland. Esther also reveals a balance between the hostland as land of opportunity and a land of danger. While this appears to be a constant throughout all three books, one can discern different responses to this relationship to the hostland. In Ezra-Nehemiah the response is for the community to abandon the hostland and return to the homeland, while in Daniel and Esther the response is to remain within the hostland. For Daniel, the focus is consistently on relying on miraculous interventions from God,[58] while for Esther there is greater reliance on human ingenuity.[59] This may reflect chronological developments. In the first phase of diasporic life one has little option but to remain, especially in the case of victim diaspora. The passivity of the diasporic community is evident in the need for Daniel and his friends to rely on God for miraculous interventions. As time progresses, however, one can discern a development. Growth in power and resources within the hostland[60] opens up two possibilities: return to the homeland as in Ezra-Nehemiah (facilitated by working within the hostland system) or remain in the land and learn to function successfully within the hostland by working within its system, as in Esther.

---

certain streams that show "the development of a new creative energy in a challenging, pluralistic context outside the natal homeland." For the "astonishing theological creativity" that came with the exilic crisis, see Brueggemann, *Cadences of Home*, 115.

57. Cf. Humphreys, "Life-Style for Diaspora," 216, 222, who speaks of "the possibility of living a creative and rich life," "a life both rewarding and creative within the pagan setting." The use of the term "Diaspora" is more conducive than the term "exile" to discerning the positive dimension of life away from the land; cf. Oded, "Exile—the Biblical Perspectives," 85.

58. Humphreys, "Life-Style for Diaspora," 219–21, contrasts the passivity of the courtiers in Daniel, who rely on "the miraculous intervention of the deity," to the active stance of Esther and Mordecai.

59. Collins, "Court-Tales," 225. See Berg, *Book of Esther*, 176, who notes that "each individual Jew . . . must use his/her power and authority to assist the people of Israel," an emphasis that "restrict[s] the role played by God in the narratives."

60. As well as shifts in political configurations, such as the defeat of the Babylonians by the Persians.

CONCLUSION

The Writings of the Old Testament contain key literary riches that not only reflect the diasporic reality of post-monarchial Israel and Judah, but provide direction for life in diaspora. Both of these aspects are foundational for Christian theology and ethics. First, the diasporic reality of post-monarchial Israel and Judah represents a key transition in the history of redemption. While many Christians ignore post-monarchial Judaism as irrelevant to Christian theology,[61] this period is essential in redemptive history for the formation of the Christian community. Not only would the Messiah rise from and be recognized within this community, but this community would experience the covenantal traditions sociologically in ways more conducive to the historical and religious realities of the early church (as well as post-70 CE Judaism).[62] When books like Acts depict the church as emerging from returnees from diaspora (Acts 2) who are then being dispersed again from Jerusalem to Judea, to Samaria, and to the uttermost parts of the earth (Acts 1:8; 8:1) due to persecution, one can see how books depicting post-monarchial diasporic experience provide a theological foundation for such a phase in redemptive history.

Second, the diasporic reality of post-monarchial Israel and Judah also provides ethical direction for Christian communities seeking to live within this world. Each of these books, however, provides a different perspective on faithful living. Such diversity is key to the enduring relevance of the canonical traditions for confessional communities, for the diversity enables the Scriptures to continue to speak relevantly into the ever-changing social realities and challenges of the people of God.[63] One needs wisdom to discern which of these books provides the necessary resources for the present state of a particular community of faith. These Old Testament books reveal various approaches to the perspective of Christ that his community would be in the world (John 17:11) and not of the world (John 17:14).

---

61. Typified by the frontispiece in Heaton, *Everyday Life in Old Testament Times*, 26, entitled: "The Closing Scene of Old Testament Times: The Babylon of Nebuchadnezzar," which pictured Judean exiles being marched under Babylonian guard through the famous Ishtar gate of Babylon; cf. Boda, *Haggai/Zechariah*, 21.

62. Thus, the claim of Blumenthal, "Book of Daniel," 73, that the destruction of the temple does not mean "that Judaism underwent any drastic changes, only that its mainstay changed from state religion to one accepted and perpetuated by its adherents as individuals," seems naïve, since that sociological shift is so radical.

63. See especially Sanders, "Adaptable for Life."

BIBLIOGRAPHY

Barton, John. "Theological Ethics in Daniel." In *The Book of Daniel: Composition and Reception*, edited by John J. Collins and Peter W. Flint, 660–70. Leiden: Brill, 2001.

Beach, Lee. *The Church in Exile: Living in Hope after Christendom*. Downers Grove, IL: IVP Academic, 2015.

Bechtel, Carol M. *Esther*. Interpretation. Louisville, KY: Westminster John Knox, 2002.

Bedford, Peter R. "Diaspora: Homeland Relations in Ezra-Nehemiah." *VT* 52 (2002) 147–65.

Berg, Sandra Beth. *The Book of Esther: Motifs, Themes, and Structure*. Missoula, MT: Scholars, 1979.

Berlin, Adele. *Esther*. JPS Bible Commentary. Philadelphia: Jewish Publication Society, 2001.

Blumenthal, Fred. "The Book of Daniel: A Guide for Judaism in Exile." *Jewish Bible Quarterly* 29 (2001) 73–79.

Boda, Mark J. "Flashforward: Future Glimpses in the Past of Ezra 1–6." In *Let Us Go Up to Zion: Essays in Honour of H. G. M. Williamson on the Occasion of His Sixty-Fifth Birthday*, edited by Mark J. Boda and Iain Provan, 247–60. Leiden: Brill, 2012.

———. *Haggai/Zechariah*. Grand Rapids: Zondervan, 2004.

———. "Prayer as Rhetoric in the Book of Nehemiah." In *New Perspectives on Ezra-Nehemiah: History and Historiography, Text, Literature, and Interpretation*, edited by Isaac Kalimi, 279–96. Winona Lake, IN: Eisenbrauns, 2012.

———. *A Severe Mercy: Sin and Its Remedy in the Old Testament*. Siphrut: Literature and Theology of the Hebrew Scriptures 1. Winona Lake, IN: Eisenbrauns, 2009.

Bottomley, Gillian. "Culture, Ethnicity, and the Politics/Poetics of Representation." *Diaspora: A Journal of Transnational Studies* 1 (1991) 303–20.

Boyarin, Daniel, and Jonathan Boyarin. "Diaspora: Generation and the Ground of Jewish Identity." *Critical Inquiry* 19 (1993) 693–725.

Brubaker, Rogers. "The 'Diaspora' Diaspora." *Ethnic and Racial Studies* 28 (2005) 1–19.

Brueggemann, Walter. *Cadences of Home: Preaching among Exiles*. Louisville, KY: Westminster John Knox, 1997.

Clifford, James. "Diasporas." *Cultural Anthropology* 9 (1994) 302–38.

———. *Routes: Travel and Translations in the Late Twentieth Century*. Cambridge, MA: Harvard University Press, 1997.

Cohen, Robin. *Global Diasporas: An Introduction*. 2nd ed. Global Diasporas. New York: Routledge, 2008.

Collins, John J. "The Court-Tales in Daniel and the Development of Apocalyptic." *JBL* 94 (1975) 218–34.

———. *Daniel: A Commentary on the Book of Daniel*. Hermeneia. Minneapolis: Fortress, 1993.

Costas, Orlando. "The Subversiveness of Faith: Esther as a Paradigm for a Liberating Theology." *Ecumenical Review* 40 (1988) 66–78.

Davies, P. R. *Daniel*. Old Testament Guides 4. Sheffield: JSOT Press, 1985.

Dempster, Stephen. "An 'Extraordinary Fact': Torah and Temple and the Contours of the Hebrew Canon." *TynBul* 48 (1997) 23–56.

Dufoix, Stéphane. *Diasporas*. Translated by William Rodarmor. Berkeley: University of California Press, 2008.

Fox, Michael V. *Character and Ideology in the Book of Esther.* Studies on Personalities of the Old Testament. Columbia, SC: University of South Carolina Press, 1991.

Gerleman, Gilles. *Studien zu Esther: Stoff, Struktur, Stil, Sinn.* Biblische Studien. Neukirchen-Vluyn: Neukirchener Verlag, 1966.

Giri, Bed Prasad. "Diasporic Postcolonialism and Its Antinomies." *Diaspora: A Journal of Transnational Studies* 14 (2005) 215–35.

Goldingay, John. *Daniel.* Word Biblical Themes. Dallas, TX: Word, 1989.

———. "Daniel in the Context of Old Testament Theology." In *The Book of Daniel: Composition and Reception,* edited by John J. Collins and Peter W. Flint, 639–59. Leiden: Brill, 2001.

Heaton, Eric William. *Everyday Life in Old Testament Times.* New York: Scribner, 1956.

Humphreys, W. Lee. "Life-Style for Diaspora: A Study of the Tales of Esther and Daniel." *JBL* 92 (1973) 211–23.

Laniak, Timothy S. "Esther's *Volkscentrism* and the Reframing of Post-Exilic Judaism." In *The Book of Esther in Modern Research,* edited by Sidnie White Crawford and Leonard J. Greenspoon, 77–90. London: T. & T. Clark, 2003.

———. *Shame and Honor in the Book of Esther.* SBL Dissertation Series 165. Atlanta: Scholars, 1998.

Lucas, Ernest. *Daniel.* Apollos Old Testament Commentary. Leicester, England/Downers Grove, IL: Apollos/InterVarsity Press, 2002.

———. "Daniel: Resolving the Enigma." *VT* 50 (2000) 66–80.

Oded, Bustenay. "Exile—the Biblical Perspectives." In *Homelands and Diasporas: Greeks, Jews and Their Migrations,* edited by Minna Rozen, 85–106. International Library of Migration Studies. London: I. B. Tauris, 2008.

Porteous, Norman W. *Daniel: A Commentary.* Philadelphia: Westminster, 1965.

Rose, Jacqueline. *The Last Resistance.* London: Verso, 2007.

Safran, William. "Diasporas in Modern Societies: Myths of Homeland and Return." *Diaspora: A Journal of Transnational Studies* 1 (1991) 83–99.

Sanders, James A. "Adaptable for Life: The Nature and Function of Canon." In *Magnalia Dei, the Mighty Acts of God: Essays on the Bible and Archaeology in Memory of G. Ernest Wright,* edited by Frank Moore Cross, Werner E. Lemke, and Patrick D. Miller, 531–60. Garden City, NY: Doubleday, 1976.

Scobie, Charles H. H. *The Ways of Our God: An Approach to Biblical Theology.* Grand Rapids: Eerdmans, 2003.

Seow, C. L. *Daniel.* Westminster Bible Companion. Louisville, KY: Westminster John Knox, 2003.

Sheffer, Gabriel, ed. *Modern Diasporas in International Politics.* New York: St. Martin's, 1986.

Smith-Christopher, Daniel. *A Biblical Theology of Exile.* Overtures to Biblical Theology. Minneapolis: Fortress, 2002.

———. "The Book of Daniel." In *The New Interpreter's Bible,* edited by Leander E. Keck, 7:17–152. Nashville: Abingdon, 1996.

———. *The Religion of the Landless: The Social Context of the Babylonian Exile.* Bloomington, IN: Meyer-Stone, 1989.

Stern, Elsie R. "Esther and the Politics of Diaspora." *Jewish Quarterly Review* 100 (2010) 25–53.

Sweeney, Marvin A. "Tanak versus Old Testament: Concerning the Foundation for a Jewish Theology of the Bible." In *Problems in Biblical Theology: Essays in Honor of*

Rolf Knierim, edited by Henry T. C. Sun and Keith L. Eades, 353–72. Grand Rapids: Eerdmans, 1997.

Tölölyan, Khachig. "The Nation-State and Its Others: In Lieu of a Preface." *Diaspora: A Journal of Transnational Studies* 1 (1991) 3–7.

Towner, W. Sibley. *Daniel*. Interpretation. Atlanta: John Knox, 1984.

Valeta, David M. "Court or Jester Tales? Resistance and Social Reality in Daniel 1–6." *Perspectives in Religious Studies* 32 (2005) 309–24.

White, Sidnie Ann. "Esther: A Feminine Model for Jewish Diaspora." In *Gender and Difference in Ancient Israel*, edited by Peggy Day, 161–77. Minneapolis: Fortress, 1989.

2

Who Says "You Can't Go Home"?
Reconsidering the Models of Exile and Diaspora as Metaphors for the Church Today in Light of Recent Exilic Research

Paul S. Evans

INTRODUCTION

THE PHRASE "YOU CAN'T go home again" is an expression in popular culture suggesting that once you have left your hometown and moved to the "big city" you never really return to your home and expect it to be the same.[1] Of course, the phrase applies more broadly than this, and points to the common experience of longing for a return to the way things were that can never really be actualized. As Susan Matt has observed, "The idea that it is impossible to return home and to the past is commonplace today and a hallmark of modern consciousness."[2] Nevertheless, this does not stop one from longing for such a return home,

---

1. The phrase derives from a novel by Thomas Wolfe entitled *You Can't Go Home Again* (1940), which tells the fictional story of George Webber who writes a novel that refers to his home town frequently. While Webber's novel was a great success it essentially alienated him from his town, as the residents found his references to the town distorted and they resented him for it. Thus Webber found he could not "go home again." Ultimately, the character, Webber, discovers "You can't go back home to your family, back home to your childhood . . . back home to a young man's dreams of glory and of fame . . . back home to places in the country, back home to the old forms and systems of things which once seemed everlasting but which are changing all the time—back home to the escapes of Time and Memory" (706).

2. Matt, "You Can't Go Home Again," 469.

or to the way things were. Emotions of homesickness or nostalgia[3] and yearnings to return have existed from time immemorial and naturally persist in the modern world.

Unsurprisingly these emotions are expressed in literature and film where themes of displacement, homesickness, and return are widely found. Typically in such stories, a character(s)—for one reason or another—is displaced from home (or home planet in the case of science fiction) and is unable to return. In such stories, the attempt to return home is often a key plotline. The motifs of leaving home—whether by choice, necessity, or coercion—and returning home are also prominent in the Old Testament where the theme of exile subsumes both. In fact, exile is a leading theme in the Old Testament, being found in the very fabric of the Old Testament from beginning to end.

Initially exile is seen in the conclusion of the Garden story where the first man and woman are exiled from their home in the Garden in Eden (Genesis 3). In the next chapter, Cain is cursed to wander in exile (Genesis 4). Later, the builders of Babel are exiled from their land (Gen 11:1–9). Abraham leaves his home in Ur (Gen 11:30—12:9) to enter the Promised Land, only to go into brief exile in Egypt, followed by his exodus back to the Promised Land (Gen 12:10–20). The motif surfaces again as Jacob goes into exile in fear of the wrath of his brother Esau (Genesis 28–32), but then eventually returns to the land (Genesis 33). Joseph is exiled to Egypt (Genesis 37) as a slave and never returns to the Promised Land. Jacob and his descendants follow Joseph to Egypt, abandoning the Promised Land (Genesis 46). Eventually these descendants are enslaved (Exod 1:8–14) and only return to the Promised Land through *the* Exodus. In his life David experiences multiple exiles due to the murderous intentions of Saul, and the coup led by his son; twice David even sojourns in a foreign land (1 Sam 21:10–15; 27:2–7) with the Philistines (in Gath and Ziklag) but eventually returns to claim the throne of Israel. After the division of the Israelite kingdom, the northern nation is eventually exiled by Assyria (2 Kgs 18:9–12) to other lands. Finally, Judah—the last of the Israelite kingdoms—is exiled to Babylon by Nebuchadnezzar (2 Kings 24–25). During this same crisis, other Judean groups flee to Egypt (2 Kgs 25:26).[4] The exiled Babylonian

---

3. Matt defines homesickness as "the longing for a particular home" and nostalgia as "a longing for a lost time" (ibid.).

4. As Carroll, "Exile! What Exile," 63, notes, this flight to Egypt is almost a "reversing the exodus."

community (or *Golah*), empowered by Cyrus of Persia, then returns to the land with leaders such as Sheshbazzar (Ezra 1:8, 11), Zerubbabel (cf. Hag 1:12; Ezra 3:2, 8), Ezra, and Nehemiah (e.g., Ezra 7:6, 10; Neh 8:9).[5]

Biblical scholars have long recognized the importance of the exile for Israel's theological thought. As J. A. Sanders writes: "Out of the Exile, Judaism was born. The Exile is at the heart of the biblical understanding of divine judgment and revelation. It was the crucible of Israel's faith."[6] Similarly R. Albertz writes: "I venture to claim that without the experience of the exile, Israel would never have made the discovery of monotheism in the strict sense; without it, Israel would never have transcended the limits of its national religion."[7] Furthermore, some have suggested that exile is one of the main themes of the entire Scriptures. N. T. Wright has even suggested that the "exile" that began with the Babylonians did in fact not end with Cyrus but continued into Jesus' day.[8] While there have been detractors regarding this thesis, Wright does mount a good case that at least *some* Jews would have perceived the situation this way.[9] In fact, going forward it is essential to realize that one's perspective is an extremely important aspect in understanding what exactly constituted exile. (We shall return to this point again below.)

Besides being a perennial topic of interest for historians and biblical scholars, the metaphorical usefulness of the exile as relevant for the church today has been underscored by theologians and biblical scholars alike.[10]

---

5. The threat of exile is found in the law before Israel even has a land from which to be exiled, with the covenant curse threatening being scattered to the nations (Lev 26:33; Deut 28:64) or even reversing the exodus by sending them back to Egypt (Deut 28:68). This threat is kept in mind even at the pinnacle of Israelite power under Solomon. When he prays for the people he is aware that if the people sin it might result in being exiled from the Promised Land (1 Kgs 8:46).

6. Sanders, "Exile," 188.

7. Albertz, *Israel in Exile*, 435–36.

8. Cf. Wright, *New Testament and the People of God*; Wright, *Jesus and the Victory of God*; Wright, "Theology, History and Jesus."

9. Wright points to Neh 9:36, which laments that the returnees are "slaves to this day," and Tob 14:5–7, which predicts that sometime in the future "they will all return from their exile" even though the book is a postexilic production. Similarly, Bar 3:7–8 states, "we will praise you in our exile" even though it is written well into the postexilic period. Cf. 2 Macc 1:27–29.

10. E.g., Klein, *Israel in Exile*; Hauerwas and Willimon, *Resident Aliens*; Suleiman, *Exile and Creativity*; Radner, "From Liberation to Exile," 931–34; Brueggemann, *Cadences of Home*.

Fairly recently some have considered the metaphor of exile as a helpful analogy for reflection on the relationship of the church to the postmodern culture of the West. Unfortunately, the appropriation of the metaphor of exile often lacks sophistication and sometimes has failed to take into account the contributions of academic research on the exile. Therefore, this paper will follow the lead of such studies in considering the theme of exile as a metaphor for the church today, however, it will also critique and nuance such an approach and suggest that the findings of recent exilic scholarship may provide some new insights for those wishing to apply this metaphor to today's de-centered church. Furthermore, based on this research I will suggest that the metaphor of diaspora may be a more appropriate metaphor than exile for a new generation of Christian "exiles."

RECENT APPROPRIATION OF EXILE AS METAPHOR

Walter Brueggemann has been one of the chief advocates for the appropriation of the metaphor of exile for the church today.[11] Brueggemann's approach is to understand the Bible as "a set of models (paradigms) of reality made up of images situated in and contextualized by narratives."[12] Brueggemann downplays the importance of history behind the exile theme, emphasizing that the historical reality (Babylonian exile) does not have to match the situation to which he is applying the metaphor.[13] Drawing on previous scholarship, Brueggemann emphasizes the theological crisis that the exile created for ancient Israel. Yet despite (or perhaps because of) these trau-

---

11. He first made this provocative suggestion in Brueggemann, "Disciplines of Readiness." But see also his "Rethinking Church Models," and "Preaching to Exiles." These three essays were reprinted in his book, *Cadences of Home*.

12. Brueggemann, "Preaching to Exiles," 11.

13. Initially he stated that one of the main reasons the metaphor is useful is that it "is largely paradigm and model, not extensive historical fact" (Brueggemann, "Disciplines of Readiness," 6). At the time of his writing, the historicity of the exile was being called into question (cf. Carroll, "Myth of the Empty Land," and Barstad, *Myth of the Empty Land*), however, that ship has largely sailed. There has been extensive work investigating the exile as historical fact, and despite the theories of Torrey and Carroll, its historicity is beyond reasonable doubt. Brueggemann also emphasizes, "These narrative renderings of reality in the Bible (as elsewhere) are not factual reportage, but are inevitably artistic constructs that stand a distance from any 'fact,' and are filtered through interest of a political kind" ("Preaching to Exiles," 11). In other words his emphasis on the lack of historicity is not so much an acceptance of fictitiousness but an awareness of the distance all historical reportage has from historical event itself and the inevitable creativity employed by historians in presenting their story.

matic experiences, this time period proved to be a theologically creative and generative period for Israel through which the faith of Judaism and Christianity emerged.

Brueggemann emphasizes the cultural and spiritual aspects of exile rather than those of geographical displacement.[14] The exiles found themselves in a "hostile, alien environment where the predominant temptation is assimilation."[15] Brueggemann draws analogies with the Western church (initially he was applying it specifically to the Presbyterian Church in the United States of America), which has similarly lost power and prestige and finds itself in an environment with similar challenges.[16] According to Brueggemann, in the modern cultural and religious context, the Western church finds its "central faith claims ... increasingly unwelcome and ... received, if not with hostility, at least with indifference" and the church is increasingly "alienated from the dominant value system."[17] Therefore, the metaphor of exile seems quite appropriate.

Brueggemann finds fitting responses to such a situation in the way in which ancient Jews responded to their exile and draws on many different exilic texts to illustrate what type of response the Western church might have to the present situation of exile. Brueggemann has suggested that the "theological vocation" of the church is, like that of these ancient Jews, to resist both "assimilation and despair."[18] Many of Brueggemann's suggestions are lucid, productive exhortations, replete with valuable insights. Brueggemann explicitly suggests that by following such biblical examples, the church, like ancient Israel, might be "converting exile into homecoming."[19]

Brueggemann's approach has been picked up by writers from various fields and has proved a fruitful and generative perspective. The model of the exile has undoubtedly aided further theological reflection on the postmodern situation of the de-centered church in the West. In some ways Brueggemann's suggestions have helped to balance what biblical models are utilized by the church. Traditionally, models like the Exodus, the Conquest—or

---

14. Brueggemann writes, "exile is not primarily a geographical phenomenon, but is a liturgical, cultural, spiritual condition; one may indeed be an exile while being geographically at home" ("Disciplines of Readiness," 6).

15. Ibid.

16. Ibid.

17. Ibid.

18. Ibid.

19. Ibid., 9.

David defeating the Philistines—have been more commonly employed as analogies for the church. By and large the biblical model of exile had been overlooked in the church. For these reasons (as well as others) we are in Brueggemann's debt. However, the present paper contends that more work needs to be done in nuancing our use of this metaphor. Therefore, what follows is a survey of several important contributions made by recent exilic scholarship, followed by some reflection on their implications for appropriating the biblical metaphor of exile for today.

DIFFICULTIES IN PRECISELY DEFINING AND DELIMITING THE EXILE

As noted above, throughout the Old Testament there is a repeated motif of leaving home or homeland, often followed by a return. However, it must be pointed out that most of those displaced *do not return*. The first humans do not return to the Garden. Cain apparently wanders away from his family for good. The northern kingdom of Israel is never re-gathered to Palestine and many who are exiled to Babylon never return to the land. In the books of Esther and Daniel we see examples of Jews who remained in Persian territories and did *not* return to Jerusalem under Cyrus's authorization.[20] Large Jewish populations remained in Babylon itself (and eventually produced the Babylonian Talmud). Substantial Jewish communities remained in Egypt (and eventually produced the translation of the Old Testament into Greek known as the Septuagint).[21]

This situation leads us to question what exactly is meant by "exile" and what it would mean when the "exile" is over. Robert Carroll has put the question well. He writes:

> How then are we to define this exile? How are we to explain its nature? When did it end? If so many people remained in a state of deportedness, can the exile be said to have ended? What kind of exile is it where the bulk of the people never did return to their

---

20. Ahn, *Exile as Forced Migrations*, 28, points out that "the period involves at least three generations in Babylon, a remnant community or communities back in Judah, a group of Israel migrants previously displaced during the Neo-Assyrian period, and Judean refugees in Egypt, Pathros, Ethiopia, Elam, Hamath, and presumably the coastlands."

21. These Egyptian Jewish populations are also attested in extra-biblical evidence like the Elephantine papyri, which point to Egyptian Jewish communities even having their own temple.

own land, but only a token number went back as if those who were left behind did not count at all?[22]

While Carroll's questions were intended to cast doubt on whether there really was a Babylonian "exile" historically—something he argues against—his comments bring some clarity to the discussion. This again brings to the fore the importance of perspective (noted briefly above) for defining the exile. Perhaps the existence or persistence of the "exile" depended upon the perspective of individuals.

Implications

The extent to which using the metaphor of exile will resonate with individuals or individual churches will depend considerably upon the perspectives of each. Second, in light of Brueggemann's stated goal of turning exile into homecoming, one might question what "homecoming" means in the modern ecclesiastical context. In light of the historical realities of the various exiles and displaced persons in ancient Israel, what home means is not an easy question, and neither is defining when exile truly ends.

THE PLURALITY OF EXILIC PERSPECTIVES

It has long been acknowledged in critical biblical scholarship that the Old Testament does not contain a monolithic perspective but contains within its pages much theological diversity. Unfortunately, this is not well known outside of academic scholarship (and is virtually unheard of in popular understanding of the Bible). A clear strength of Brueggemann's work on the Old Testament has been his underscoring of the diversity found within the biblical text. His magnum opus, *Theology of the Old Testament*, was organized around different and divergent voices contained within the text, which he labeled as "Israel's Core Testimony," "Israel's Countertestimony," and "Israel's Unsolicited Testimony."[23] For our purposes here, it is important to note that this polyphony of perspectives in the Old Testament is also evinced in differing views on, and portrayals of, the exile. This can be seen in both narrative and non-narrative portions of the Old Testament.

For example, the narrative description of the destruction of Jerusalem and subsequent exile of the people in the book of 2 Kings is uniformly negative. This is especially evident when compared with the account of the

---

22. Carroll, "Exile! What Exile," 66.
23. Brueggemann, *Theology of the Old Testament*, 115, 315, 405.

same historical events in the narrative portion of the book of Jeremiah. In fact, much of the language and phraseology is verbatim with that of 2 Kings (cf. 2 Kgs 24:18—25:30 and Jeremiah 52), however, in Jeremiah there appears to be a more optimistic perspective maintained.[24] In many ways the Jeremianic account of Jerusalem's destruction is *more* detailed than that in Kings, yet there is *no reference* to the temple being burned.[25] Given that to an ancient Israelite the burning of the temple was one of the greatest tragedies of all, omitting this appears to be a purposeful move to downplay the negative aspect of the exile. Furthermore, while in both 2 Kings and Jeremiah the Babylonians are said to "leave some of the poorest in the land to be vinedressers and tillers of the soil" (2 Kgs 25:12; Jer 52:16), in Jeremiah it also records that the Babylonians actually "gave vineyards and fields" to the poor (Jer 39:10). Furthermore, Jeremiah himself is treated well by the Babylonians (in contrast to how his own people treat him!) who offer him the choice of going to Babylon with them (where they promise to take good care of him) or remaining in the land or going anywhere he would choose to go (Jer 40:4–6). In Jeremiah 40 some Judahites are said to return to Palestine during the exile and to have "gathered wine and summer fruits *in great abundance*" (Jer 40:12; my emphasis), a very positive development indeed.[26] As Ahn asserts, in the book of Jeremiah, in contrast to the book of Kings, "The authors or editors are clearly trying to show something less damaging or caustic."[27]

Divergent perspectives appear in non-narrative biblical literature as well. Lamentations vehemently complains about the exile, even to the extent of viewing Yahweh as enemy.[28] However, Second Isaiah emphasizes God as caring for them in exile (Isa 40:27–31). The exilic prophet calls the readers to "forget" the "former things," which appear to be the sins that necessitated the exile.[29]

---

24. Ahn, *Exile as Forced Migrations*, 3, writes, "Jeremiah desperately wants to inject some optimism."

25. Ibid.

26. Ibid., 4, Ahn calls this a "remarkable passing injection of optimism—to harvest an abundance of wine and summer fruit during a time of socio-economic uncertainty and political annexation."

27. Ibid.

28. Klein, *Israel in Exile*, 9–18.

29. Ahn, *Exile as Forced Migrations*, 5.

> Do not remember the former things, or consider the things of old.
> I am about to do a new thing; now it springs forth, do you not
> perceive it? I will make a way in the wilderness and rivers in the
> desert (Isa 43:18–19).

This is in stark contrast to the Deuteronomistic History, which clearly emphasizes the culpability of Israel and underscores the sins that send them into exile (e.g., 2 Kgs 24:3–4). Furthermore, in the oracles of Jeremiah, the prophet declares that the exile is part of Yahweh's will and is meant for good, not harm (Jer 29:11).[30]

Implications

An awareness of the divergent perspectives on the exile in the Old Testament can be beneficial when applying the metaphor to the de-centered church of today. Not everybody will have the same perspective on the "exile" of the church. Some will think it is the result of the sin of church leadership. Others will see it as an unfair negative situation. Still others may view it as a chance for revival and a new creation. All of these perspectives are reflected in the biblical text as well.

JUDEO-BABYLONIAN GENERATIONAL CONSCIOUSNESS

Recent scholarship on the exile has brought to light the significance of the different generations who experienced exile at the hand of the Babylonians. The dissertation of John Ahn was groundbreaking in this regard.[31] Drawing on modern sociological studies of similar phenomena of displaced peoples, Ahn introduced the nomenclature of "forced migration," and "displacement and resettlement" into the discussion. The exile of Judah is more accurately called a "forced migration." This perspective has helped to reframe and focus academic discussion of the Babylonian exile.

The Old Testament records three different "forced migrations" wherein Judeans were exiled to Babylon. The first displacement occurred in 597 BCE. Jehoiakim, king of Judah, became a vassal to the Babylonians, but three years later (relying on Egypt for aid) he rebelled against Nebuchadnezzar. While the Babylonians moved to quell the rebellion, Jehoiakim died and his son

---

30. For further examples of the diversity of biblical responses to exile, see Klein, *Israel in Exile*.

31. Ahn's 2006 Yale dissertation was eventually published in 2011 as *Exile as Forced Migrations*.

Jehoiachin succeeded him. The Babylonians subsequently took Jehoiachin and thousands of others (the royals, princes, and warriors) into exile.[32]

The second displacement occurred in 586 BCE when Jehoiachin's successor, Zedekiah, rebelled against Babylon (against Jeremiah's prophetic advice). Nebuchadnezzar laid siege to Jerusalem for three years and eventually sacked the city, burning its temple, capturing the king, slaughtering the royal family, and taking Zedekiah to Babylon along with another wave of exiles (though a smaller number of exiles than in the first wave). A third displacement is recorded in Jeremiah 52 (though not referenced in the book of Kings) and dates to 582 BCE, wherein further Judeans were exiled to Babylon (though involving a considerably smaller number of exiles than in the previous two waves).

Before Ahn's work it was common to conflate the 597 BCE and 586 BCE groups of exiles together (and commonly to ignore the 582 BCE group). However, Ahn's analysis has helped to distinguish the different concerns of each group of exiles.[33] (Most likely these people were brought to Babylon as laborers for the irrigation-canal projects or other building projects. The decreasing number of exiles with each wave represents changing needs of the projects, and perhaps less demand for new workers.)[34]

Drawing on modern sociological studies of displaced peoples, Ahn isolates general issues and concerns that arise in forced population transfers. He notes many of these issues as:

---

32. Second Kings 24:14 records 10,000 exiles at this point, while Jeremiah records 3,023. Second Kings 24 contains three sets of numbers for exiles: 10,000 (v. 14); 7,000 (v. 16); and 1,000 (v. 16). Ahn suggests the three figures represent the three different waves of exiles. He writes, "Although this pair of the statistical rounded figures in the [sic] 2 Kings 24 is slightly larger than the ones in Jer 52, both figures nevertheless line up together in decreasing fashion" (ibid., 6).

33. Technically, it is only correct to speak of the first wave of migrants as "exiles," since when the second and third group migrated they were already part of the Babylonian empire, so that what really took place in the second and third waves "was in fact an internal displacement of peoples from the periphery of the Babylonian empire (Judah) to the center (Babylon) not another exile" (Ahn, "Exile," 199).

34. The number of people brought to Babylon doubtless was tied to labor needs. As Ahn (ibid., 200) writes, "The Neo-Babylonians imposed forced migration on conquered persons to work on their extensive and numerous primary, secondary and tertiary canals. This repeated systematic and calculated move would have prevented any immediate overpopulation. Such an oversupply of laborers would have had the domino effect of shortages in housing, problems with food distribution, issues with water supply as well as the risk of serious health problems."

(1) tensions between local and central politics; (2) clashes between cultural/traditional values and new ones; (3) struggles of socio-economic classes; (4) challenges of preserving one's first language (Hebrew) in the immediacy of one's family or community while dealing with the language or languages of the dominant culture (e.g., Aramaic for speaking and Akkadian/Sumerian for reading or writing); (5) restrictions of food or diet; (6) issues of gender and marriage (e.g., at what generational point does intermarriage become a realistic possibility[?]); (7) problems of raising children and grandchildren in a bifurcated or dual culture; (8) questions of partial or full acculturation or assimilation; (9) struggles to maintain religious practices, including those for the sake of social identity; (10) defining the concept of home (is it Babylon or Judah/Yehud?).[35]

These issues have some significant analogues *mutatis mutandis* with the situation of the church in the post-Christian West, many of which Brueggemann and others have skillfully pointed out. However, what can add some precision to this discussion is an awareness of "generational consciousness" that has been underscored in recent exilic scholarship.

Ahn has pointed out that sociological studies that trace these generational concerns do not trace further than the third generation, since the fourth generation has usually completely assimilated.[36] Ahn suggests that this three-generational consciousness is visible in biblical texts. Even the length of the exile described as 70 years reflects this generational consciousness. Each generation is 20 years (as suggested in the book of Numbers) so 70 years marks 3.5 generations. The first generation of 20 years is followed by a transitional generation—the so-called 1.5 generation—of 10 years, followed by the second generation of 20 years, and concluding with the third generation of 20 years, thus accounting for the 70 years of Jeremiah.

Thus, the first generation (597–577 BC) of exiles were Judean adults displaced and brought to Babylon. Their voices may be heard in a text like Psalm 137 ("By the rivers of Babylon—there we sat down and there we wept when we remembered Zion"). These would have experienced hardships common to all first-generation forced migrants: loss of prestige and social status, subjection to insults, and strong yearnings to return home.

---

35. Ibid., 201.
36. Ibid., 203.

By contrast, the 1.5 generation, the adolescents or teenagers from Judah who were brought to Babylon, had different social issues. Their social issues may be addressed by Jeremiah 29, which exhorts them to:

> Build houses and live in them; plant gardens and eat what they produce.
>
> Take wives and have sons and daughters; take wives for your sons, and give your daughters in marriage, that they may bear sons and daughters; multiply there, and do not decrease (Jer 29:5–6).

The second generation of exiles were those born to both the first and the 1.5 generation. Their social issues are slightly different, including issues of "assimilation through education, in-group and out-group, economic issues within the second generation between the descendants of 597, 587, 582 BC."[37]

The third generation (those born to the second generation) are the ones who are given the opportunity to return under Cyrus, many of whom become "the first generation of Judeo-Persians."[38] Unique to this generation is the issue of defining what constitutes home. Having been born and raised in Babylon (by parents who also were born in Babylon) the issue of whether to return home would not have been as straight-forward as it would have been for the exiles of earlier generations. A relevant social issue would have been whether they could justify staying in Babylon or justify "returning" to Judah.

Ahn's generational demarcation is immensely helpful in identifying issues and concerns of the different generation units of the Judean exiles. Furthermore it helps us understand the different responses to exile found in the biblical text as perhaps coming from different generations of exiles and evincing their varying perspectives due to their social location(s). As Ahn writes, "This Judeo-Babylonian generational consciousness is an integral aspect of contemporary exilic scholarship."[39]

Implications

In considering implications of this recent exilic scholarship for theological appropriation of the metaphor of exile today, it is important to keep in

---

37. Ibid.
38. Ibid.
39. Ibid., 204.

mind Brueggemann's qualification regarding correspondence of historical reality to the metaphor. He writes, "Note well, I have made no argument about the one-to-one match between metaphor and reality. I have proposed only that this metaphor mediates our experience to us in fresh ways, and gives access to scriptural resources in equally fresh ways."[40] Keeping this in mind, I propose that recognizing the generational differences for those experiencing exile may *mutatis mutandis* underscore some realities in the church today. The first generation of Christians who experienced "exile" felt first-hand the loss of cultural influence and the marginalization from the powers of society. The 1.5 generation, that is, those who were children at the time this de-centering of the church occurred, may have had a slightly different perspective. Their reaction as they matured would have been more about how to succeed in this new cultural environment, rather than continuing to lament the change itself. However, their closeness to the "turning of the times," and their close relationship to the first generation may have kept the sense of loss close to their heart.

The second generation faced more issues of assimilation than previous generations. This generation, the children of the first and 1.5 generations, faced issues of assimilation through education. In this regard, the influence of education, whether "secular" or "Christian" (including both Sunday School and Christian schools) cannot be underestimated. This group is somewhat removed from the *Event* of the de-centering of Christianity, having never experienced "North American Christendom" in any way, but having grown up with a marginalized Christianity being the norm.

The third generation faces issues of what exactly constitutes home. Having been born and raised in a post-Christian North America they have a different perspective on what exactly was "lost" in the "exile." This generation may intuitively see the value in postmodern culture. They may see themselves as having the best of both worlds as Christians and postmoderns. In fact, they likely would not feel at home in the preexilic Christendom in which their grandparents lived. Furthermore, unlike their forbears, the new generation is so accustomed to rapid change that their capacity for "homesickness/nostalgia" has been diminished. As Matt writes, for them "the past is the past" and the new generation does "not believe it is possible to return to [the past], *nor do they mourn it*, as earlier generations did"

---

40. Brueggemann, "Preaching to Exiles," 12.

(emphasis mine).[41] For them the image of exile with its longing to return home may not be the best metaphor. (We shall return to this below.)

THE LANGUAGE OF EXILE

While the exile event indelibly looms large in Old Testament history and was the locus of the production of many biblical texts, a close look at the language of exile in the Old Testament proves beneficial in delineating more precisely the themes of the text. Furthermore, lexical study suggests that the prominence of the image of exile in the Old Testament has been somewhat overstated. This can be seen in the preoccupation with the Hebrew גלה (and its cognates) to the near exclusion of other vocabulary of displacement in the Old Testament. An example of this can be seen in Ahn's book, *Exile as Forced Migrations*, where he briefly sets out to define גלה in his introduction (suggesting that "to migrate" or "emigrate" fits the reality)[42] but does not consider *any* other relevant Hebrew terms. This evinces a common methodological problem.

Similarly, in his article on exile in the IVP *Dictionary of the Old Testament: Prophets*, Ahn notes that the most common lexeme for exile in the Old Testament is גלה but notes eight different "synonyms" found in the Old Testament.[43] While it is true that גלה (including both verbs and nouns drawn from its root such as גלות, גולה, etc.) is most common (appearing 60 times with this meaning),[44] many other expressions rival its prominence (e.g., נדח appears 51 times with this meaning; פוץ appears 32 times regarding exile explicitly). In fact, the numerical prominence of גלה is not consistent but dependent upon different biblical books, with some preferring one of the

---

41. Matt, "You Can't Go Home Again," 497.
42. Ahn, *Exile as Forced Migrations*, 34–35.
43. Ahn, "Exile," 197.
44. גלה appears 187 times in the Old Testament, but more often has the meaning of "uncover/expose" or "reveal" (Gen 9:21; 35:7; Exod 20:26; Lev 18:6–19; 20:11, 17–21; Num 22:31; 24:4, 16; Deut 23:1; 27:20; 29:28; Judg 18:30; 1 Sam 2:27; 3:7, 21; 4:21–22; 9:15; 14:8, 11; 20:2, 12–13; 22:8, 17; 2 Sam 6:20; 7:27; 15:19; 22:16; 2 Kings 15:29; 16:9; 17:6, 11, 23, 26–28, 33; 18:11; 24:14–15; 25:11, 21; Isa 5:13; 16:3; 22:8, 14; 23:1; 24:11; 26:21; 38:12; 40:5; 47:2–3; 49:9, 21; 53:1; 56:1; 57:8; Jer 1:3; 11:20; 13:19, 22; 20:4, 12; 22:12; 24:1; 27:20; 29:1, 4, 7, 14; 32:11, 14; 33:6; 39:9; 40:1, 7; 43:3; 49:10; 52:15, 27–28, 30; Ezek 12:3; 13:14; 16:36–37, 57; 21:29; 22:10; 23:10, 18, 29; 39:23, 28; Hos 2:12; 7:1; 10:5; Amos 1:5–6; 3:7; 5:5, 27; 6:7; 7:11, 17; Mic 1:6, 16; Nah 2:8; 3:5; Ps 18:16; 98:2; 119:18; Job 12:22; 20:27–28; 33:16; 36:10, 15; 38:17; 41:5; Prov 11:13; 18:2; 20:19; 25:9; 26:26; 27:5, 25; Ruth 3:4, 7; 4:4; Lam 1:3; 2:14; 4:22; Esth 2:6; 3:14; 8:13; Dan 10:1; Ezra 2:1; Neh 7:6; 1 Chr 5:6, 26, 41; 8:6–7; 9:1; 17:25; 2 Chr 36:20).

so-called "synonyms" or in some cases not using גלה at all. For example, גלה is not found in the Pentateuch, whereas Ahn's so-called "synonyms" נדה (found eight times),[45] and פוץ (found in the covenant curses in Deut 4:27; 28:64; 30:3) are used instead. In fact, גלה is not found in the Old Testament until 2 Kings 15:29, when it is used of Tiglath-pileser exiling many Israelites to Assyria. The term is used frequently from this point on in the book to refer to the actions of Assyria and Babylon.[46] The book of Jeremiah uses גלה 19 times[47] but uses 18 נדה times.[48] Significantly, the exilic book of Ezekiel employs the root גלה only twice with this meaning (Ezek 39:23, 28),[49] while it uses the so-called synonym 18 פוץ times.[50]

Interestingly, of the eight "synonyms" of גלה that Ahn lists, he finds that five of them (כדר, בזר, זרה, פוץ and נפץ) have the meaning "to scatter."[51] To call these terms synonyms of גלה seems inaccurate and unhelpful at best. While גלה refers to the deportation or immigration to a specific place, scattering has connotations of a spreading out to different locations. In fact, many occurrences of these "scatter" words refer to the plural "nations" (גוים) as the destination for those scattered (as opposed to one nation—Babylon or Assyria).[52] Therefore, these "scatter" terms do not seem to fit best with

45. Deut 4:19; 13:6, 11, 14; 22:1; 30:1, 4, 17.

46. Second Kings 16:9; 17:6, 11, 23, 26, 27, 28, 33; 18:11; 24:15; 25:11, 21.

47. Jer 1:3; 13:19(2x); 20:4; 22:12; 24:1; 27:20; 29:1, 4, 7, 14; 39:9; 40:1, 7; 43:3; 52:15, 27, 28, 30.

48. Jer 8:3; 16:15; 23:2–3, 8; 24:9; 27:10, 15; 29:14, 18; 30:17; 32:37; 40:12; 43:5; 46:28; 49:5, 36; 50:17.

49. Contra Reimer's work on this ("Exile, Diaspora, and Old Testament Theology," 12), which claims that the occurrences of this word for exile are "split almost evenly between Jeremiah and Ezekiel." While the root is used frequently in Ezekiel (14 times) it almost always means "to expose" or "to uncover" (cf. Ezek 13:14; 21:24 [MT 21:29]) and is frequently used for the shaming exposure of nakedness (cf. Ezek16:36–37, 57; 22:10; 23:10, 18, 29; 39:23, 28) and only twice means "exile" (Ezek 39:23, 28).

50. Ezek 11:16–17; 12:15; 20:23, 34, 41; 22:15; 28:25; 29:12–13; 30:23, 26; 34:5–6, 12; 36:19.

51. Ahn, "Exile," 197. He defines פוץ as "scatter," החד as "be pushed," and נדה as "forced out." (For the latter term BDB notes the meaning of "dispersed"). For an exhaustive study of vocabulary relating to exile see the second chapter of Kiefer, *Exil und Diaspora*.

52. E.g., Jer 9:16, "I will scatter them among nations [בגוים]." Cf. Ezek 4:13; 6:8, 9; 11:16; 12:15; 20:23; 22:15; 29:12; 30:23, 26; 32:9; 36:19. Reimer ("Exile, Diaspora, and Old Testament Theology," 11) has drawn attention to the fact that in regard to the "scattering" language in the Old Testament "there is a pronounced bulge in the prophets of the period around the fall of Jerusalem, Jeremiah and Ezekiel. Between them they account for almost half of the 'scattering' language in the Hebrew Bible (47.5%)."

the unified exile to Babylon, but with the notion of diaspora. In fact, the lexical evidence as a whole would indicate that notions of diaspora are just as common as those of exile. While the unified "exile" did occur, threats and fears of "scattering" are widespread and in some ways more pervasive than those of exile.[53]

This brings us back to some of the questions about the exile posed earlier in this paper. Many of those exiled or scattered did not return, so how do we know when the exile is over? Perhaps this focus on "exile" has overlooked another important and prominent theme in the Old Testament, that of diaspora. Returning to the generational view of the exile, it must be remembered that many of the third generation of exiles did *not* return to the Promised Land but remained in the foreign land (e.g., Esther etc.). In these instances this generation cannot really be referred to as exiles at all. Instead these people represent those living in the diaspora.

Implications

The pervasive nature of "scattering" or "diaspora" language in the Old Testament calls for a reassessment of the tremendous attention that the exile has received in scholarship vis à vis the neglected theme of diaspora. Noting this imbalance, Reimer calls for "a deliberate nuance of the dominance of the 'exilic' period, and 'exile' as theological symbol" and asserts that the "importance of exile (both as history and symbol) has been overplayed, and that of diaspora undervalued."[54]

As noted above, the idea that "you can't go home" has become a part of modern consciousness. Common experience has shown that those who attempt to return home are often frustrated by the results. The returnees often suffer from reverse culture shock as they find that either they or the homeland has changed so significantly that it does not feel like home any longer. This reverse culture shock may reflect the experience of the third generation of Christian "exiles" (those living in the post-Christian West). Not surprisingly then, as we noted above, this third generation of "exiles" may have need of a new metaphor. Like the third generation of exiles in Babylon, many of whom never returned but instead became the diaspora, the new generation of Christians born into a postmodern secular pluralistic society may not resonate with a metaphor like "exile," which longs for a return to the way things were (as Brueggemann writes, to convert

53. Ibid., 14.
54. Ibid.

"exile into homecoming").[55] In my judgment this new generation might find the model of diaspora more useful and appropriate, given their social and cultural locations.

Exile has connotations of a forced existence away from home and of punishment; diaspora does not. Exile would seem to speak solely of judgment, but diaspora communicates both judgment and grace. What initially was punishment (exile) becomes a new creation (diaspora) where the faithful can serve. The new situation evinces God's grace and calling.[56]

It is important to remember that many in the diaspora chose to stay in the foreign land rather than return home. The situation was no longer a forced displacement or exile. While exile longs for a return to the way it was, diaspora can view its new situation as a divine calling. So the new generation of Christians may not wish to return to the Christians-at-the-center ideal that supposedly existed in the mid twentieth century. Instead, diaspora suggests a home in a foreign land where one is a true resident and can have influence. Perhaps the "exile" of the Western church from the centers of power was providential, what God intended. Perhaps going back is not an option. Turning "exile" into homecoming may involve remaining in the foreign land, as Jeremiah says: "Seek the *shalom* of the city to which I have carried you into exile. Pray to Yahweh for it, for its *shalom* will be your *shalom*" (Jer 29:7).

Recalling our insights into the different social issues that affected different generations of exiles, the third generation has issues regarding what constitutes *home*. What is home? To the first "exiles" this is an easy question with an obvious answer. To the third generation it is much more complex. Having been born and raised in the current post-Christian culture, it might be difficult for them to define home as something else. Those in the Jewish diaspora who chose to remain behind did maintain a distinct faith-identity (with the synagogue and their tight knit faith community), however, they were not exiles but residents in the land. As Reimer writes:

> Diaspora implies a different and more complex relationship between where-I-live, and where-I-belong . . . the model of "diaspora," which recognizes only a qualified belonging and articulates no sharp impulse to "return," seems to me a better metaphor for

---

55. Brueggemann, "Disciplines of Readiness," 9.

56. As Reimer, "Exile, Diaspora, and Old Testament Theology," 16, notes, "the roots of grace-in-judgment go down deep in the biblical witness."

Christian biblical theology than that of "exile," in which the desire for a "return home" remains urgent.[57]

We have previously referred to the different perspectives on the exile found in the Scriptures. Second Isaiah uses the metaphor of new creation in regards to the effect of the exile (Isaiah 40–48, 51:9–11).[58] Ahn suggests that this fits with the generational view of exile. He writes,

> They have the best of both worlds as Judeans and Babylonians; a new generation that has preserved that which was passed down, experiencing the fullness of monotheism, reflecting on oral and written traditions, and coming to an understanding that they are God's beloved and chosen in a vastly pluralistic Babylonian society.[59]

So the new generation of Christians born into the postmodern situation may have the best of both worlds. Drawing on the legitimate insights of postmodernism, while embracing the Scriptures and the truths passed down through the church, these Christians can be in the world but not of it (John 17:15–16).

Yet the model of diaspora should still caution against assimilation. Not all in the diaspora remained faithful. Not all maintained their faith. Similarly, the new generation of Christians faces temptations of assimilation and rootlessness. In diaspora studies today there is some debate about what the term "diaspora" means, but generally it has been defined as "communities with shared identities" like "language, religion, custom or folklore" who have "settled outside their natal (or imagined natal) territories" but they continue to "maintain some sort of loyalty and emotional links with 'the old country.'"[60] Without that shared identity, faith, and links with the past, one is no longer part of the diaspora. Diaspora Jews maintained their identity through their faith, their tight-knit community, synagogues, and commitment to the Scriptures. In this regard, the "diaspora" believer is behooved to remain rooted in the faith community, the traditions passed down, and God's Word. The diaspora model contains within it many of the same cautions, exhortations, and insights to Christian identity as those that have been brought to the fore through theological reflection on the model

---

57. Ibid., 17.

58. Second Isaiah's use of creation imagery is widely recognized as "one of the most salient features" of the book (Blenkinsopp, *Isaiah 40–55*, 107). Cf. Haran, "Literary Structure," 134; von Rad, *Old Testament Theology*, 1:137; Westermann, *Isaiah 40–66*, 25.

59. Ahn, *Exile as Forced Migrations*, 5.

60. Rubesh, "Diaspora Distinctives," 114. Cf. Cohen, *Global Diasporas*, ix.

of exile. However, diaspora may prove a more appropriate model for new generations who are rethinking the nature of the "exile" of the de-centered church and whether a return "home" is justifiable.

CONCLUSION

Brueggemann's provocative suggestions and observations have led us to this point. As he writes:

> [P]ondering this metaphor helps us think again about a rich variety of metaphors in Scripture that can function as a kaleidoscope, to let us see our life and faith in various dimensions. Such an exercise may move us past a single, frozen metaphor which we take as a permanent given.[61]

While Brueggemann doubtless wrote to counter the hegemony of the application of biblical metaphors representing the triumphant church (as mentioned above), today, twenty years after he wrote these words, the "single, frozen metaphor" could also be exile. While exile may still be an appropriate metaphor in some circumstances, this paper has suggested that diaspora may be a more appropriate model for the de-centered church in the twenty-first century.

This is not to say that diaspora is the ultimate ideal. The metaphor of diaspora reminds us we are not *truly* home. We belong, but it is a qualified belonging. In many respects we are still "aliens and strangers on earth" (Heb 11:13). Ultimately, the expression "you can't go home" that has become a hallmark of modern consciousness is *not* true. Unlike exiles who long to return to the way it was, we are looking forward to a new home. As the writer of Hebrews notes: "If they had been thinking of the country they had left, they would have had opportunity to return. Instead, they were longing for a better country—a heavenly one" (Heb 11:15–16). We all as one body await our bridegroom to be revealed, that one day we may all live together in the heavenly Jerusalem and hear the words "Now the dwelling of God is with people, and he will live with them. They will be his people, and God himself will be with them and be their God." (Rev 21:3).

BIBLIOGRAPHY

Ahn, John J. "Exile." In *Dictionary of the Old Testament: Prophets*, edited by Mark J. Boda and J. Gordon McConville, 196–204. Downers Grove, IL: IVP Academic, 2012.

---

61. Brueggemann, "Preaching to Exiles," 12.

———. *Exile as Forced Migrations: A Sociological, Literary, and Theological Approach on the Displacement and Resettlement of the Southern Kingdom of Judah*. BZAW 417. Berlin: de Gruyter, 2011.

Albertz, Rainer. *Israel in Exile: The History and Literature of the Sixth Century B.C.E.* Atlanta: SBL, 2003.

Barstad, Hans M. *The Myth of the Empty Land: A Study in the History and Archaeology of Judah during the "Exilic" Period*. Symbolae Osloenses. Oslo: Scandinavian University Press, 1996.

Blenkinsopp, Joseph. *Isaiah 40–55*. AB 19A. New York: Doubleday, 2002.

Brueggemann, Walter. *Cadences of Home: Preaching among Exiles*. Louisville, KY: Westminster John Knox, 1997.

——— "Disciplines of Readiness." In *Occasional Paper No. 1*, 1–25. Louisville, KY: Presbyterian Church (USA), 1989.

———. "Preaching to Exiles." *Journal for Preachers* 16, no. 4 (1993) 3–15.

———. "Rethinking Church Models through Scripture." *Theology Today* 48, no. 2 (1991) 128–38.

———. *Theology of the Old Testament: Testimony, Dispute, Advocacy*. Minneapolis: Fortress, 1997.

Carroll, Robert P. "Exile! What Exile? Deportation and the Discourses of Diaspora." In *Leading Captivity Captive*, edited by Lester L. Grabbe, 62–79. Sheffield: Sheffield Academic, 1998.

——— "The Myth of the Empty Land." *Semeia* 59 (1992) 79–93.

Cohen, Robin. *Global Diasporas: An Introduction*. Seattle: University of Washington Press, 1997.

Haran, Menahem. "The Literary Structure and Chronological Framework of the Prophecies in Is. XL–XLVIII." In *Congress Volume: Bonn, 1962*, 127–53. VTSup 9. Leiden: Brill, 1963.

Hauerwas, Stanley, and William H. Willimon. *Resident Aliens: A Provocative Christian Assessment of Culture and Ministry for People Who Know that Something Is Wrong*. Nashville: Abingdon, 1989.

Kiefer, Jörn. *Exil und Diaspora: Begrifflichkeit und Deutungen im antiken Judentum und in der hebräischen Bibel*. Arbeiten aur Bibel und ihrer Geschichte. Leipzig: Evangelische Verlagsanstalt, 2005.

Klein, Ralph W. *Israel in Exile: A Theological Interpretation*. Overtures to Biblical Theology. Philadelphia: Fortress, 1979.

Matt, Susan J. "You Can't Go Home Again: Homesickness and Nostalgia in U.S. History." *The Journal of American History* 92 (2007) 469–97.

Radner, Ephraim. "From Liberation to Exile: A New Image for Church Mission." *Christian Century* 30, no. 18 (1989) 931–34.

Reimer, David J. "Exile, Diaspora, and Old Testament Theology." *Scottish Bulletin of Evangelical Theology* 28, no. 1 (2010) 3–17.

Rubesh, Ted. "Diaspora Distinctives: The Jewish Diaspora Experience in the Old Testament." *Torch Trinity Journal* 13, no. 2 (2010) 114–36.

Sanders, James A. "Exile." In *The Interpreter's Dictionary of the Bible*, edited by Keith R. Crim, 1:188. Nashville: Abingdon, 1976.

Suleiman, Susan Rubin, ed. *Exile and Creativity: Signposts, Travelers, Outsiders, Backward Glances*. Durham, NC: Duke University Press, 1996.

von Rad, Gerhard. *Old Testament Theology*. Trans. D. M. G. Stalker. 2 vols. New York: Harper & Row, 1962.
Westermann, Claus. *Isaiah 40-66: A Commentary*. The Old Testament Library. Philadelphia: Westminster John Knox, 1969.
Wolfe, Thomas. *You Can't Go Home Again*. New York: Harper, 1940.
Wright, N. T. *Jesus and the Victory of God*. Minneapolis: Fortress, 1996.
———. *The New Testament and the People of God*. Minneapolis: Fortress, 1992.
———. "Theology, History and Jesus: A Response to Maurice Casey and Clive Marsh." *JSNT* 69 (1998) 105–12.

3

Identity and Identification in Israel's Diaspora
Socio-Cultural and Biblical Perspectives
A Response to Mark J. Boda and Paul S. Evans

GORDON K. OESTE

WHETHER BY DESIGN OR happy accident, Boda's and Evans's papers are quite complementary, as both papers use developmental, socio-cultural approaches to understanding diaspora, both emphasize the diversity of Old Testament understandings of exile and diaspora, and both see that diversity as a helpful resource for the church. They even answer each other's questions: when Boda asks how long it takes for a diaspora consciousness to develop (p. 4), Evans answers: up to three generations (p. 32).

One of the things I found helpful in Boda's analysis was his combination of Cohen's socio-cultural model with a synchronic-canonical approach, though a diachronic reading would almost certainly yield different results.[1] This approach allows him to trace developments and perspectives on diaspora life reflected in Daniel, Ezra-Nehemiah, and Esther, though the tenor of these perspectives would change significantly if the

---

1. While the book of Daniel is set during the exilic and early post-exilic period, some have located the composition of the book in the sixth century BCE, shortly after the time-period of the book's setting (Longman, *Daniel*, 22–24; Lucas, *Daniel*, 313–15). Others, however, situate Daniel 1–6 in the third century BCE or earlier, and Daniel 7–12 in the first third of the second century (Towner, *Daniel*, 5–6). Collins, *Daniel*, 24–38, sees five stages in the composition of the book, three of which precede the second century. The compositions of the books of Ezra-Nehemiah and Esther are generally dated to the fourth or third centuries (e.g., Williamson, *Ezra-Nehemiah*, xxxvi; Levinson, *Esther*, 26).

book of Esther reflects homeland satire of life in exile instead of a positive diaspora perspective.[2]

Boda's synchronic-canonical approach allows him to spotlight some of the differing perspectives that appear in the exilic- and post-exilic diaspora, like a decreasing emphasis upon the retention of Jewish names, increasing assimilation of Persian mores, and a persistently hostile host culture that is both "a place of troubled relationship and a place of creative, enriching life" (p. 21). One of the places where we might expand (and so modify) Boda's observations is in regard to Cohen's seventh characteristic feature of diasporas—a troubled relationship with exilic hostlands—noting particularly the role that threat plays in shaping diasporic Jewish identity.

Boda notes that each of the diaspora narratives portrays a balanced portrait of life under foreign rule, where threats to the Diaspora community are balanced by opportunities for growth and advancement (p. 22). As Boda indicates, in Ezra-Nehemiah, the Persian administration is portrayed as largely sympathetic to Jewish concerns and there is far greater danger to the community *after* returning to the homeland than while in exile.[3] Yet danger may even arise while transitioning from Persian exile to the Jewish homeland, though Ezra and Nehemiah utilize different strategies for handling this peril. While Nehemiah is happy to allow the king's soldiers and horsemen to accompany his troupe (Neh 2:9), Ezra, while transporting the gold and silver riches from the temple, refuses to request soldiers and horsemen for protection "from the enemy" (Ezra 8:22), and uses the opportunity to draw attention to God's provision for those who trust him (Ezra 8:23), reinforcing reliance upon the God of Israel instead of the power of the empire.

In Daniel, threats from the host culture eventually serve not only to advance the career track of Daniel and his three friends (taking Daniel to virtually the pinnacle of the empire by the end of his life [Dan 6:3, 28]),[4]

---

2. See for example Stern, "Esther and the Politics of Diaspora."

3. These dangers include: physical threats (Neh 4:21–23), psychological threats (Neh 6:5–9), false accusations (Ezra 4:12–16), character defamation (Neh 2:19), and threats of robbery (Ezra 9:22), among others.

4. Daniel, Hananiah, Mishael, and Azariah enter the king's service (Dan 1:19–20) after refusing to defile themselves (1:8); Daniel is placed in a high position after interpreting the king's dream (2:48); the three friends are promoted after refusing to bow to the king's image (3:30); Daniel is promoted to the rank of third highest in the kingdom after interpreting the writing on the wall (5:29); Daniel serves as one of three administrators over all the satrapies of the Persian kingdom (6:2), but so distinguishes himself that the king is ready to set Daniel over the entire kingdom (6:3). His competitors attempt to

but also serve as opportunities to reinforce Jewish identity, distinguishing Daniel and his three friends from their peers (Dan 1:12–19) and from pagan idolaters (Dan 3:14–18), and showing them as determined to pray only to their God (6:10). Daniel's God-given ability to interpret the king's dream not only spares the lives of Daniel and his three friends, but results in Daniel's model prayer of thanksgiving to God (Dan 2:20–23) and the king's exaltation of Daniel's God as "God of gods and Lord of lords" (Dan 2:47; cf. 3:28–29; 4:34b–35; 6:26–27).

In Esther, in the aftermath of the neutralization of the threat of annihilation, not only does Mordecai rise to second in rank to the king (10:3), but the deliverance is memorialized in the annual celebration of Purim, a festival promoting Jewish identity by commemorating the community-wide response to Haman's attempt to annihilate "all the Jews" (Esth 3:6, 13; 9:20, 24) in the Diaspora, pitting the Jews against all other opponents (Esth 8:11, 13; 9:1, 5, 16, 22). Diaspora communities need, at times, to be mobilized in the formation of group-identity.[5] The threats to Jewish life and existence in exile become key mobilizing "events" that serve as defining moments of individual and collective Jewish identity, though the diasporic narratives show that there are a variety of ways to handle these dangers.

One of the areas where Boda's appropriation of Cohen's characteristics of diasporic communities may be in need of some minor amendment is in relation to Cohen's sixth characteristic of sustained group consciousness. Kinship affiliation in the ancient Near East and in biblical post-exilic narratives played a key role in developing and maintaining a strong sense of group consciousness and the formation of group identity. Boda rightly notes that there is a group consciousness that develops among Daniel and his three friends, but then goes on to state that "there is no sense, however, of the broader community" (p. 21). However, an examination of kinship terminology reflects some recognition of the larger community by both Daniel and others.[6] Daniel, Hananiah, Mishael, and Azariah are not identified by a patronymic, but by their relationship to the Babylonian administration

---

end Daniel's life by having him thrown into the lion's den, but after his divine deliverance, Daniel continues to prosper in the Persian Empire (6:28).

5. Cohen, *Global Diasporas*, 15.

6. Israelite conceptions of kinship affiliation viewed the entire nation as a series of nested households extended from the individual household through to a national level of affiliation as the people of Israel (עם ישראל) (King and Stager, "Of Fathers, Kings and the Deity," 42–45, 62).

(Dan 1:3–7), which is atypical in Old Testament narrative,[7] but typical of the named individuals in the book of Daniel.[8] However, the four men are introduced as "sons of Israel" (1:3) and "sons of Judah" (1:6), and Daniel self-identifies with "my people, Israel" in his prayer of confession (9:20; cf. 9:7, 11). Moreover, three different Babylonian characters view Daniel as one of the exiles "from Judah" (Dan 2:25; 5:13; 6:13), identifying him with larger, "national" kinship structures. This seems to indicate an increasing national and tribal consciousness coupled with diminishing ties to more local sources of identity like the household (בית אב) and clan (משפחה), levels of Jewish society most closely tied to the land.[9]

On the other hand, the use of kinship terminology in Ezra-Nehemiah reflects a strong sense of group consciousness, as seen for example by the references to the community as the people of Israel (עם ישראל)[10] or the sons of Israel (בני ישראל),[11] reflecting an ideal of national-level kinship bonds among the returnees.[12] However, Ezra-Nehemiah also sees the development of a new social structure that the returnees brought with them from exile, the "fathers' house" (בית אבות), which seems to have taken the place of the clan (משפחה) in some cases.[13] The fathers' house seems to be an outgrowth

---

7. Anderson, "Israelite Kinship Terminology," 29–31.

8. Jehoiakim, King of Judah (Dan 1:1); Nebuchadnezzar, king of Babylon (1:1); Ashpenaz, chief of the royal officials (1:3); Arioch, commander of the king's guard (2:14); Belshazzar the king (5:1; 8:1) or Belshazzar, king of Babylon (7:1); Darius the Mede (5:31; 11:1) or Darius the king (6:6, 25); Gabriel the man (9:21; cf. 8:16 where he is introduced simply as Gabriel); Jeremiah the prophet (9:2); Cyrus, king of Persia (10:1) or the Persian (6:28); Michael, one of the chief princes (10:13) or "your prince" (10:21). The exception is Darius the son of Ahasuerus, but he is also identified positionally by "from the seed of the Medes" and "was made king over the kingdom of the Chaldeans" (9:1). Belshazzar is described in relation to Nebuchadnezzar as "his father" (5:2), "your father" (5:11, 18), and "my father" (5:13), but not using a patronymic.

9. Block, "Marriage and Family," 37–38. Vanderhooft, "The Israelite משפחה, the Priestly Writings and Changing Valences," 490–91, similarly notes how the משפחה lost its concrete connection to the spatial dimensions of Israel's earlier kinship organization in the Persian period.

10. Ezra 2:2; Neh 7:7.

11. Ezra 6:16, 21; Neh 1:6; 8:14, 17; 9:1; 10:40; 13:2.

12. Cf. King and Stager, "Of Fathers, Kings and the Deity," 45. Significantly, "Israel" only occurs four times in Daniel (Dan 1:3; 9:7, 11, 20) and not at all in Esther, but occurs 51 times in Ezra-Nehemiah, while "Judah" only occurs once in Esther (Esth 2:6 in relation to Jehoiachin, king of Judah) and four times in Daniel (Dan 1:1, 2, 6; 9:7), but occurs 41 times in Ezra-Nehemiah.

13. Collins, "Marriage, Divorce, and Family," 105. Similarly, Levine, "Clan-Based

of the concept of the father's house (בית אב), expanding the extended family represented by the traditional father's house.[14] The fathers' house became a way of preserving a sense of communal identity in exile and developed into a marker of authentic Jewish identity for those returning from exile (Ezra 2:59).[15] At the same time, a national consciousness as the people of Israel still served as a key orienting principle for Ezra-Nehemiah,[16] evidenced by the offering of twelve males goats "for the number of the tribes of Israel" (Ezra 6:17; cf. 8:35) at the celebratory dedication of the house of God.

In the book of Esther, Esther and Mordecai's kin are never identified as the people of Israel,[17] but by the exilic and post-exilic gentilic, "Jews."[18] Boda has already noted Mordecai's three-generation Benjaminite lineage and his battle for survival with Haman the Agagite, reprising Saul's battle with the Amalekite king Agag (1 Samuel 15) and Israel's ancient blood-feud with the Amalekites (Exod 17:14; Deut 25:17–19). Not only can homeland identity not be ignored (Boda, p. 10), but it inextricably links diaspora identity to homeland identity, even for those who may attempt to hide it (Esth 4:14), yet orienting that identity not to the father's house, clan, or even the tribal levels of affiliation, but towards an ethnic-group consciousness that finds its origin and expression outside of the homeland (Esth 9:27–28). Consequently, identity in the Diaspora is still tied to kinship, but exigencies of diaspora existence form new ways of understanding and ramifying that identity.

Economy," 451–53, notes the fragmentation of the clan in the post-exilic period.

14. Collins, "Marriage, Divorce, and Family," 105, suggests the בית אבות encompassed from 800 to 1000 people. Weinberg, "*Beit 'Abot*," 410–13, holds that the post-exilic בית אבות grew out of splinters of pre-exilic family and/or clan structures.

15. Williamson, "Family in Persian Period Judah," 477–78. Knoppers, "Ethnicity, Genealogy, Geography, and Change," 162, notes how identification with the house of the fathers ties together various waves of returnees from exile.

16. Ezra 2:2, 59; 3:11; 4:3; 6:16, 17; 7:10, 11, 28; 8:25, 29, 35; 9:1; 10:2, 5; Neh 1:6; 7:7, 67; 10:33, 39; 12:47; 13:3, 18; cf. 13:26 in reference to the days of Solomon.

17. "The people of Israel" reflects a kinship ideology above that of the tribal level. Cf. Cross, *From Epic to Canon*, 12–13.

18. Esther uses the term "Jew" 58 times (about 63 percent of all occurrences in the Hebrew Bible), while the term is used 19 times in Ezra-Nehemiah and only twice in Daniel (3:8, 12), where it primarily reflects the perspective of the Babylonians towards Daniel and his people. The term in Ezra-Nehemiah serves chiefly to designate Israel from a Persian perspective, but also becomes a self-designation in the first person sections of the book (e.g., Neh 1:2; 2:16; 4:12; 5:1, 8, 17).

One of the stimulating contributions that Evans makes to these discussions is his explanation of why the term "diaspora" may be both a helpful way of understanding some biblical texts and also a more fruitful metaphor for the modern Western church as it considers its relationship to the broader culture. Evans gives at least four reasons why the metaphor of "exile" is inadequate. First, exile is difficult to define, particularly the question of when exile ends (p. 32). Second, the biblical text itself records very different reactions to exile (e.g., Ezek 12:1–15; cf. Ezek 36:24–28 [pp. 33–35]). Third, utilizing the work of Ahn, Evans highlights how the biblical texts themselves reflect a "generational consciousness" highlighting the different perspectives, issues, and questions related to successive generations of exiles (pp. 35–38). Fourth, while the biblical text reflects a significant linguistic emphasis upon exile, a closer examination of the lexical field reveals a concomitant emphasis upon scattering, so that the term "diaspora" better reflects the more rounded terminology found in the Hebrew Bible (pp. 41–42). And so, by implication, diaspora serves as a more fruitful metaphor with which the Western church may identify.

However, I am not quite ready to set aside the metaphor of exile, in part because of the expectation in the Hebrew Bible of return to the homeland for *every* exilic "generation." Evans asks, "Who says you can't go home?" and notes that the defining question for third generation exiles centers around the definition of home and the need or desire to return to their grandparents' natal homeland (pp. 39, 43). While the reality of this issue may be reflected by the many Jews who remained in exile,[19] the biblical texts addressing each successive exilic generation reflect a consistent hope, and even expectation, of return.

Ezekiel and Jeremiah address the first generation of exiles. Even in the midst of dire warnings of impending judgment and exile, Ezekiel can still tell Israel that Yahweh "will gather you from the peoples and assemble you from the lands where you have been scattered" (Ezek 11:17; cf. 16:51–63; 20:30–44)[20] and Jeremiah similarly addresses the exiles going to Egypt say-

---

19. The fact that many chose to define "home" apart from the Jewish homeland is reflected in the biblical texts in the successive waves of returnees described in Ezra-Nehemiah and in Ezra's need to recruit and convince an adequate number of Levites to return with him to Jerusalem (Ezra 8:15–20). This may have been in order to comport with the Exodus narratives (so Williamson, *Ezra-Nehemiah*, 116), but it is just as likely that they struggled to find Levites willing to leave Persia for Jerusalem.

20. Schwartz, "Ezekiel's Dim View of Israel's Restoration," 52, notes that this passage and others like it cannot be dismissed as merely redactional on literary grounds, even

ing[21] that Yahweh "will save you from far away and your offspring from the land of their captivity" (Jer 30:10–11; 46:27–28; cf. 50:18–20). So, not surprisingly, both prophets emphasize the hope and expectation of return for the first generation of exiles.

Jeremiah 29, which addresses the children and teenagers (or the 1.5 generation) carried to Babylon, promises to give the captives a hope and a future by holding out the expectation of return after seventy years (Jer 29:10–14; cf. 25:11–12; 2 Chr 36:21; Dan 9:2; Zech 1:12; 7:5). Similarly Isa 43:4–7, in a passage that Evans connects with the second generation of exiles that have grown up in exile (p. 38), describes how Yahweh, who has already announced his planned return to Jerusalem (Isa 40:1–5), also promises those in Babylon that he will bring their offspring from all four points of the compass to himself out of exile.

Maybe most surprisingly, the same hope of return is held out for the third exilic generation that has been most thoroughly exposed to the hostland culture, religion, and values. Isaiah 49 attempts to persuade this generation wrestling with orientation towards home that Yahweh will say "to the captives, come out, to those who are in darkness, show yourselves," using language reminiscent of Yahweh's own return to Jerusalem to describe the return of the exiles from all points of the compass (Isa 49:8–12).[22] This is powerful rhetoric attempting to convince those liable not to return. The hope of return even extends well into the post-exilic period (cf. 2 Chr 36:22–23) to the time of Ezra and Nehemiah (Neh 1:8–9), so that when members of the third (and following) exilic generation might ask, "Who says you can't go home?" the voices of the prophets chime in to advocate for a return to the homeland.[23] Thus, while each generation faces different issues and questions, they *each* are addressed by the prophetic expectation and hope that they will return to their ancestral homeland. Each must

though it is situated among the oracles from before the fall of Jerusalem.

21. Lundblom, *Jeremiah 21–36*, 229.

22. Blenkinsopp, *Isaiah 40–55*, 306. Baltzer, *Deutero-Isaiah*, 316, connects this passage to the time of Nehemiah (Neh 5:1–13), holding that the exile's lands are not devastated and the exiles are not in chains in Babylon, though the allotment of patrimonial lands (49:8) is not easily connected to this period and the language here is poetic hyperbole (cf. Isa 49:11).

23. The book of Daniel does not explicitly describe a return from exile, but Daniel 6:10 orients the exiles to Jerusalem and the visions of Daniel 7–12 presume restored life in Jerusalem and the temple (Dan 11:31; 12:11), so that while not explicitly expecting a return, the book of Daniel at the very least orients diaspora life and concern towards Jerusalem.

decide its relationship to the homeland, whether exile becomes diaspora and whether hostland becomes home. Each generation must also make its peace with the expectation of return.

Therefore, it seems to me that both exile and diaspora can serve as helpful metaphors for different church communities as they reflect upon the nature of their relationship with the culture in which they are situated. However, there are other images that the church may also draw upon as it seeks biblical resources for relating to its larger cultural context. For example, the biblical prophets provide models of interaction with Israel's social, cultural, and political institutions from both positions of influence deeply embedded within central institutions (e.g., Nathan, Isaiah) and from the periphery of those institutions (e.g., Amos, Elijah).[24]

In this light, Evans's emphasis upon the metaphor of diaspora, and particularly his use of Ahn's generational model, can provide very helpful theological resources for pastors and church leaders in the Western church as they endeavor to minister to different generations with different experiences and expectations of the church's relationship to its surrounding culture(s). The metaphors of exile and diaspora can also be very helpful for the North American church as it seeks to minister in multi-cultural, multi-ethnic settings, where church and community members may be in various generations of "dispersion" from their own physical and spiritual homelands.[25] Additionally, if home is understood in terms of the forging of a new identity marked by the adaptation of homeland forms and traditions to new, diaspora realities as they take shape, this may provide the church with a body of resources to meet the ever-changing demands of life in spiritual diaspora.

BIBLIOGRAPHY

Anderson, Francis I. "Israelite Kinship Terminology and Social Structure." *The Bible Translator* 20 (1969) 29–39.

Baltzer, Klaus. *Deutero-Isaiah*. Hermeneia. Philadelphia: Fortress, 2001.

Bibby, Reginald W. *A New Day: The Resilience and Restructuring of Religion in Canada*. Lethbridge: Project Canada Books, 2012. Online: http://projectcanadabooks.com/images/A_NEW_DAY_Sept_12_2012.pdf.

Blenkinsopp, Joseph. *Isaiah 40–55*. AB. New York: Doubleday, 2002.

---

24. See Wilson, *Prophecy and Society*, 69–88, for a summary of the social role of central and peripheral intermediation.

25. This will also be impacted by regional differences, where regions will experience greater and lesser degrees of the "de-centering" of the church. See for example Bibby, *New Day*, 15.

Block, Daniel I. "Marriage and Family in Ancient Israel." In *Marriage and Family in the Biblical World*, edited by Ken M. Campbell, 33–102. Downers Grove, IL: InterVarsity, 2003.

Cohen, R. *Global Diasporas: An Introduction*. 2nd ed. New York: Routledge, 2008.

Collins, John J. *Daniel*. Hermeneia. Philadelphia: Fortress, 1993.

———. "Marriage, Divorce, and Family in Second Temple Judaism." In *Families in Ancient Israel*, edited by Leo G. Perdue et al., 104–62. Louisville, KY: Westminster John Knox, 1997.

Cross, Frank Moore. *From Epic to Canon*. Baltimore: The Johns Hopkins University Press, 1998.

King, Philip J., and Lawrence E. Stager. "Of Fathers, Kings and the Deity: The Nested Households of Ancient Israel." *Biblical Archaeology Review* 28, no. 2 (2002) 42–45, 62.

Knoppers, Gary N. "Ethnicity, Genealogy, Geography, and Change: The Judean Communities of Babylon and Jerusalem in the Story of Ezra." In *Community Identity in Judean Historiography: Biblical and Comparative Perspectives*, edited by Gary N. Knoppers and Kenneth A. Ristau, 147–71. Winona Lake, IN: Eisenbrauns, 2009.

Levine, Baruch A. "The Clan-Based Economy of Biblical Israel." In *Symbiosis, Symbolism, and the Power of the Past: Canaan, Ancient Israel and Their Neighbors from the Late Bronze Age through Roman Palestina*, edited by W. G. Dever and S. Gitin, 445–53. Winona Lake, IN: Eisenbrauns, 2003.

Levinson, Jon D. *Esther*. Old Testament Library. Louisville, KY: Westminster John Knox, 1997.

Longman, Tremper, III. *Daniel*. NIV Application Commentary. Grand Rapids: Zondervan, 1999.

Lucas, Ernest C. *Daniel*. Apollos Old Testament Commentary. Downers Grove, IL: InterVarsity, 2002.

Lundblom, Jack. *Jeremiah 21–36*. AB. New York: Doubleday, 2004.

Schwartz, Baruch J. "Ezekiel's Dim View of Israel's Restoration." In *The Book of Ezekiel: Theological and Anthropological Perspectives*, edited by Margaret S. Odell and John T. Strong, 43–67. SBLSymS 9. Atlanta: SBL, 2000.

Stern, Elsie R. "Esther and the Politics of Diaspora." *Jewish Quarterly Review* 100 (2010) 25–53.

Towner, W. Sibley. *Daniel*. Interpretation. Atlanta: John Knox, 1984.

Vanderhooft, David S. "The Israelite, the Priestly Writings, and Changing Valences in Israel's Kinship Terminology." In *Exploring the Longue Durée: Essays in Honor of Lawrence E. Strager*, edited by J. David Schloen, 485–96. Winona Lake, IN: Eisenbrauns, 2009.

Weinberg, Joel P. "Das Beit 'Abot im 6.–4. Jh. v. u. Z." *VT* 23 (1973) 400–14.

Williamson, H. G. M. *Ezra-Nehemiah*. WBC 16. Waco, TX: Word, 1985.

———. "The Family in Persian Period Judah: Some Textual Reflections." In *Symbiosis, Symbolism, and the Power of the Past: Canaan, Ancient Israel and Their Neighbors from the Late Bronze Age through Roman Palestina*, edited by William G. Dever and S. Gitin, 469–85. Winona Lake, IN: Eisenbrauns, 2003.

Wilson, Robert R. *Prophecy and Society in Ancient Israel*. Philadelphia: Fortress, 1980.

4

Coping with Alienating Experience
Four Strategies from the Second Temple Period

LOREN T. STUCKENBRUCK

INTRODUCTION

A LARGE BODY OF writings from the Second Temple period—they are often though not exclusively "apocalyptic" in worldview—are thought to have been composed in order to address a crisis, whether real or perceived. In such writings authors were attempting, both for themselves and, presumably, for their respective communities, to come to terms with a world in which circumstances are not what they "ought" to be, or are at least acknowledged to be less than ideal.

In recent years we have been learning a great deal about religious attitudes among Jews living in the Diaspora, mostly through literature composed in Greek in the eastern Mediterranean world.[1] In addition, from a body of literature composed in Aramaic and (mostly) Hebrew, such as texts recovered from the Dead Sea, we have become acquainted with not only spatial but also metaphorical notions of "exile" arising from a real or

---

1. See Barclay, *Jews in the Mediterranean Diaspora*, and the recent study of Tuval, "Doing without the Temple." Cf. further Gafni, *Land, Center, and Diaspora*; Gruen, *Diaspora*; the essays collected in Barclay, *Negotiating Diaspora*. While Barclay's study of a large body of literature is organized around a sociological approach, Tuval deals with, in addition to the works of Philo and Josephus, the following writings: 2 *Enoch, Prayer of Joseph, Ezekiel the Tragedian, Testament of Abraham,* Stephen's speech in Acts 2, *Sibylline Oracles* 1–5, *Pseudo-Phocylides, Testament of Job,* 2 Maccabees, 3 Maccabees, *4 Maccabees,* Wisdom of Solomon, *Hellenistic Synagogal Prayers, Joseph and Aseneth,* and *Letter of Aristeas.*

Rejection

profound sense of remoteness from the center of Jewish life in Jerusalem.[2] Certainly the geographical and metaphorical issues of diaspora and exile continue to merit discussion. Identified in this way, however, these issues have sometimes not offered a basis for considering a more fundamental question: what it would have meant for some Diaspora Jews to understand themselves as living at a distance from Jerusalem and what this meant for an attempt to remain religiously loyal, on the one side, and to live in tension with the dominant socio-religious and political context, on the other. Indeed, a sense of "rejection" or "alienation" would have been especially acute in some apocalyptic and related texts, whatever their geographical distance or proximity to Jerusalem and the temple cult may have been. In an effort to focus on this dimension of experience, the present discussion will focus on several works originally composed in Aramaic or Hebrew that, together, offer a series of alternatives some pious Jews devised in order to address and cope with apparently overwhelming challenges. These works are (a) the Book of Watchers (1 *Enoch* chs. 1–36); (b) the Book of Tobit; (c) the Epistle of Enoch (1 *Enoch* 92; 93:11—105:2); and (d) *4 Ezra*. While the historical circumstances behind these works varied, it should be remembered that the ideas they espoused were not merely intended as a by-product or function of the external circumstances that initially inspired them. The writers of these (and other) documents believed they had something to say of import that extended beyond their social boundaries; they set before their immediate audiences and, potentially, others beyond them, a larger theological *worldview* that could put the problems they encountered into perspective. In broader terms, the writers of these texts designed their ideas in such a way as to make "the way the God of Israel sees things" less elusive for their audiences than before. The fissures between themselves, the broader Gentile culture, and other Jews they deemed unfaithful gave rise to several kinds of answers and perspectives that sought to reconcile God's purposes with (a) oppression from the dominant socio-political system, (b) remoteness from one's homeland and, with it, from participation in the defining religious institutions, and (c) removal from core values of the sacred tradition. By looking at these different models, we encounter people who struggled with the charge, whether potential or real, that their bleak circumstances were the result of rejection by or alienation from God.

---

2. See Hacham, "Exile and Self-Identity," who offers insightful comparisons between Greek writings of the Diaspora and the Dead Sea texts. On the community associated with Qumran itself, see further Dimant, "Not Exile in the Desert."

THE BOOK OF WATCHERS:
THE PRAYER OF COMPLAINT IN 1 ENOCH 9:4-11

Though the Enochic Book of Watchers, in its present form (*1 Enoch* 1–36), goes back to at least the latter part of the third century BCE, its oldest section, found in *1 Enoch* 6–11, can be dated to perhaps as early as the late fourth century.³ It is well known that this section, which took shape before being integrated into traditions associated with the patriarch Enoch (*1 Enoch* 1–5; 12–16; 17–19; 21–36), offers a narrative relating to events prior to the time of the Great Flood. As such, these chapters preserve a core myth around which much of the emerging Enoch tradition would be organized. This does not mean, however, that the additional traditions, beginning with *1 Enoch* 12–16, simply expanded the content of chs. 6–11 on the latter's own terms; whereas chs. 6–11 make no mention of Enoch and refer briefly to the figure of Noah (10:1–3), chs. 12–16 give Enoch considerable prominence while no mention is made of Noah. In addition, whereas the earlier traditions comprising chs. 6–11 articulate several basic themes that would play a role in compositions that would subsequently be added to *1 Enoch*, the inclusion of "Enoch" within the follow-up narrative indicates a shift in the initial phase of reception. With this in mind and without dealing with the Book of Watchers as a whole, the following comments will focus on the two units in *1 Enoch* 6–11 and 12–16.

With the question of "rejection" in view, what is one to make of the narrative about the rebellious angels in *1 Enoch* 6–11? To filter the text through this question illustrates something of the diverse ways in which rejection (here applied as an etic category of thought) could be understood. The text, especially of the tradition associated with rebellious angel Asael, would have left its intended readers and hearers to understand that their values were being threatened by the introduction of objectionable practices. The skills introduced by the rebellious angels, recounted in *1 Enoch* 7:1 and 8:3, fall into three main categories: (1) weaponry; (2) beautification techniques (including the fashioning of jewelry and decorative treatments for the eyes); and (3) medico-magical arts (including the application of

---

3. Scholarly attempts to date the work have varied, depending to some extent on whether or not *1 Enoch* 6–11 is thought to be an interpretation of Genesis 6–9 or, alternatively, contains tradition that Genesis (esp. 6:1–4) presupposes. For the latter view, see Milik, *Books of Enoch*, who in this respect is followed by Davies, Review of *The Origin of Evil Spirits*, and Reeves, "Manichaeans." 264. In any case, a later date, i.e., just before or in the middle of the second century BCE, is highly unlikely, on grounds of the manuscript evidence (esp. 4Q201); cf. Stuckenbruck, "Early Traditions Related to *1 Enoch*," 44–47.

herbs, astrology, incantations, and the casting and loosing of spells). The early transmitters and recipients of this tradition were confronted by a dominant culture, an overwhelming force that was dictating how people should live; this cultural program is deemed in the text as being contrary to God's design for the created order. The wayward angels have not simply introduced bad practices or conducted themselves inappropriately; the text presents them as having fundamentally and irretrievably departed from the order with which creation was endowed. In effect, they have violated creation itself, both through their cultural program and through the activities of their giant-sized offspring, who, according to the text, engaged in the destruction of animated life created by God (1 En 7:3–4: birds, land animals, fish, people; the text may allude to Gen 1:11–13, 20–22, 24–30 and Ps 146:6).

George Nickelsburg is perhaps correct to posit behind the reprehensible teachings of the fallen angels expressions of culture associated with the socio-political might in the Levant wielded by the successors of Alexander the Great.[4] In order to put up resistance to this unwanted, culturally progressive incursion into a Jewish setting, the text attempts to unmask its character as "demonic, monstrous, violent, destructive, or rapacious," to underscore its "transience," and to assert that it is "subject to the greater power of God and accountable to divine judgment."[5] More profoundly, the political and social ruling powers are objectionable because they are an aberration from the way God has set things up to be. This claim on the part of 1 Enoch 6–11 is significant. By attributing a rejection of the created order to the rebellious angels—to the extent that they function as ciphers for bringers of Hellenistic culture—the text gives expression to a painful awareness and sense of alienation from the experienced world. The text reflects a world in which values and traditions are perceived as being under threat, perhaps even through the agency of other Jews prepared to accommodate their lifestyle and teachings to such external stimuli.[6]

In its accessible form, the text is thus produced within a context in which God-given religious foundations of pious Jews are being rejected by those who are in power, not only among the Hellenistic overlords (more

---

4. Nickelsburg, *1 Enoch 1*, 161–71.

5. Cf. Portier-Young, *Apocalypse against Empire*, 45.

6. Suter, "Fallen Angel, Fallen Priest," has plausibly—though in my view, too one-sidedly—argued along these lines and has regarded the Enochic text as a response to a progressive priestly group that has disregarded marriage laws; see Wright, *Origin of Evil Spirits*, 46–47, 133–36.

immediately the Seleucid and Ptolemaic rulers near the beginning of the third century BCE) but also among Jews themselves. Faced by an inability to address the problem through a program of institutional reform, the scribal community behind this tradition resorts to the telling of a story that serves to define unwanted expressions of culture outside the bounds of their God's activity and rule. Those who have been rejected as upholders of an ancient tradition out of devotion to God are here turning the tables on their oppressors by rejecting, in principle, everything they stand for. The "myth"[7] of the fallen angels and the punishments they incur functions as more than a way to counter one set of cultural preferences by advocating another (the latter of which the text does not describe). By appealing to and updating ancient tradition to speak to the present, the narrative seeks to redefine reality in order to leave the dominant carriers of culture out of the picture in the larger scheme of things.

The power of myth, though, does not consist in the storyline itself, but in the way it is fused with and arises out of the critical circumstances of those who tell it. There is little in the text to suggest that God's rejection of political, military, and cultural oppression was perceived as a reality in the experienced world. The authors thus narrate the myth as a process. Both humans and even the earth itself, in a state of having been robbed of their existence (whether metaphorically or actually), are given the voice of lament (1 En 7:5; 8:4; 9:2–3, 4–11) that, mediated through four archangels to God (9:1), overcomes the remoteness from God that their present conditions seem to indicate. The text of the lament itself in 9:4–11 may be translated as follows:[8]

> (9:4) "O Lord of lords, God of gods, King of Kings! The throne of your glory endures through all generations of the world, and your name (is) holy and to be praised and glorified into all eternity. (5) You have made everything, and with you is authority over all things; everything is laid bare and revealed before you; you see all things, and nothing is able to hide from before you. (6) You have seen what Asa'el has done, how he has taught every kind of wickedness on the earth and has divulged eternal secrets that are

---

7. It is very important to emphasize that this term in no way connotes something false; rather, I use it to refer to a storyline that, from the perspective of its tellers, is intended to express something fundamentally true.

8. I follow the Ethiopic text, negotiated critically with the Greek versions and substituting the angels' names with their equivalents as they appear among the Aramaic fragments.

in heaven, (7) (and) how Shemiḥazah has conveyed knowledge to human beings—to him you had given authority to rule over those who belong to him. (8) And they came to the daughters of humanity on the earth and have lain with them—with those women—and they have corrupted themselves and have revealed through them all kinds of sins. (9) And the women have given birth to giants, and in this way the whole earth has been filled with blood and iniquity. (10) And now behold, the souls of those who are dead are crying out and complaining to the gates of heaven, and their sighing has gone up and does not cease in the face of the iniquity that has happened on the earth. (11) And you know everything before it happens, and you know this and allow it to happen, yet you do not speak to us. And what should we do about this?"

The text is not a petition; rather, it raises a complaint about God's apparent inaction in the face of what the rebellious angels have done and about the consequences of their activities. What the text refers to, however, reflects the world as perceived by the community trying to resist those who bear Hellenistic culture and impose it on them. In the face of socio-cultural subjugation and the violence it brings, God appears to be silent and without response.

The compilers of 1 Enoch 6–11 do not let the matter rest with the complaint. As the following narrative demonstrates (10:1—11:2), the ancient storyline about the divine destruction of evil through the Great Flood (cf. Gen 6:5—8:22) is adapted in order to address the tumultuous circumstances around the turn of the third century BCE. The narrative looks back to God's intervention against evil in the ideal past, not only to declare what will ultimately happen in the future when the world order is restored to its original integrity (10:16–22), but also to affirm that God's rejection of an apparently ineradicable form of oppression is a process that has already begun.

The truly pious, the legitimate heirs of Noah, who in the sacred past was not only saved from the clutches of evil but rescued from the measures brought by God against it, can conduct their lives as a community (called "the plant of truth"; cf. 10:3, 16) in relation to both the future and the present. The future is one in which the created order and all that it was set up to be will be more than merely the God-given reality that reverses current experience; the world will be transformed in such a way that God's plan for it will become the *only* reality. With this *telos* in view, the community, whose piety and loyalty to God is under threat, can know the present as a time in which they are not as alienated as their circumstances indicate.

The Book of Watchers, whether in its earliest tradition (*1 Enoch* 6–11) or from traditions that accumulated to it (chs. 12–16, 17–19, 20–36, and 1–5), does not provide much obvious information about its socio-religious provenance. Several clues may nonetheless suggest that the circle that generated the tradition was priestly, in which case at least some concern with Jerusalem is likely. First, the text of *1 Enoch* 10:9 brands the giant offspring as the products of an illegitimate union; indeed, in the Greek Codex Panopolitanus they are called "bastards" (μαζηρεους, a transcription for the Hebrew word *mamzerim*) and "sons of fornication" (οἱ υἱοὶ τῆς πορνείας). If the term, which refers to those of (forbidden) mixed origin, is an allusion to Deut 23:2 (cf. also Zech 9:6), and if the text is concerned with marriages between Jewish priests and non-Jewish women, then the critical attitude adopted towards the giants may, on one level, be a veiled protest against socio-religious and cultural accommodation in the priesthood.[9] Second, as has been argued by Martha Himmelfarb, Enoch's ascent to the heavenly throne room in *1 Enoch* 14, with the initial intent of making intercession on behalf of the fallen angels, is best understood in relation to the priest's entry into the holy of holies of the temple cult.[10] To the extent that Enoch is granted a priestly role and that this role is based on a religious office, the Book of Watchers lays claim to a superior priesthood that invalidates other expressions of that institution. There is, however, no concrete evidence that the circle(s) behind the text were priests in any formal sense. The location of Enoch's dream vision at "the waters of Dan in the land of Dan" near Mount Hermon (*1 En* 13:7–9) is not only remote from Jerusalem, it is where the angels' descent leading to the illegitimate birth of the giants is placed as well (6:6). If, then, the traditions—of not only the angels' sin but also the ascent to the heavenly throne—are placed there, it is difficult to see how the narrative, in its acquired form (*1 Enoch* 6–16), is immediately concerned with the Jerusalem cult. In this light, we are faced by the possibility that priestly language could be used by circles without a functioning priesthood on the ground.[11] Without gainsaying priestly connections entirely, a more immediate context for the tradition, then, would be a scribal community[12]—or at

9. So the argument of Suter, "Fallen Angel, Fallen Priest."

10. Himmelfarb, *Ascent to Heaven*, 14–20.

11. For this important nuance, see Angel, *Otherworldly and Eschatological Priesthood*, 23–35, 297–310.

12. Note the designation "scribe" is applied to Enoch in *1 En* 12:2–3 and 15:1, who writes a petition on behalf of the angels as they beg God for mercy (13:4) and who, in this role (15:1), is commissioned to announce to the angels that their punishment is

least a community in which a scribe or scribes were prominent—a community that recalled and interpreted sacred tradition in order to undermine the appeal of a dominant "foreign" culture that violated human dignity, destroyed the environment, and fundamentally distorted the created order. The socio-religious horizon of this early part of the Enoch tradition is broad; the tradition locates Judaism within the larger world of myth and sacred history known in the Levant during the years following Alexander the Great's conquests.

In relation to such a framework the complaint, indeed lament, of *1 Enoch* 9:4–11 conveys more than disappointment at the apparent inactivity of God. It functions to align the values of those behind the text with God who has acted before in the sacred past to ensure that oppressive forces of evil have no ultimate place in the future world. The relativizing of tradition attributed to incursions defined as being from the "outside" constituted the critical problem for *1 Enoch* 6–11, and in this vein, only an appeal to the highest authority is seen as an effective way to defy and combat the cultural overtures of a powerful regime. Those who think themselves rejected (by those in power and, initially, even by a God who does not respond) herewith repudiate the wicked activities of their contemporaries by profiling them as being unconditionally rejected by God.

THE BOOK OF TOBIT: NEGOTIATING LIFE AT A DISTANCE

If the earliest Enoch tradition met a sense of rejection with an understanding of God who has invalidated the holders of socio-political and cultural power, the Book of Tobit actually comes to terms with rejection itself. Although the book is framed by an awareness of the central role that the temple cult in Jerusalem plays in the lives of Jews (Tob 1:1–7; 13:1–18; 14:5–7),[13] the piety of its main characters manifests itself in the eastern Diaspora, that is, in Ecbatana and Nineveh. The fictional story of Tobit is set in the late tenth and eighth centuries BCE, but it was in fact authored sometime

---

inevitable (15:2—16:4).

13. Despite occasional doubts that these sections originally belonged to the story and should be read together, Fitzmyer has advanced strong arguments in favor of the literary integrity of the book as a whole; cf. Fitzmyer, *Tobit*, 42–45, and Nickelsburg, Review of *Studien zum Buch Tobit*.

within the early third and the second century BCE, and so addresses issues faced by Jews outside the land at this time.[14]

By declaring the temple and Jerusalem to be God's own dwelling place (1:4; 13:16) and having life take shape under God's direction so far away (1:10—12:22), the author and early transmitters of the story expressed a tension that, once introduced by the event of "exile" (1:10; cf. 1:2–3),[15] is never resolved within the narrative itself. Tobit's piety is marked at the beginning by acts that relate to the temple (1:4-8). Unlike others from the tribe of Naphtali, he visits Jerusalem and while there goes beyond what is expected in dispensing charitable acts. Nevertheless, both the marriage of Tobias to Sara and the healing of Tobit's blindness are told without any overt mention of Jerusalem (7:10—11:19).[16] This, however, is only a provisional "happy ending"; the main characters and their families remain in exile throughout the story until their deaths in Nineveh (14:4—Tobit and his wife) and Ecbatana of Media (Tobias—14:14), respectively. The situation of exile as a mark of the characters of the story, who represent Israel in the Diaspora, is expressed by Tobit in his anguished prayer as he confesses his and Israel's sins in Tob 3:3–4:[17]

> Now remember me, O Lord, and look kindly upon me.
> Do not punish me for my sins or for my oversights,
> or for those of my ancestors.
> I sinned against you, and disobeyed your commandments;
> you have given us over to plunder, captivity, and death
> so that we have become a byword, a proverb, and a taunt
> in all the nations among which you have scattered us.

As this prayer indicates, the book takes the location of exile so seriously that it would be misleading to regard the temple cult as the defining component of the story, even though it is mentioned at the beginning and end. Even the frame itself relativizes its own claim to the principle centrality of Jerusalem. First, just prior to the description of Tobit's regular visits

14. See on the date, Moore, *Tobit*, 40-42, and Fitzmyer, *Tobit*, 50-54.

15. Although the term "exile" only occurs here, it characterizes the setting of the story and the plight that the book seeks to address.

16. Only in 3:12, when Sara turns her eyes towards God, the text implies that she is facing Jerusalem.

17. I follow Fitzmyer's translation of the earlier, longer recension, which negotiates the Dead Sea fragments with the texts of Codex Sinaiticus and part of the Old Latin version (Fitzmyer, *Tobit*, 129).

to Jerusalem as a young man, the story introduces him as a man from the tribe of Naphtali that had already been captured by the Assyrians (1:2). It is here that the first description of Tobit's piety is given; it takes the form of charitable giving: Tobit would donate money to both his relatives and to others from Israel who had been captured and taken away to Nineveh (1:3). Having introduced Tobit's character this way, only in a flashback to the days of his youth does the story describe how Tobit engaged in pious acts when visiting Jerusalem during religious holidays in obedience to what is prescribed for Israelites through tradition (1:6–8). To be sure, the throwback to Tobit's youth underscores, as mentioned above, the primacy of temple as the place of God's presence in the world; however, it functions as a way to describe the extent of his righteousness, which went beyond that of his Jewish contemporaries. The audience of the book is thus from the beginning in no doubt that the authenticity of Tobit's piety in the main part of the story does not depend on its connection to Jerusalem in any immediate sense.

Second, at the end of the book, the hymn that exults in Jerusalem (13:9–18) and in the predictions of Israel's restoration to Jerusalem, including the recognition of the God of Israel among the Gentiles (14:5–7) is not integrated into the experiences of the characters in the book. Admittedly, the hymn in ch 13, which opens with the praise of God and calls upon Israel to worship him (13:1–2), is placed on the lips of Tobit himself (13:1). Significantly, however, the second half of the hymn relates to the *heavenly* Jerusalem, not to Jerusalem as it currently exists. The descriptions of Jerusalem are idealizing: its features are bejeweled (13:16–17), its components are animate (13:18), and it is the place where the exemplary worship of God takes place (cf. 13:16, 18). This Jerusalem is, by implication, superior to the present one known to the writer(s) and audience.

The burden of "exile" borne by Tobit and the other characters in the book would initially seem to involve remoteness from the Jerusalem in the land of Israel. However, when Jerusalem is envisioned as heavenly, this distance no longer applies in the same way. Israelites everywhere, including Tobit in a place of exile, can through prayer and thanksgiving engage in a form of hymnic worship (without the offering of sacrifices) that, in effect, closes the gap; indeed, at the beginning of the hymn, Tobit identifies himself as one who acclaims God "in the land of my captivity" (13:6—so the Old Latin and shorter Greek recension). The text does not expressly state so, but Tobit's hymn at the end of the narrative, which punctuates the uttering of prayers of petition (3:2–6, 7–15) and thanksgiving (esp. 8:5–8; 11:14–15) throughout the story, offers a climax that assures continuity between piety in the Diaspora with the purposes of God who has made his name to dwell in Jerusalem. Rather than being placed at a disadvantage due to living in the Diaspora, those who live out pious lives can engage authentically in the worship of God by focusing on Jerusalem in its heavenly dimension. The text thus implies that this Jerusalem above is what ultimately counts and that genuine piety is not exiled from this reality. As the final predictions of the dying Tobit in ch. 14 indicate, the book does not forget about the earthly Jerusalem in the land of Israel, nor does it overlook the importance of the theme of a return from the exile (14:5). If ch. 13 places the reality of Jerusalem for Tobit in heaven, ch. 14 envisions the working out of divine purpose for the city as occurring at an unspecified time in the future. However, this future ingathering of Israel to Jerusalem, as well as the acknowledgement of Israel's God by the Gentiles (14:6–7), as much as they constitute a suitable end to the book itself, do not diminish the importance of the values presented in the main part of the book. Indeed, these events lie *outside of and future to* the piety attributed to Tobit, his wife Anna, Tobias, and Sara. While Jerusalem is of huge importance to the writer(s) of the text, the text shows no real enthusiasm for the present Jerusalem.[18] The restoration to come is going to be one that will come about through human agency; it will happen as God again shows mercy upon his people (14:5).

How, then, does the Book of Tobit deal with the problem of alienation and exile of Jews from the place of God's presence in the world? The answer is: pragmatically. *Life under less than ideal conditions outside the land of Israel is embraced.* The book acknowledges the problem of geographical and social displacement, but at the same time makes no attempt to fix it by forging a narrative that locates the characters in Jerusalem at the end of the story. Though no clear definition is offered in the text about what an earthly Jerusalem as the place of God's indwelling should now involve, the book redirects the audience's focus in both spatial and temporal terms. Since the Jerusalem that counts is heavenly and future and since this Jerusalem is distinct from the one from which the story's characters have been exiled, the narrative can in the meantime direct the audience's focus to the importance of almsgiving, family loyalty, and prayer as acts that God rewards in the lives of Israelites who persist in them despite challenging odds. Conditions of exile, which pose socio-religious and economic threats to the

---

18. The future Jerusalem predicted by Tobit in 14:5 is "not like the first (i.e., present) one."

survival of God's people, are not to be wished away. They can, instead, be negotiated with a measure of confidence that, whether in the present or in the ultimate future, God's plan for Israel within the larger world will not be frustrated. Rather than demonizing the Gentile world, the text inspires readers to adopt a realistic pattern of life that God can reward in the present, while leaving the ultimate resolution of things, which was predicted by the prophets of Israel (14:5), to a time that only God can determine.

THE EPISTLE OF ENOCH: WHEN THE SACRED TRADITION STRIKES

Although the Epistle of Enoch[19] forms part of what today is designed *1 Enoch* and, like much of the Book of Watchers, draws on the patriarch Enoch to present its message, it bears a very different character. Composed either during the years preceding the Maccabean crisis or during the time of socio-religious upheavals under the reign of Alexander Jannaeus (104-76 BCE),[20] the work reflects on the experience of rejection at a profound level and battles to find a place for God's people over against a complexity of odds. In doing this, the Epistle departs from the Book of Watchers in a number of ways. Unlike the Book of Watchers, which transmits a narrative about angelic rebellion (*1 Enoch* 6–16) and has Enoch travel the cosmos to envision present and future realities (chs. 17–36), the Epistle offers little in the way of storyline or visionary experience (cf. only 103:2). Instead, after a brief introduction that identifies the work as communication from the patriarch to his son Methuselah (so the Aramaic text of 92:1 in 4Q202 [= 4QEnochg] 1 ii 22) and following a few introductory sections (92:2-5; 93:11-15; 94:1-4), the main body of the text consists in a series of passages that reinforce the respective fates of punishment and reward for the wicked and the righteous (94:5—104:8). In addition, whereas the Book of Watchers attributes the ultimate source of oppression to an "outside" source, exem-

---

19. The name for the work derives from the concluding title found at the end of Chester Beatty-Michigan Papyus (fifth century), where it follows immediately upon the Enochic story about the birth of Noah in *1 Enoch* 106-107. The manuscript, which preserves much of the Enoch text in Greek from 97:6, probably originally included the Enochic tradition beginning at *1 En* 91:1. Given that the title relates better to the Epistle than to the immediately preceding account of Noah's birth, it is applied to the prior work. The Epistle, however, is not in fact the whole of *1 Enoch* 91-105. As an Exhortation (91:1-10, 18-19) and the Apocalypse of Weeks (93:1-10 plus 91:11-17) form two distinct literary units, the Epistle to be discussed here is 92:1-5, 93:11—105:2.

20. For a discussion of the possible dates, see Stuckenbruck, *1 Enoch 91-108*, 211-15.

plified by wayward angels, the Epistle seems more immediately concerned with an inner-Jewish conflict that in large part can be traced to differences in social class. As we shall see below, these differences manifest themselves in the way the two documents within the Enoch tradition formulate their respective laments (*1 En* 9:4–11; 103:9–15).

The twin themes of reward and punishment that so characterize the entirety of the Epistle are considered a stock element in ancient Jewish apocalyptic thought.[21] Due to the repetition of this emphasis in the main part of the text, the deeper theological problems being addressed in the work have not always been appreciated. At first blush, it would seem that the writer wanted to ensure that the wicked will be held accountable for the terrible things they have done during their lifetime, while the righteous, who have been subject to maltreatment by the wicked, will be rewarded, again beyond the bounds of their earthly lives. The aim of the work thus appears to be orientated around the future. It is one thing, however, to observe how much the Epistle is given over to the eschatological honoring of the faithful and shaming of the "sinners," but another to ask what sociological function such language had for those who produced and initially received the book's message. Is the purpose of the work merely to remind an audience of the ultimate fates awaiting the loyal and unfaithful, or is there something more profound at work?

In looking for the latter, we do well to inquire about the "sinners," against whom no less than eight woe-oracles are directed (94:6—95:2; 95:4–7; 96:4–8; 97:7–10; 98:9—99:2; 99:11–16; 100:7–9; 103:5–8) and who are repeatedly denounced.[22] As mentioned above, unlike the Book of Watchers, the target of the Epistle's invectives are not so much Gentiles or non-Jews (with some Jews complicit in their activities); the work, rather, focuses most of its complaints against other Jews. What kind of profile does the text allow us to reconstruct in relation to those who are also called "rich" and "wicked ones"? Clues in the text suggest that the opponents are not simply Jews who have blatantly engaged in Gentile practices or have deliberately rejected their religious identity. On the contrary, they are fellow-Jews who hold a coherent theology of their own based on traditions that the writer of the Epistle also holds sacred. When the author of the Epistle declares the

---

21. Such is especially the case for those whose understanding of "apocalyptic" has focused on eschatology; see, e.g., Charles, *Eschatology*; Rowley, *Relevance of Apocalyptic*; Hanson, *Dawn of Apocalyptic*.

22. On no less than 44 occasions does the Epistle mention punishments that will come upon the wicked; for a list, see Stuckenbruck, *1 Enoch 91–108*, 196–97.

instructions of other wicked Jews to be false (cf. especially 98:9—99:2), he does not wish to call the traditions underlying their teachings into question so much as to reject the inferences they have drawn from them.

In the case of the wicked, it seems that Deuteronomistic tradition played a significant role. In particular, the covenant blessings and curses found in Deuteronomy 28–30 may have functioned for them as an ideological underpinning for the social privileges they enjoyed. If according to the Torah, for example, loyalty to God is to be rewarded by relative wealth, social wellbeing, and economic flourishing, then the religious who find themselves relishing such conditions can argue logically that their standing is the God-given and entitled outcome of their piety. What the tradition, taken at face value, dictates as advantageous for one segment of Jewish society does not appear to offer anything constructive to say to those whose piety and covenant faithfulness has not resulted in social advantage. Is one to infer that the less fortunate, the economically enslaved and oppressed, find themselves in such a state *because*, as suggested in Deuteronomy 28, they have not kept the covenant?

The acute problem for the writer of the Epistle is rejection. On one level, he is keenly aware that many of his Jewish contemporaries have endured economic and cultural abuse at the hands of more privileged classes. Such injustices reflect the exclusion of one group of Jews by others from full participation in the society's wellbeing. This circumstance raised an acute theological problem for the writer. Does the sacred tradition of the Torah side with the well-to-do while offering no legitimate theological space for "the righteous" who are dispossessed of the social dignity they should have? By implication, is the God of Israel, who is deemed to speak through the words of tradition, rejecting the faithful who are being subjected to such suffering? The writer does not wish to short-circuit the problem by offering a quick solution. Near the end of the work, he formulates a lament at 103:9–15, attributed to the righteous who are still alive, that draws heavily on the text of Deuteronomy 28 (allusions to which are given in italics below):[23]

---

23. The translation below is based on the fuller Ethiopic version since the preserved Greek text in the Chester-Beatty Michigan Papyrus, which, except at the very beginning of the cited text, does not essentially depart from the Ethiopic, is more fragmentary. For a translation of the Greek, along with text-critical notes, see Stuckenbruck, *1 Enoch 91–108*, 537–47 (the critical Ethiopic translation in which is reproduced here).

(9) Do not say about the righteous and chosen ones who were in life,[24] "In the days of our toil we labored hard; and we have seen every (manner of) toil, and have found many evils. And *we have become exhausted and few* (Deut 28:62) and our spirit is weak. (10) And we were destroyed, and the one who would help us in word was powerless in deed, and we did not find anything. And *we were crushed and destroyed* (Deut 28:7, 48) and *we have not hoped to see life from day to day* (Deut 28:66). (11) *We had hoped to become the head, and became the tail* (Deut 28:13, 44). *We labored while working, but did not have authority over our work* (Deut 28:33); and *we became food for the sinners and the iniquitous ones* (Deut 28:36), and *they have made their yoke heavy upon us* (Deut 28:48). (12) There attained authority over us those who hated us and beat us, and *to those who hated us we bowed our neck, and they did not show us mercy* (Deut 28:48). (13) *We wanted to go away from them, so that we might escape and have rest, but we did not find any place to escape to and to be safe from them* (Deut 28:65). (14) And we complained about them to the rulers in our suffering, and we cried out against those who consumed us, but they did not recognize our cry and did not want to hear our voice. (15) And *they helped those who robbed and devoured us* (Deut 28:29) and those who made us few; and they hid their wrongdoing, and did not remove from us the yoke of those who devoured us and scattered us and murdered us; and they hid our murder, and did not remember that they had raised their hands against us.

The passage in itself is a remarkable piece of irony, for which there is nothing comparable in Second Temple literature. The author has the righteous formulate their plight by alluding densely to that very tradition that seems to have excluded them. The circumstances of the covenant faithful are described in precisely those terms that are applied to the wicked in Deuteronomy 28. The lament is thus an admission not only that conditions for the righteous are not as they ought to be, but also—and more profoundly—that the lives of the wicked are in line with the blessings pronounced in Deuteronomy upon the faithful. For all appearances, the righteous, in suffering oppression at the hands of other Jews, have been excluded from a dignified form of participation in society; even more than this, however, *they find themselves rejected by the very traditions they hold dear.*

---

24. The Greek text more clearly puts the lament into the mouth of the righteous who are alive: "For do not say, O rig[hteous] (and) holy ones who are in life . . ."

Rejection

How can comfort come to God's people when their own Scriptures seem so clearly turned against them? Rather than rejecting Deuteronomy outright, the Epistle adopts a hermeneutic that places it within a wider framework and uses the notion of time to redefine the scope of its application. First, it is important to note that for the writer, the Deuteronomistic tradition is not one that stands in isolation from others. While the blessings and curses of Deuteronomy might be taken to sanction the *status quo* that divides society into "haves" and "have-nots," with the inadvertent result that the former can abuse the latter, two other sources of tradition take up the cause of the oppressed who live as victims of injustice; here both the prophetic and Enoch tradition known to the writer play a formative role. Among the prophets of the Hebrew Bible, the traditions of Amos and Jeremiah give the author words with which to describe the wicked: they "build their houses through sin" (*1 En* 94:7; cf. Jer 22:13), gorge on natural resources and trample on the lowly (*1 En* 95:5–6; cf. Amos 5:11; 6:6) and gain their wealth by iniquitous means (*1 En* 97:8; cf. Jer 17:11). Given that the circumstances of "the righteous" serve the author of the Epistle as the point of departure, it is the prophetic traditions that offer the most immediate interpretive framework and it is around them that the covenant blessings and curses have to be organized. The earlier Enoch tradition in the Book of Watchers likewise served the Epistle with language that declares oppression to be subject to divine judgment. Of the 55 possible allusions in the Epistle to the Book of Watchers, 25 alone pick up on language found in *1 Enoch* 6–11.[25] Though the Epistle's emphasis on where sin originates (cf. *1 En* 98:4–6) is conspicuously different from the explanation offered in the Book of Watchers (6:1—8:3), the essential socio-political and cultural concerns remain the same: *any* abuse of power, especially that which compromises what is perceived as authentic Jewish piety, has no enduring place within the world order and will be destroyed.

If the promises of Deuteronomy for the loyal and woes on the unfaithful are, despite appearances, not rejected, how does the *Epistle* go about retaining them at all? The writer shows himself capable of using Deuteronomy in another passage in order to criticize those whose clothing and self-decoration breach boundaries that mark off sexual identity (*1 En* 98:2; cf. Deut 22:5). To the extent, however, that the covenant blessings and curses remain of any value, the Epistle cannot adopt them at face value;

---

25. See the listing of these instances and discussion in Stuckenbruck, *1 Enoch 91–108*, 206–11.

they do not, in fact, hold as far as life on this side of death is concerned. Rather than doing away with the blessings and curses altogether, the Enochic writer adopts a strategy that simply delays them. Although the wording from Deuteronomy does not shape most of the descriptions of future reward and punishment in the text, it is clear that the assignment of justice to an eschatological court assumes the profound and ongoing validity of God's covenant with his faithful people.

FOURTH EZRA: WHEN THE PLACE OF WORSHIP NO LONGER EXISTS

Fourth Ezra is one of the theologically most profound non-Christian Jewish compositions from antiquity and, therefore, merits some detailed discussion in relation to the problem of rejection. Divided into a series of seven episodes consisting of dialogues and visions, the document was written by someone who adopted a name associated with the post-exilic lawgiver while locating the narrative in the more immediate aftermath of the destruction of the first temple (4 *Ezra* 3:1–3). The literary framework of the distant past allows the writer to address the crisis of his own time, at or near the end of the first century CE: if Jerusalem, along with the temple, stands at the center of Israel's worship, how is one now to cope with the fact that both the city and the cult have been undeniably destroyed? The work attaches to this problem a number of other questions that implicate God (cf. 4 *Ezra* 3:3–35; 5:23–30; 6:55–59; 9:26–37). If God has held evil accountable in Israel's past, why is it that God seems to be doing nothing about sin in the present? Why, for example, are Israel's enemies (Babylon, which is Rome) who have destroyed Zion, not being punished? If the destruction of Jerusalem is a punishment for sin, what is the meaning of God's covenant with Israel? Despite having the covenant and the Torah, Israel is just as much subject to the "evil heart" of Adam as the rest of humanity and thus equally accountable. Is there then no advantage for Israel as God's covenant people? In short, the value of God's election cannot be discerned, and it seems that God is treating God's people unfairly. The critique is not merely leveled at overlords, as in the Book of Watchers, or at the abuse of sacred tradition, as in the Epistle of Enoch, but rather takes aim at the character of God himself. The trauma of recent events at the hands of Rome leads the writer of 4 *Ezra* to imply that God has set up his people for disappointment: Israel is alienated from her place of worship at the temple (which lies in ruins), unable for the most part to keep the Torah (which remains

Rejection

an unalterable standard), and no less accountable before God than anyone else (because of the nature they share with the rest of humanity). In short, Israel looks like a rejected people, not so much because of what they have suffered at the hands of Rome, but because God has dealt unfairly with them. In the face of these questions, can any identity for Israel as God's elect people be retained?

The writer behind the seer Ezra does not easily accept answers from Uriel, his angelic interlocutor. The angel's principled statements that Israel will be held accountable to the Torah, that only the very few will be able to be obedient to the Torah, and that justice will only take place in the next age do little to bring Ezra any insight or perspective through which he can find comfort. Ezra is, in effect, inconsolable. Despite some narrative progression and clarifying of Ezra's exemplary status, the first three of the seven episodes show little sign that the seer has gained any degree of understanding from the angel's responses to his questions.

A decisive turn in the storyline, however, takes place in the fourth episode (4 Ezra 9:25—10:59), in which Ezra has a vision of a woman who is in mourning over the death of her son and, having left her husband to go out into the countryside, declares her wish to die (10:18).[26] As the text makes clear to the audience, the woman's anguish is symbolic: she represents the heavenly Jerusalem who mourns the destruction of its earthly counterpart. The protagonist of the story finds himself thrust into the unexpected role of one who attempts to comfort the woman.

Ezra's role as consoler takes the form of two speeches (10:5–17, 19–24), with the second one following the woman's flat refusal to listen to his advice that she return to the city and to her husband (cf. 10:18–19). The initial "consolation" speech, which the woman does not heed, advances an argument through comparison. Ezra initially focuses on the woman's suffering as a matter of *individual grief* that cannot be compared with the greater, more collective grief that "Zion, the mother of us all"[27] (10:7) is undergoing in relation to the whole world (10:10).[28] The seer asks in 10:11, "Who then

---

26. For a fuller accounting of this encounter, see Stuckenbruck, "Ezra's Vision of the Lady."

27. The English translation cited in the present discussion follows that of the Latin version by Metzger, "Fourth Book of Ezra."

28. The reference to "Zion" here is enigmatic, since its function is not bound up with Israel *per se*, but rather with humankind as a whole; cf. the discussion in Hogan, *Theologies in Conflict*, 164–65 and n. 12. It should be remembered, however, that the term translated as "earth" can also refer more specifically to "the land."

ought to mourn the more, she who lost so great a multitude, or you who are grieving for one?" After a brief imaginary dialogue with the woman (vv. 12–14), Ezra exhorts her to bear her troubles bravely, while acknowledging that God's decree (for her) is in fact just (v. 16).

Though this speech presents Ezra as a consoler and so portrays him as active in this new role, the shift it represents in the narrative does not seem to translate into any real or new understanding or insight on his part. To put what Ezra says in perspective, it is necessary to take the angel's interpretation of the vision (10:38–54) into account. As the audience is soon to learn by hindsight through Ezra's discussion with the angel (10:29–54), the seer's words here to the woman are both misconceived and ironic. They are misconceived because they contrast the woman with "Zion, the mother of us all," that is, Ezra regards the woman as essentially different from Zion while the interpreting angel in the following pericope is going to identify her as Zion itself (10:44)! Here, then, Ezra does not know he is speaking to "Zion," and so argues mistakenly that the woman's grief cannot be compared to the even greater grief being suffered by Zion. His argument is also ironic. Ezra's downgrading of her grief to that of a mere individual not only misunderstands the scale of the grief that she embodies, but also steers away from the kind of comfort and understanding he has been seeking for himself (and, implicitly, for his Jewish contemporaries) from the angel in the first three episodes. In addition to these points, there is a further one: any expectation that Ezra's shift in role to being a consoler includes an increase in understanding will be disappointed. Ezra's concern with the multitude "destined for destruction" (10:10) shows that even in his new role, he remains troubled by the problem of why it is that so many on the earth (apart from the question of Israel who has received the Torah) are going to perish (cf. the end of the third episode at 9:17–22).

Ezra's second speech to the woman (10:19–24) should be read in tandem with the first since, on its own, it makes little sense. For example, at the start, he exhorts her, "[L]et yourself be persuaded because of the troubles of Zion, and be consoled because of the sorrow of Jerusalem." It is not troubles in themselves that provide the consolation, but rather the relative weight of Zion's troubles in comparison with those of the woman whom Ezra (wrongly) regards as but an individual. The catalogue of terrible events (10:21–23), which brings together both descriptive and conventional sufferings, underscores the overwhelming magnitude of grief in Zion and Jerusalem:

Rejection

> For you see how our sanctuary has been laid waste, our altar thrown down, our temple destroyed; our harp has been laid low, our song has been silenced, and our rejoicing has ended; the light of our lampstand has been put out, the ark of our covenant has been plundered, our holy things have been polluted, and the name by which we are called has been almost profaned; our children have suffered abuse, our priests have been burned to death, our Levites have gone into exile, our virgins have been defiled, and our wives have been ravished; our righteous men have been carried off, our little ones have been cast out, our young men have been enslaved, and our strong men made powerless. And worst of all, the seal of Zion has been deprived of its glory, and given over into the hands of those that hate us.

From this bleak account of things, the woman is presumably to infer that her sufferings are by comparison of lighter weight, and she can be told, "*Therefore*, shake off your great sadness and lay aside your many sorrows, so that the Mighty One may be merciful to you again, and the Most High may give you rest, a relief from your troubles" (10:24).

There is no indication that any understanding has been achieved on the part of Ezra as he consoles the woman. Indeed, his attempt to act as a comforter seems inadequate at best. The seer thinks he has been trying to console an individual, while the woman is in fact (as the audience is about to learn) representative of a heavenly reality, the city of Zion (10:44). Despite this misperception, the text relativizes the significance of this error in understanding. How does *4 Ezra* resolve the dilemma posed by the questions that implicate God and give voice to the alienation felt by God's people? The text does not so much do so through the argument of logic or reason that has characterized the angel's responses during the first three episodes. Instead, in being made to act as comforter, Ezra (and by extension, the audience) is put into a position of seeing and being a witness to transformation as it takes place. Following his illogical, almost insensitive words of comfort, the woman is transformed from a grief-stricken and ashen figure into someone with a bright, dazzling, and frightening appearance (10:25) before she disappears from sight, leaving visible the foundations of a city (10:27). Taken together with Ezra's reaction of fright and his need to be strengthened before any further dialogue takes place,[29] this visual en-

---

29. Ezra's continuing troubled feelings, even after the change of the woman's appearance, suggests that it would be premature to agree entirely with Longenecker, *2 Esdras*, 62, that from the point of 10:20, "Gone is any sense of Ezra's complaining, indicting

counter marks the first (and only) occurrence in *4 Ezra* of a scene that is so common to Second Temple apocalyptic texts (though the latter are usually either theo- or angelophanic).[30] Whereas it is more common for visionary encounters to involve bedazzling figures from the outset,[31] *the transformation of a grief-stricken figure into one invested with divine glory is conspicuous.* Significantly, this transforming moment belongs to the woman, not to Ezra (or to his audience); and yet, this is the moment in which one might think the lack of understanding that has thus far characterized the seer could finally be in the process of being addressed. It is, then, not surprising that Ezra is made to call for the angel Uriel's help to interpret what he has seen, not only the mourning woman but also the appearance into which she was transformed.

The interpretation offered by the angel (10:33–54) discloses the woman's identity as that of the city of Zion (10:44), while her son's death is linked to the destruction of Jerusalem (10:48; from the author's viewpoint, the recent destruction by Rome in 70 CE). Several aspects of the angel's explanation to Ezra are of note. First, corresponding to the woman mourning for her son, Zion and Jerusalem are distinguished. The horrible outcome of the Jewish war against Rome does not reflect the ultimate purpose of God for Israel. Though Zion mourns (and does not trivialize) the destruction, Zion ultimately stands outside the destruction and remains distinct. Second, the interpretation remains aware of the place where Ezra has had the vision: he is still in a rural field "where there was no foundation of any building" (10:53). This field is both the place to which the angel had instructed Ezra to go for a diet of flowers and plants and for continuous prayer in preparation for the next episode (9:23–27) and the place to which the lady had come— away from the city of her mourning—to mourn and contemplate her wish to die (10:3, 18). Combined with the identification of the woman as Zion, the angel's emphasis in 10:53 that this rural field is not located where the foundations of a building had ever been laid supports the possibility that the woman represents something essentially new; what she symbolizes (Zion) can be anticipated as a manifestation of God's purpose and justice in the world, even as it relates to Israel. The possibility that here

---

spirit, and there is no sense of an inner struggle in affirming what he previously could not bring himself to accept."

30. Hence the significance of Humphrey's study, *The Ladies and the Cities*, which isolates a series of visions involving women who symbolize cities.

31. For a listing of examples, see Stuckenbruck, *Angel Veneration and Christology*, 275–83.

the audience is given to perceive that Zion is not complete (so the Latin to 10:27; cf. also the versions to 10:42), though it already bears a magnificence to be seen and heard by Ezra (10:55–56), also draws attention to the ongoing, present—and, in principle, tangible—activity of God whose building, in contrast to that of humans, will result in something permanent and indestructible (10:54; cf. also the city to appear in 7:26). Third, taken into consideration within the larger literary context, the interpretation marks the angel Uriel's last speech in the work. From here on, Ezra's interpretations and dialogues are more directly with God (12:7, 10; 13:14, 21, 51–52; 14:2–3, 19–20, 23). This is consistent with the character Ezra's shifting role. A fourth, and perhaps most important point from Uriel's interpretation emerges. It has to do with the degree to which Ezra has achieved understanding by the end of the interpretation. To be sure, Ezra has learned in the text that the mourning and transformed woman who has appeared to him is Zion, and that, as such, this new city is the embodiment of a divine purpose to be anticipated in the eschatological future.[32] However, despite a statement to the contrary ("the Most High has revealed many secrets to you," 10:38), *it is not clear whether Ezra has actually received answers in the terms in which he has posed questions* during the first three episodes of the book. The logic of the questions and the logic of the answers mediated by the angel do not connect up. Paramount instead is what the writer has the angel observe about Ezra: "you have sorrowed continually for your people, and mourned greatly over Zion" (10:39); in addition, with regard to the woman, the angel states (10:50):

> [y]ou saw her likeness, how she mourned for her son, and you began to console her for what had happened. For now the Most High, seeing that you are sincerely grieved and profoundly distressed for her, has shown you the brightness of her glory, and the loveliness of her beauty.

Ezra may have been seeking understanding, but God's perspective is more concerned with the importance of uttering a genuine lament. Although the number of shifts in the fourth episode is unmistakable, the basis for these—and this includes the measured amounts of understanding

---

32. One should resist the temptation simply to describe this Zion as "heavenly," as it is not clear that the writer operates with any explicit contrast between "heaven" and "earth." On the other hand, the contrast between the present and the coming age is more pronounced, and Zion—as a city whose foundations are laid and is being built—is more the reflection of a future, yet assured, reality.

that the seer has acquired—remains essentially the same and, indeed, has been sustained in the storyline: Ezra repeatedly expresses his overwhelming grief and refuses to be consoled by anything the angel has said. It is not even clear that when the angel exhorts Ezra "do not be afraid, and do not let your heart be terrified" (10:55), that Ezra therefore finds himself in just such a state; the narrative leaves this result unsaid, and it is an open matter whether readers can infer that the very consolation that he has been seeking has finally come about.[33] In this sense, his mourning and that of the woman—she also refuses consolation and is never portrayed as one who has been consoled—are mirrors of one another.[34] Of course, in the rest of the book, the audience will learn that the character Ezra is endowed with a special place in the chain of revelation from God to Israel (10:56–57; 14:1–48). But the importance attached to Ezra's lamenting and its convergence with the woman's plight (in the midst of which she is transformed, as Ezra unwittingly describes that plight to her) embrace what the writer of *4 Ezra* enjoins upon the audience. *The ultimate value of cognitive understanding is relativized, while more immediate place is given for lament that, in the midst of illogical and unreasonable suffering,* is *in itself* the essential prelude to any disclosures of understanding that may or may not follow.

In the remainder of *4 Ezra*, the seer has two visions of messianic activity (11:1—12:51; 13:1–58) and finds himself catapulted into a Moses-like status as a recipient of revelation (14:1–48) that begins with a call that is reminiscent of the burning bush episode in Exodus 3. None of this material, for all the resolution it offers, discloses how alienation from the temple—the very place where God should be worshiped—and, indeed, from God himself—is ultimately dealt with. I have focused my attention therefore on the point of the story in which the shift towards an answer takes place. Significantly, the answer to a profound sense of having been rejected by God is twofold: (1) in the face of remoteness from God, there is the need to utter a lament that describes and expresses honestly the destitute state of things as they are and (2) there is the need to turn away from one's own grief to address the grief of others. In relation to the second point, *4 Ezra*

---

33. One may note Ezra's continuing "perplexity of mind and great fear" and "fear" following the visions in the fifth and sixth episodes (12:3–5; 13:13).

34. I am reticent to read the text as depicting the seer's attempt to console the woman as successful and his reception of comfort as a result; cf. Stone, *Fourth Ezra*, 336. Although Stone notes that Ezra no longer mourns in the narrative, this does not mean that he has, simply, been comforted here and, with the readers, leaves his troubles completely behind.

recognizes that the suffering and alienation, when experienced by God's people, is *shared*. As such, the anguish of the individual offers the basis for recognition of the anguish of others. To the extent that the shift in Ezra's character in *4 Ezra* is paradigmatic, the text invites members of the audience to seek out what they hold in common and to place themselves in the role of those who comfort, that is, as those who can convey the mercy and comfort to one another.

CONCLUSION

We have reviewed above several ways through which Jewish writers attempted to deal with the problem of rejection and alienation. The theological strategies these writers adopted are intertwined with the socio-political, economic, and cultural conditions they and their immediate audiences faced. In the Book of Watchers a definitive judgment of God in the sacred past functions to guarantee that the present injustices and violations of Jewish values will be held to account. The compilers of this early Enochic tradition locate their program of resistance on the stage of world myth and engage in open criticism of a splintering regime that is undergoing a turmoil of its own. The text looks forward to a renewed world order, patterned after the reconstitution of things at the end of the Noachic deluge (*1 En* 10:16—11:2).

By contrast, in addressing Jewish life in the Diaspora that is remote from Jerusalem, the Book of Tobit does not look to a future life in order to find God's ways operative in the world. Instead, it embraces the rejection inherent to life in the Diapora (cf. Tob 3:4); it does so by advocating prayer, almsgiving, and family loyalty, which compensate for the geographical distance from the place of the divine presence and make it possible for Jews to come to terms with their status as refugees, knowing that they are not bearers of a less authentic form of religious loyalty.

In comparison to the Book of Watchers and the Book of Tobit, the Epistle of Enoch combats socio-economic and religious rejection as primarily being carried out by contemporary Jews. The problem is upfront and close and, with only a small exception (cf. *1 En* 105:1–2), the text offers little room to think about the larger world arena in which the injustices are being carried out and for which one can anticipate the achievement of divine purpose. Since the writer cannot image how the dire conditions of the righteous can be rectified in this life as the covenant would lead one to expect, he finds an answer in the future, a future that—unlike the case in the Book of Watchers—does not so much involve a return to original things but is essentially discontinuous with the present order. The covenant's validity is not so much lost as it is postponed to what will happen at the final judgment.

In *4 Ezra*, we encounter a different scenario altogether. Unlike the previous three writings, which were composed during a time when the Jerusalem cult was in existence, the seer is challenged by the complete removal of the temple, that very place that was supposed to have functioned as the *axis mundi* for all authentic worship of the God of Israel. The writer asks hard questions of God that are never quite answered in the way they have been put. Nonetheless, an answer to the institutional absence of God and to God's apparent rejection of his people emerges that is at once *experiential* and *theological*. It is experiential in the transformation that occurs when one focuses on helping others who mourn, and it is theological in the utterance of an honest lament that does not shy away from declaring "things as they are." As in the other writings, eschatology comes into play, but it is not eschatology that in the narrative of *4 Ezra* explains the transformation towards understanding that takes place.

Suffering, rejection, and remoteness from God play a role in all four of the documents we have reviewed. None of the ways their writers have faced their respective dilemmas is obviously "Christian." Yet, the depth of the relationship they exhibit between people and the God of Israel furnishes resources for those whose Christian outlook involves faithfulness to the one whom Jews worshiped then and continue to worship now.

BIBLIOGRAPHY

Angel, Joseph. *Otherworldly and Eschatological Priesthood in the Dead Sea Scrolls*. Studies on the Texts of the Desert of Judah 86. Leiden: Brill, 2008.

Barclay, John M. G. *Jews in the Mediterranean Diaspora: From Alexander to Trajan (323 BCE to 117 CE)*. London: T. & T. Clark, 1996.

———, ed. *Negotiating Diaspora: Jewish Strategies in the Roman Empire*. Library of Second Temple Studies 45. London: T. & T. Clark, 2004.

Charles, R. H. *Eschatology: The Doctrine of a Future Life in Israel, Judaism, and Christianity*. 1899. Reprint, New York: Schocken Books, 1963.

Davies, Philip R. Review of *The Origin of Evil Spirits*, by Archie Wright. *Journal of Semitic Studies* 55 (2010) 273.

Dimant, Devorah. "Not Exile in the Desert, but Exile in Spirit: The Pesher of Isaiah 40:3 in the Rule of the Community and the History of the Qumran Community." In *Connected Vessels: The Dead Sea Scrolls and the Literature of the Second Temple Period*, edited by Moshe Bar-Asher and Devorah Dimant, 40–53. Megillot 2. Jerusalem: Haifa University Press and Bialik Institute, 2010.

Rejection

Fitzmyer, Joseph A. *Tobit.* Commentaries on Early Jewish Literature. Berlin: Walter de Gruyter, 2003.

Gafni, Isaiah. *Land, Center, and Diaspora: Jewish Constructs in Late Antiquity.* JSPSup 21. Sheffield: Sheffield Academic, 1997.

Gruen, Erich. *Diaspora: Jews among Greeks and Romans.* Cambridge, MA: Harvard University Press, 2002.

Hacham, Noah. "Exile and Self-Identity in the Qumran Sect and Hellenistic Judaism." In *New Perspectives on Old Texts: Proceedings of the Tenth International Symposium of the Orion Center for the Study of the Dead Sea Scrolls and Associated Literature, 9–11 January, 2005,* edited by Esther G. Chazon, Betsy Halpern-Amaru, and Ruth A. Clements, 3–21. Studies on the Texts of the Desert of Judah 88. Leiden: Brill, 2010.

Hanson, Paul D. *The Dawn of Apocalyptic: The Historical and Sociological Roots of Jewish Apocalyptic Eschatology.* Revised ed. Philadelphia: Fortress, 1979.

Himmelfarb, Martha. *Ascent to Heaven in Early Jewish and Christian Apocalypses.* Oxford: Oxford University Press, 1993.

Hogan, Karina. *Theologies in Conflict in 4 Ezra: Wisdom, Debate, and Apocalyptic Solution.* JSJSup 130. Leiden: Brill, 2008.

Humphrey, Edith McEwan. *The Ladies and the Cities: Transformation and Apocalyptic Identity in Joseph and Aseneth, 4 Ezra, the Apocalypse and The Shepherd of Hermas.* JSPSup17. Sheffield: Sheffield Academic, 1995.

Longenecker, Bruce W. *2 Esdras.* Guides to Apocrypha and Pseudepigrapha. Sheffield: Sheffield Academic, 1995.

Metzger, Bruce M. "The Fourth Book of Ezra." In *The Old Testament Pseudepigrapha,* edited by James H. Charlesworth, 1:516–59. 2 vols. Garden City, NY: Doubleday, 1983–85.

Milik, Józef T. *The Books of Enoch from Qumrân Cave 4.* Oxford: Clarendon, 1976.

Moore, Carey A. *Tobit: A New Translation with Introduction and Commentary.* AB 40A. New York: Doubleday, 1996.

Nickelsburg, George W. E. *1 Enoch 1.* Hermeneia. Minneapolis: Fortress, 2001.

———. Review of *Studien zum Buch Tobit,* by M. Rabenau. *JBL* 116 (1997) 348–50.

Portier-Young, Anathea E. *Apocalypse against Empire: Theologies of Resistance in Early Judaism.* Grand Rapids: Eerdmans, 2011.

Reeves, John C. "Manichaeans as *Ahl al-Kitāb*: A Study in Manichaean Scripturalism." In *Light against Darkness,* edited by Armin Lange, Randall Styers, and Eric M. Myers, 249–65. JAJSup 2. Göttingen: Vandenhoeck & Ruprecht, 2011.

Rowley, H. H. *The Relevance of Apocalyptic: A Study of Jewish and Christian Apocalypses from Daniel to Revelation.* 3rd ed. New York: Association, 1963.

Stone, Michael E. *Fourth Ezra: A Commentary on the Book of Fourth Ezra.* Hermeneia. Philadelphia: Fortress, 1990.

Stuckenbruck, Loren T. *Angel Veneration and Christology: A Study in Early Judaism and in the Christology of the Apocalypse of John.* WUNT 2.70. Tübingen: Mohr Siebeck, 1995.

———. "The Early Traditions Related to *1 Enoch* from the Dead Sea Scrolls: An Overview and Assessment." In *The Early Enoch Literature,* edited by Gabriele Boccaccini and John J. Collins, 41–63. Leiden: Brill, 2007.

———. "Ezra's Vision of the Lady: The Form and Function of a Turning Point." In *Fourth Ezra and Second Baruch: Reconstruction after the Fall,* edited by Matthias Henze and Gabriele Boccaccini, 137–50. Leiden: Brill, 2013.

———. *1 Enoch 91–108*. Commentaries on Early Jewish Literature. Berlin: Walter de Gruyter, 2007.

Suter, David W. "Fallen Angel, Fallen Priest: The Problem of Family Purity in *1 Enoch* 6–16." *Hebrew Union College Annual* 50 (1979) 115–35.

Tuval, Michael. "Doing without the Temple: Paradigms in Judaic Literature of the Diaspora." In *Was 70 CE a Watershed in Jewish History?*, edited by Daniel R. Schwartz and Zeev Weiss, 181–239. Ancient Judaism and Early Christianity 78. Leiden: Brill, 2012.

Wright, Archie T. *The Origin of Evil Spirits: The Reception of Genesis 6.1–4 in Early Jewish Literature*. WUNT 2.198. Tübingen: Mohr Siebeck, 2005.

5

Cities of Refuge
The Role of the Jewish Christian Communities in the Spread of Christianity

CYNTHIA LONG WESTFALL

INTRODUCTION

IF AN APPROPRIATE THEME for the Diaspora is the rejection of God's refugees, then we may say with confidence that Jewish Christianity in the Diaspora epitomized the experience of that rejection, not only in terms of its treatment by Rome, Jews, and other Christians extending beyond the first and second centuries, but also in terms of its neglect in church history and in the history of Western biblical interpretation. Until recently, the consensus of scholarship has assumed that Gentile Christianity and Judaism separated early in "the parting of the ways." It has been believed generally that the first major separation was supposed to have occurred when the temple was destroyed in 70 CE, and became finalized in 132–36 CE with the Bar-Kochba Revolt.[1] The Jewish leadership of the early

---

1. See the model of the consensus view of the parting of the ways in Goodman, "Modeling the 'Parting of the Ways,'" 121. See also fig. 2 on p. 122 for dating of the key events that were thought to cause the split. The evidence that the split was inevitable and was complete by either 70 CE or 135 CE is pervasive, and the split is often depicted as a fact in popular level dictionaries and encyclopedias. Since World War II, scholarly discussion has shifted to re-evaluate the traditional view, though the traditional view is still often assumed by scholars who are not part of the discussion, even though the consensus has discarded the presupposition that rabbinic Judaism represents first-century Judaism. For a succinct articulation of the traditional position before the shift (1946) see Dix, "Ministry in the Early Church." He asserts that the turning point was in the first or second century, after which "there were no relations between Jews and Christians except

church was supposed to have been disabled and disrupted, and leadership allegedly passed to the Gentile-led and dominated churches. Therefore, the formation of the canon is often believed to have been determined by the Gentile churches. The apostolic nature of the non-Pauline/non-Lukan canon (e.g., Matthew, the Johannine corpus, and the Petrine epistles) has largely been disputed and assigned a late date that would place it after the alleged parting of the ways, or has been neglected altogether.

However, these narratives behind the texts are tangled and inconsistent, and in conflict with the evidence. First, there are indications that some variations of Jewish Christianity continued to exist, even into the fourth century. Second, the apostolic mission to the Jews spread throughout the Diaspora, and neither these communities in the Diaspora nor their leadership would have been disbanded as a result of revolts in Palestine. If anything, they were strengthened in leadership and numbers if not in resources, because Jewish Christian immigrants who fled or were forced out of Palestine joined their communities. Third, the non-Pauline/non-Lucan New Testament corpus is consistent with Second Temple and/or Jewish Hellenist concerns and literary style. Furthermore, besides the Johannine Epistles and possibly Revelation, the epistles explicitly claim to be written by the apostolic "pillars" of the church or close associates, so regardless of the actual authorship, one can argue that they are meant to be understood as literature within the context of apostolic Jewish Christianity. Furthermore, though the apostolic origin of Revelation is contested, its Jewish nature is self-evident, and one can make a similar argument for the Johannine Epistles. In other words, evidence has been brought to light that indicates the ongoing existence and influence of Jewish Christianity, rather than its eradication, in the period of the early church at least until Constantine.[2]

Scholars who have advocated the New Perspective on Paul have demonstrated that Luther conflated first-century Judaism with Medieval Catholicism, and consequently Protestant scholarship adopted Luther's anachronistic description of Paul's opponents.[3] Similarly, it has been sug-

---

hostile ones" (228).

2. For example, this is the entire gist of the argument of Becker and Reed, *Ways that Never Parted*.

3. For a good introduction to the New Perspective on Paul (NP), see Thompson, *New Perspective on Paul*. The background for the NP is Sanders's ground-breaking work in 1977, *Paul and Palestinian Judaism*. However, the NP discussion truly began with Dunn, "New Perspective on Paul" in 1983 (but see also Dunn, *New Perspective on Paul: Collected Essays*). The NP has been promoted by Wright (e.g., *Paul: In Fresh Perspective*).

gested that much of the New Testament has been wrongly understood because the texts were interpreted by the Western church within fourth-century contexts that were radically different from the contexts in which the texts were written.[4] In the fourth century, Roman Christian leadership began to wield political power, extend its power base, and promote uniformity under its umbrella, not only in doctrine and practice, but in its historic reconstruction of apostolic succession and other aspects of early Christianity. For example, the apostle Peter was described by Paul as the apostle who was entrusted with the gospel to the circumcised (Gal 2:7–9). Later, Peter was instead re-presented as primarily the first pope of the *Gentile* church of Rome. Western interpretation and historical perspectives were further distorted by the effects of the Muslim conquest of many of the areas that had been evangelized by the apostolic Jewish Christian witness. The evidence of Jewish Christianity has been typically ignored or erased until recently, and consequently the Jewish nature of early Christianity has been little examined and rarely emphasized until recently.

It has been convincingly argued by Skarsaune and others that the mission "to the circumcised" (Gal 2:9) spread through the Diaspora through apostolic witness; it had significant success and produced the church's earliest theologians.[5] Acts and the Pauline corpus indicate that thousands of practicing Jews were believers (Acts 21:20), that the apostles were actively engaged in mission (Gal 2:8–9; 1 Cor 9:5), and other Christians were actively preaching the gospel in all areas but the extreme West (Rom 15:20–24). The church probably spread to Rome through Jewish Christian witness, and Paul felt compelled to push further east to Spain so that he would not be "building on someone else's foundation" (Rom 15:20). This paper will argue that Jewish Christians in the Diaspora converted Gentiles and incorporated them into believing Jewish communities and culture that were metaphoric cities of refuge consistent with certain philosophies and practices in the Second Temple Diaspora, in contrast to Paul, who established indigenous

---

4. See, for example, Frederiksen, "What 'Parting of the Ways'?"; Reed, "Jewish Christianity," 227–28. The christianization of the Roman Empire and the process of promotion, institutionalization, and legislation of Western Christianity under the umbrella of the Roman papacy has framed our understanding of the early church. This development was parallel to and directly related to the formation of Rabbinic Judaism.

5. See, for example, Skarsaune and Hvalvk, *Jewish Believers in Jesus*; Jackson-McCabe, *Jewish Christianity Reconsidered*; Broadhead, *Jewish Ways*. Broadhead (28–42) gives samples of key contributors to the re-definition of Jewish Christianity.

churches within the Gentile culture, under the influence of alternative trajectories within the Second Temple Diaspora.

METHODOLOGY AND ASSUMPTIONS

This paper defines Jewish Christianity as the communities of believers that followed Jesus in lifestyles and worship patterns that were consistent with first-century Jewish cosmologies and liturgies.[6] They lived in what David Frankfurter describes as "continuous communities of halakhically-observant Jewish groups," and proclaimed Jesus as their Messiah.[7] They saw themselves as the "True Israel" in continuity with the Law and the Prophets. Paul distinguished their mission from his own in Gal 2:9, saying that Paul and Barnabas should "go to the Gentiles" (εἰς τὰ ἔθνη), and the apostles represented by Peter, James, and John should "go to the circumcised" (αὐτοὶ δὲ εἰς τὴν περιτομήν). Jewish Christianity was spread by the twelve apostles in Judea, Galilee, Samaria, and throughout the Diaspora. Luke depicts James as claiming that there were many thousands of Jews who were believers and that they were "*all* zealous for the law" (πάντες ζηλωταὶ τοῦ νόμου ὑπάρχουσιν [Act 21:20]). Though it was led by the Jerusalem church, the mission to the Jews came to reflect different trajectories or philosophies that were already present among the Diaspora Jewish communities about how believing Gentiles could be in relationship with God's people, while the Pauline mission extended the implications of other trajectories from the Second Temple Diaspora.

If we can begin with the assumption for the sake of argument that the Jewish Christian communities in the Diaspora were in continuity with Second Temple Judaism, then we will be able to further throw light on certain aspects of Jewish Christianity that affect our readings of the Jewish Christian New Testament corpus, and our understanding of the nature of the difference between the Pauline mission to the Gentiles and the rest of first-century Christianity, as well as some of the primary points of conflict. The focus in this paper will be differing views and practices concerning how the Gentiles should be included in the communities of believers that

---

6. This definition is pragmatic and not meant to obscure the complexity and difficulty of articulating "an accurate and useful definition" (Broadhead, *Jewish Ways*, 28). See ibid., 28–58, for an overview of the quest for a definition of Jewish Christianity and the issues involved. Even the term "Jewish Christianity" is questioned, and some prefer "Christian Judaism" to describe the first believers in Jesus, considering the movement to be part of the diversity of Judaism during the Second Temple Period.

7. Frankfurter, "Beyond 'Jewish Christianity,'" 134–35.

can be traced through the literature of the Diaspora and related to practices in the first century and the early church.[8]

The methodology consists of placing the practices of Jewish Christianity in regard to Gentile conversion in the Diaspora in the context of the beliefs and practices of Second Temple Diaspora Judaism. First, relevant features in the Diaspora experience will be identified that belong to paradigms current among Jews, some of which can be distinguished from the paradigms in Palestine, though there was certainly a mutual influence and exchange. Second, philosophies and practices concerning the spiritual status of the Gentiles and their conversion will be traced through Second Temple literature from the Diaspora. Third, the philosophies and practices will be correlated to the practices of Jewish Christianity primarily through Luke's description of apostolic mission, Paul's descriptions and criticisms of the practices of Jewish believers, and the Jewish Christian New Testament corpus.[9] These will be contrasted with Paul's practices. Finally, the implications for the relationship of Christianity to Judaism and biblical models for missions will be discussed.

RELEVANT DIASPORA PARADIGMS

The Diaspora brought Jewish communities into relationship with Gentiles in the surrounding dominant cultures that were significantly different in nature from Jewish-Gentile relationships in Palestine. The experience of the Diaspora stimulated new paradigms for how the Jews understood and experienced their faith as it was directly influenced by relationships with the dominant Gentile culture, and, in turn, influenced relationships with Gentiles.

The widespread concern and interest in the issue of the Gentiles' relationship to Israel's God emerged out of several aspects in the Jewish experience. Positive daily social interaction with Gentiles led some Jews to hope that Gentiles might recognize the truth and prompted them to make connections with positive types or examples of Gentile believers in the Old Testament. The disrupted connection of the Diaspora community to the land shifted their self-definition to more of a metaphor of citizenship in a

---

8. This work is indebted to Donaldson's study *Judaism and the Gentiles*, and extends his conclusions to Jewish Christian relationships with the Gentiles.

9. The Jewish Christian canon consists of the books in the New Testament that are not Pauline or Lucan: Matthew, Mark, John, Hebrews, James, 1 and 2 Peter, 1, 2 and 3 John, Jude, and Revelation.

community with shared ancestral customs that consisted of "socialization, education and patrimony," and ideology that included ethical qualities and the exclusive worship of the God of Israel.[10] The metaphor of citizenship could then be extended to include an ethnic identity that could be adopted, as in the case of Roman citizenship. Negative interactions with the dominant culture highlighted the refugee experience of the Diaspora. This led to a "reverse Diaspora" [11] where the Diaspora communities formed networks of "civic bodies and households and friendships"[12] that were cities of refuge in exile. An understanding then developed that Gentiles also could take refuge with God by joining the Diaspora communities.

Gentile criticisms of Judaism and attraction to Judaism in terms of attitudes and actions stimulated the discussion of the issue. Gentiles criticized the Jews in the Diaspora on the grounds of exclusivity and misanthropy, accusing them of poor citizenship and atheism because they refused to honor the local gods. This led to apologetic literature such as Josephus's *Against Apion*, the *Letter of Aristeas*, and the *Sibylline Oracles*, which describe Jewish traditions in Hellenistic terms. The attraction of Gentiles to Judaism and the Diaspora synagogue pushed the issue much further. Religion in the Greco-Roman world encompassed all aspects of life, public and private. The Diaspora community worshipped and lived openly in a culture that was polytheistic in practice, form, and function. In the Roman Empire, religious inclusivity was a value and an intentional imperial policy. For a Gentile, there were almost unlimited religious options that he or she could experience, so that any Gentile would feel free to enter a synagogue during a service or for prayer. Inevitably, some Gentiles wished to form a closer relationship with the Diaspora community or the God of Israel. This led to a discussion of what kind of relationship was possible between a Gentile and the God of Israel.

Donaldson suggests that the issue of how a Gentile could enter into a relationship with Israel's God was not a defining feature of Second Temple Judaism in the Diaspora.[13] Rather, the defining feature was the question of how much a Jew could adopt Gentile ways. However, while the rumors of Paul's alleged adoption of Gentile ways was a crucial issue for the Jewish

---

10. Donaldson, *Judaism and the Gentiles*, 239.
11. Ibid., 237.
12. Philo, *Spec. leg.*, 1.52: πόλεων καὶ οἰκείων καὶ φίλων.
13. Donaldson, *Judaism and the Gentiles*, 3.

Christians in Jerusalem (Acts 21:21, 28),[14] the issue of Gentile conversion became the defining feature that differentiated Pauline Christianity from Jewish Christianity. Therefore, it is helpful to look at the spectrum of philosophies and practices in the Diaspora that were concerned with the relationship of Gentiles to the Jewish community.

DIASPORA PHILOSOPHIES AND PRACTICES CONCERNING GENTILE SPIRITUAL STATUS AND CONVERSION

There were some differences of opinion concerning the spiritual status of the various categories of Gentiles and the apocalyptic future of Gentiles. However, many Gentiles were attracted to the Jewish communities and the synagogues in varying degrees, and the Jewish communities encouraged this interest. Gentiles who chose to become proselytes were incorporated into the Diaspora community, adopted the Jewish culture, and belonged to the nation of Israel rather than their nation of birth. This pattern, or variations of it, best accounts for the mission practices of apostolic or Jewish Christianity that Paul characterizes as the "mission to the circumcised." As Donaldson argues, the debates and conflicts that besieged Jewish Christianity internally, and particularly the clashes with the Pauline mission, were "variations of debates that were already established within Judaism" that concerned the patterns of universalism.[15]

Universalism versus Exclusivity

As Boda has convincingly argued, the "mission of God . . . to the nations of the world" is a dominant message in the Psalter, but is also present throughout the Old Testament.[16] Therefore, the early church was able to find biblical support for universalism in its mission, but there is also evidence of support for the universalism of Judaism in the Second Temple Period.

---

14. Luke quotes James as saying to Paul: "They have been told about you that you teach all the Jews living among the Gentiles to forsake Moses, and that you tell them not to circumcise their children or observe the customs" (Acts 21:21).

15. Donaldson, *Judaism and the Gentiles*, 9. Donaldson writes, "since earliest Christianity needs to be seen as one aspect of Second Temple Judaism broadly considered, a better understanding of these Jewish patterns of universalism will contribute to a better understanding of how and why early Jewish Christianity began to attract Gentiles and of the debates and conflicts that ensued."

16. Boda, "Declare His Glory," 14.

It has been common, due to the influence of Baur, to portray Judaism as a religion of exclusivity while Christianity is portrayed as a superior religion of universality.[17] It would appear that part of the effect of the domination by a succession of empires after the Restoration, and particularly the aggressive campaigns of Hellenization, was that some forms of Judaism in Palestine and Galilee emphasized the exclusivity of Israel in vision and practice. In the extreme, the Gentile presence in the land of Israel was contamination, and the purity laws demanded separation. The universalism and apocalyptic inclusion of the Gentiles tended to be seen as an indication of the victory of Israel, the subordination of all other nations to the God of Israel, and the punishment of the nations.

However, among the Jews in the Diaspora, one might argue that it was common, perhaps even more common, to understand the universalism in the Psalter, Torah, and the other prophets and writings as one in which the God of Israel was present among his people even when they were exiles and sojourners, and Gentiles could have some positive relationship to Israel's God. The realities of life in the Diaspora made it more difficult to espouse exclusivity to the degree that it was practiced in Palestine. The quest for theological coherence in their altered reality of different anxieties and challenges to their identity resulted in a different relationship to the dominant cultures—sometimes a more positive relationship.[18]

Centripetal Attraction versus Centrifugal Mission

Many have attempted to argue that Judaism provided a precedent for evangelistic outreach, while others have argued that there was no Jewish mission that attempted to reach out and convert Gentiles.[19] While it is beyond the

---

17. See Gerdmar, *Roots of Theological Anti-Semitism*, 113.

18. That is not to say that an argument for exclusivity was not present in the Diaspora—sociological patterns in immigrant communities show a certain amount of tension and polarization in immigrant integration and ghetto formation. Sometimes exiles from the homeland can become more intolerant of the dominant culture and vehement advocates of cultural exclusivity than those who remain in the nation of origin, which is probably exemplified in the initial conflict between Stephen and the Jews of Cyrene, Alexandria, Cilicia, and Asia in the Synagogue of the Freedmen in Jerusalem (Acts 6:8–10). For an influential study on this phenomenon, see Meyer-Ortmanns, "Immigration, Integration and Ghetto Formation," 311.

19. For those who argue for a mission in Judaism, see Bamberger, *Proselytism*; Braude, *Jewish Proselyting*; Boccaccini, *Middle Judaism*, 252; Feldman, "Was Judaism a Missionary Religion?"; Feldman, *Jew and Gentile*, 106, 289–93; Georgi, *Opponents of Paul*; Harnack, *Mission and Expansion*, 9; Moore, *Judaism in the First Centuries*, 1:323–24; Schürer,

purposes of this paper to settle this question, Josephus reported a number of "conversions" by conquest, which indicate that at least some Jews at some points in history took initiative in "converting" Gentiles when they had political and military power to do so.[20] Similarly, pragmatic conversions occurred for the sake of alliances in marriage, which was explored positively in the pseudepigraphal story of *Joseph and Aseneth*.[21] However, in the Diaspora, not only was forced conversion not an option, but proselytizing for monotheistic Judaism was discouraged both in the polytheistic Roman Empire and in the rival neighboring Parthian Empire. The full conversion of a prominent Gentile was thought to be a dangerous move for both the Jewish community and the convert.[22] Nevertheless, there is no doubt that the Jewish Diaspora communities attracted Gentiles without taking the initiative to evangelize them. Apart from an unsolicited attraction on the part of Gentiles to the qualities of Judaism (which was consistent with the polytheistic eclecticism of the time), most reported conversions took place because of marriage. In other contexts where it was possible for Judaism to be dominant, fear or coercion were also factors. While some would not see this as mission, the denial of any Jewish mission may come out of a constricted definition of mission that is anachronistic and/or parochial, based on our modern missionary theories and practices.[23] It is difficult to find

History of the Jewish People, 3:160. For those who argue against any missionary effort, see Goodman, "Jewish Proselytizing"; Goodman, *Mission and Conversion*; Kraabel, "Roman Diaspora"; McKnight, *Light among the Gentiles*; Munck, *Paul and the Salvation of Mankind*, 264–71.

20. For conversions by force, see Josephus, *J.W.* 2.454; *Ant.* 11.285; 13.257–258; 13.318–319; 15.254–255; 16.225.

21. *Joseph and Aseneth* is a Diaspora story of romance and piety that Donaldson describes as "the longest and most elaborate conversion story to be found in the Jewish literature of the period" (Donaldson, *Judaism and the Gentiles*, 141).

22. In *Ant.* 20.34–48, Josephus tells the story of King Izates (1–55 CE) of the royal family of Adiabene, a Parthian client kingdom (the Parthian state was a rival kingdom to the Roman Empire), whose wives were converted to Judaism by a Jewish merchant named Ananias. Izates decided to convert and be circumcised, but his mother and Ananias argued against it, saying it was dangerous and unnecessary. Ananias "threatened that if he should be unable to persuade Izates, he would abandon him and leave the land. For he said that he was afraid that he would be punished, in all likelihood, as personally responsible because he had instructed the king in unseemly practices."

23. See Westfall, "Hebrew Mission," 187–91, for a broad definition of mission as opposed to a more narrow one such as a "conscious, deliberate, organized, and extensive effort to convert others to one's religion by way of evangelism or proselytization" (Köstenberger and O'Brien, *Salvation to the Ends of the Earth*, 254).

evidence of campaigns to convert, but there is ample evidence that Jews in the Diaspora were aware of the attraction of Gentiles to Judaism, welcomed the attraction, and had strategies for responding to that attraction. For example, Philo wrote:

> [Abraham] is the standard of nobility for all proselytes, who abandoning the ignobility of strange laws and monstrous customs which assigned divine honours to stocks and stones and soulless things in general, have come to settle in a better land, in a commonwealth of true life and vitality, with truth as its director and precedent (Philo, *Virtues*, 219).

Much of the Jews' sense of identity and eschatological expectation included some form of vindication of Israel in which the Gentile nations would recognize the truth and respond to it. Therefore, there was clearly a "Field of Dreams" mentality and faith in the inherent centripetal attraction of Judaism: that if they established Jewish communities that followed the ancient traditions and carried out the worship of the God of Israel in the Diaspora, then the Gentiles would come as admirers, sympathizers, and adherents. Josephus suggests that this approach to mission was successful when he claimed, "The masses have long since shown a keen desire to adopt our religious observances" (Josephus, *Ag. Ap.* 2.282). It is not as clear that there was a strong movement of Jewish groups in the Diaspora who embraced the personal responsibility to overtly persuade Gentiles in anything like door-to-door evangelism while they occupied a vulnerable position of a minority in a dominant culture. For the purposes of this discussion, we will narrow the focus to the Jewish debates on the nature of Gentile adherents or converts.

Diaspora Debates on Gentile Conversions and Spiritual Status

There were roughly three categories of Gentiles considered in the debate on the spiritual status of Gentiles: those who practiced "ethical monotheism," those who were benefactors of the Jews, and proselytes.[24]

The first category consisted of Gentiles who, apart from Judaism, perceived something about God and God's requirements from contemplating the created order.[25] Donaldson describes this pattern as:

---

24. While Donaldson combines benefaction and ethical monotheism into one category (Donaldson, *Judaism and the Gentiles*, 272), it is clear from Philo that some Gentiles who practice ethical monotheism, such as Plato, were not benefactors of Israel.

25. Besides Philo and Josephus, see, for example *Wis. Sol.* 1:1-2, *T. Ab.* 10:12-14,

Rejection

one in which Jews consider it possible for Gentiles to acquire accurate and adequate knowledge of the one true God, or to relate to this God in appropriate ways, without any knowledge of Judaism or association with the Jewish community.[26]

Some, such as Philo, believed that Gentiles such as Plato, who practiced "ethical monotheism," were on a route to the same destination as Judaism. For Philo, the destination was virtue, high worthiness, or "the blameless life of righteous people who follow nature and her ordinances" (Philo, *Spec. leg.* 2.42). Such righteous Gentiles were "indeed but a small number left in their cities like an ember of wisdom to smoulder, that virtue may not be altogether extinguished and lost to our race" (Philo, *Spec. leg.* 2.47). Furthermore, Philo believed that God communicated to Gentiles: "But we find that to good men God whispers good decisions by which they will give and receive benefits" (Philo, *Embassy* 245). Josephus suggests that Gentiles could worship the same God as the God of Israel by a different name (*Ant.* 12.22). Though some suggest that Philo had little influence on Judaism, in the area of ethical monotheism he belonged to a trajectory that was in continuity with what developed into Rabbinic Judaism. In Rabbinic Judaism, the term "righteous Gentile" referred to those who followed the Noahide Laws, which were believed to be the Seven Laws of Noah that included prohibitions of idolatry, murder, theft, sexual immorality, blasphemy, and eating live flesh, and included the maintenance of court systems that enforced the six laws.[27] Non-Jews who followed these laws were assured of a place in the world to come. There are numerous passages in the Hebrew Bible, the LXX, and the Pseudepigrapha that address the inclusion of Gentiles who are not a part of the believing community in eschatological salvation.[28] Adherents to this view believed that Gentiles were not obligated to follow the 613 commandments in the Torah, and some felt that it would be wrong for Gentiles to even attempt to keep the Law.[29]

12:12–13, *Sib. Or.* 4:24–39.

26. Donaldson, *Judaism and the Gentiles*, 493.

27. Besides Gen 9:4–6, the Nohadic Law is possibly taken from *Jub.* 7.20–28.

28. See Donaldson, *Judaism and the Gentiles*, 499–505, for a summary of the literature on the eschatological salvation of the Gentiles. The passages in the Old Testament that indicate eschatological salvation for the Gentiles include Isa 2:2–4; 9:9–10; 25:6; 66:19; Mic 4:1–3; Hag 2:21–22; Zech 8:20–23.

29. Members of this group were not necessarily included or incorporated or in relationship with Israel or the Jewish community in all of the descriptions. It could therefore be more of an abstract category in some instances since it was thought that a

The second category involved those who were Gentile benefactors of the Jewish community, who were seen as honoring the Jews and/or the God of Israel in some way, but may not have been exclusively monotheistic or following the traditions of the Jews. This can be seen as somewhat parallel to the honorific title "righteous Gentile" used by the modern state of Israel to designate Gentiles that risked their lives to save Jews during the Holocaust. Josephus describes various Romans as worshipping the God of Israel, though they were not monotheistic (e.g., *J.W.* 3.444; 5.519; *Ant.* 11.3–5). Maintaining a positive relationship with this kind of Gentile was ideal for Jews in the Diaspora, because it meant benefits and protection virtually without risk. These were relationships that one could draw on when Jews or Israel were under attack. This category would include the so-called "God-fearers" such as the centurion Cornelius. Cornelius with his family is described as devout, God-fearing, giving generously to those in need, and praying to God regularly (Acts 10:2).

The third category included the proselytes or Gentile converts to Judaism. The nature and practice of Judaism was not only religious but geographical, political, cultural, and genealogical. Therefore, there were three aspects of Judaism that were models in how Jews in the Diaspora thought of the conversion of Gentiles: (1) participation in the worship of the God of Israel; (2) membership in the ethnic group, which was often depicted as a family relationship; and (3) the adoption of the Jewish way of life that consisted of the ancient traditions based on the Torah, but that way of life was often described in the Diaspora in terms of a culture, a philosophy, or a political constitution that a Gentile could adopt. The models from the Hebrew Bible for the relationship to the Gentiles who wanted to convert and become a part of the Diaspora community included the "stranger at the gate" (or the resident alien),[30] the Gentile servants/slaves in the household,[31] and proselytes.[32] The question was: In what way can a Gentile become in-

---

true righteous Gentile who came into contact with the Jewish community would tend to become part of the second category. The categories are fluid, but this category and discussion contributed a model for a Pauline understanding of Gentile conversion, which is evident from his discussions of knowing God from the natural order (Rom 1:18–32) and Paul's mention of a Gentile's conscience that knows the Law instinctively (Rom 2:14–15).

30. Exod 20:9–10; Deut 5:13–14; 14:20–29; 16:10–14; 24:13–14; 26:11–12; 31:11–12.

31. Exod 12:43–45; Lev 25:44–46.

32. Examples of proselytes include Rahab (Josh 2:1–24) and Ruth. Boyarin argues that "this move constituted a sort of naturalization into the Jewish People more than it did a conversion in the later, religious sense. 'Conversion' in the first century still seems

corporated into the legal and corporate life of the Jewish community in the Diaspora in terms of civic bodies, households, and friendships? A closely related question was: What must Gentiles do to fulfill what God expects of them? Of course, circumcision was the primary issue, but a secondary issue for both the Jewish communities and Gentile adherents would have been open identification with Israel and the transfer of loyalty from their nation of birth, particularly if the convert was a political figure, and more so if there were political tensions between Israel and the empire of that time period.

It appears that one way the issue was side-stepped was by addressing the conversion of women, which is clear in the two most extensive discussions of conversion: the Diaspora description of the conversion of Joseph's Egyptian wife in *Joseph and Aseneth*, and an actual account reported by Josephus about a Jewish merchant Ananias who "visited the . . . wives [of the Parthian client-king King Izates] and taught them to worship God after the manner of the Jewish tradition" (Josephus, *Ant.* 2.34). Women could participate in worship and the other two issues could be side-stepped—this kind of covert practice could cultivate a beneficial and powerful patron-client relationship for Jews in the Diaspora. However, King Izates then decided not only to adopt the worship of the God of Israel, but to be circumcised, because he believed that he "would not be genuinely a Jew unless he was circumcised and decided to act accordingly." At this point, Ananias assured Izates that "The king . . . could worship God even without being circumcised if indeed he had fully decided to be a devoted adherent to Judaism, *for it was this that counted more than circumcision*." God would pardon him for the omission—it was expedient for political reasons.[33] But later, another Jew named Eleazor, "who came from Galilee and who had a reputation for being extremely strict when it came to the ancestral laws" persuaded him that he should be circumcised (Josephus, *Ant.* 20:34–48).

Josephus's account reveals a number of dynamics that represent the debates about conversion and practices in the Jewish community and that

---

semantically and socially more like becoming an Athenian or a Roman citizen" (Boyarin, "Semantic Differences," 68). This is consistent with Philo's descriptions.

33. Both Izates's mother and Ananias were afraid that there would be a dangerous political reaction if Izates's conversion to Judaism were made public. This is exactly the fear that is expressed in the story of Daniel and Bel and the Dragon in the case of Cyrus when Daniel killed Bel and Cyrus had Bel's priests put to death: "When the Babylonians heard about it, they were very indignant and conspired against the king, saying, 'The king has become a Jew; he has destroyed Bel, and killed the dragon, and slaughtered the priests.' Going to the king, they said, 'Hand Daniel over to us, or else we will kill you and your household'" (Bel 1:28–29).

are relevant to our understanding of conversion to Judaism in the first century. First, if there was not an overt initiative by groups of Jews to convert Gentiles, there should be a recognition that there was some kind of covert activity by individuals. Second, it is likely that Jewish individuals seized the opportunity to cultivate patron-client relationships in the dominant culture by some form of instruction and persuasion. Third, influential Gentile women were safer targets for some form of conversion—their practice of Judaism was not as troubling for either the Gentile community or the Jewish community and it occupied a grey area that represents a continuum between being a righteous Gentile benefactor and a proselyte. Fourth, at least some Jews in the Diaspora believed that a Gentile male could be a Jew without being circumcised—God understood the expedient circumstances and he would make exceptions for males who adopted the rest of the ancient traditions.[34] In fact, even Jews or half-Jews such as Timothy might be uncircumcised in the Diaspora.[35] Not requiring circumcision was clearly a safer route for the Diaspora communities.[36] Fifth, in contrast, devout Jews from Galilee and Judea were more likely to insist on circumcision for

---

34. Broadhead observes, "Philo, Josephus, and Jerome treat circumcision as rather non-distinctive" (Broadhead, *Jewish Ways*, 47). See particularly, Cohen, *Beginnings of Jewishness*, 39–49.

35. See Acts 16:1–3. Timothy's family was located in Lystra. Timothy's father was a Greek and his mother was a Jew. In the Hebrew Bible and at points in the Second Temple era, there is evidence that ethnic Jewishness was primarily patrilineal, but by ca. 200 CE, a matrilineal principle dominates (Cohen, *Beginnings of Jewishness*, 305–7). It is clear from Luke's account that either Paul or the Jews from that area, or both, considered Timothy to be a Jew in some sense. Typically, Jewish women took responsibility to circumcise their sons (cf. 1 Macc 1:60), but Timothy's mother had not done so. Paul had Timothy circumcised "because of the Jews who were in those places, for they all knew that his father was a Greek" (Acts 16:3). This reflects both the fact that there were diverse practices concerning circumcision in the Diaspora, and that Paul wanted those who were ethnic Jews on his team to comply with the more strict requirements as a strategy. This indicates that Paul's interest in an indigenous mission extended both to Jews and Gentiles, as he claims in 1 Cor 9:20–21: "To the Jews I became as a Jew, in order to win Jews. To those under the law I became as one under the law (though I myself am not under the law) so that I might win those under the law. To those outside the law I became as one outside the law (though I am not free from God's law but am under Christ's law) so that I might win those outside the law" (1 Cor 9:20–21).

36. On the other hand, Philo resorted to encouragement about the benefits of circumcision rather than delivering imperatives to a Greco-Roman culture that was disgusted by the thought of men mutilating their genitals (Philo, *Spec. leg.* 1.5–7). Philo gives four traditional arguments for the benefits of circumcision and two allegorical arguments about its significance.

male proselytes.[37] This stands to reason, because the forced Hellenization of Judea during the Maccabbean period targeted circumcision within the borders of Israel,[38] and because the Jews from Judea and Galilee would be more accustomed to enforcing the requirements of entrance into the temple.[39] Izates was exactly the kind of proselyte who would make a pilgrimage to Jerusalem and expect entrance into the court of men as a Jew, which could touch off an international incident if he were uncircumcised.[40]

CORRESPONDING MISSION PRACTICES OF FIRST-CENTURY JEWISH CHRISTIANITY IN THE DIASPORA

I suggest that we now understand the practices of conversion in the early church as being in continuity with the practices that we have outlined. Jewish Christians spread the gospel from Jerusalem through the Jewish communities and synagogues of the Diaspora, and Gentiles were attracted to the faith, converted, and were fully incorporated into the Jewish Christian "cities of refuge" in a similar way to how they had been incorporated into the Jewish communities. Believers from Cyprus and Cyrene had unexpected success with the Gentile population when they preached to Greeks as well as Jews in Antioch. Eventually, the same debates and issues that were a part of the Jewish discussion emerged because of Gentile conversions in the Diaspora communities such as Antioch and the Pauline mission. How the

---

37. Broadhead, following Cohen, cautions against understanding circumcision as establishing Judaism, writing, "Circumcision, which was also practiced in Egypt and in various cultures influenced by Egypt, was probably first taken as a marker of Jewishness in the Maccabean period, where it is a sign that one is not Hellenistic" (Broadhead, *Jewish Ways*, 47).

38. See, for example, 1 Macc 1:60–61; 2 Macc 6:10; 4 Macc 4:25. In reaction to the prohibition of circumcision under Antiochus Epiphanes, during the Maccabean Revolt, Matthias and his followers forcibly circumcised all uncircumcised boys within the borders of Israel (1 Macc 2:46).

39. In 2 Macc 2:21, Ἰουδαϊσμός refers to a concern for the temple, the city, and the laws, in contrast with Ἑλληνισμός in 2 Macc 4:13, which was used pejoratively to describe the ways of the foreigner.

40. Of course, there was concern about the restrictions for entrance into the temple among Diaspora Jews as is indicated in Acts 21:28–29, where it was Diaspora Jews from Asia who started a riot when they accused Paul of bringing a Gentile into the restricted area. But those were either pilgrims or residents of Jerusalem such as those who belonged to the Synagogue of the Freedmen (cf. Acts 6:9). They were present in the temple, and therefore had far different concerns and priorities than a Diaspora Jew merchant who is 2,500 kilometers from Jerusalem.

decision of the Jerusalem Council was understood by the Jewish Christians must be considered in the light of the Diaspora debates. The understanding of the Gentile presence in the Jewish Christian corpus can be understood as part of the success of the Jewish Christian mission rather than inconsistent with the gospel to the circumcised. Finally, we can contrast the gospel to the Jews with Paul's gospel to the Gentiles.

The great commission and Luke's and Mark's statements by Jesus that the gospel would be preached to all nations (πάντα τὰ ἔθνη—Matt 28:19–20; Luke 24:47; Mark 13:10) beginning in Jerusalem, are usually taken as unambiguous indication that the disciples should have understood that they were to evangelize the Gentiles. However, Luke's account of the foundation of the church at Pentecost shows that the apostolic mission would have been understood as being accomplished through bringing the gospel to the Diaspora communities, because he referred to Diaspora Jews who were in Jerusalem for the Pentecost festival as "devout Jewish men from every nation" (Ἰουδαῖοι, ἄνδρες εὐλαβεῖς ἀπὸ παντὸς ἔθνους Acts 2:5), then specified that the group included "Jews and proselytes" (Ἰουδαῖοί τε καὶ προσήλυτοι Acts 2:11). As far as Jesus' model of making disciples, the most natural application was to extend Jesus' mission and methods through these Diaspora communities that were represented at Pentecost. It is widely believed that the Roman church was founded from Roman converts who were present that day.[41] After phenomenal church growth, the stoning of Steven, and the revival in Samaria, Peter's conversion of Cornelius and his household in Caesarea (Acts 10:1–47) only took place because Peter was allegedly led in a vision (Acts 11:5). Jewish Christians in Jerusalem criticized him at that time for going into an uncircumcised person's house and eating with him (Acts 11:3), though we have seen that Jews in the Diaspora might visit in a Gentile home. It may be assumed that Cornelius was incorporated into the Jewish Christian community.[42]

It was believers from Cyprus and Cyrene who started to intentionally preach the gospel to the Gentiles (Greeks) in Antioch when they were scattered by the persecution after the stoning of Stephen (Acts 11:19–21). It was an innovative move by Diaspora Jews in a Diaspora context. So many Gentiles believed that the Jerusalem church sent Barnabas to handle the

---

41. Hvalvik concludes, "It is clear that the cradle of Roman Christianity is to be found within the Jewish community" (Hvalvik, "Jewish Believers," 184).

42. Bauckham writes, "we should probably assume that such Gentiles were required to become Jews and that initially this was uncontroversial" (Bauckham, "James and the Jerusalem Community," 73).

unusual situation, and Barnabas recruited Paul to help. Barnabas and Paul, who were Diaspora Jews themselves, did not require the Gentile converts to be circumcised. Then, in a pattern very much like the conflict between Ananias and Eleazor in Josephus's account, believers from Judea came to Antioch and told the Gentile believers that they needed to be circumcised. In the case of Izates, Eleazor said that he needed to be circumcised to be a *Jew*, but perhaps influenced by Christian terminology and concerns, the believers from Judah said that unless they were circumcised according to the custom taught by Moses, they could not be *saved* (οὐ δύνασθε σωθῆναι— Acts 15:1). This would suggest that up to this point, any Gentiles who came to faith in Judea would have been fully incorporated into the Jewish Christian community. They would have become Jews and their circumcision would be part of their adoption of Judaism.

In view of Paul's evidence and argument, and Peter's support, the Jerusalem Council determined that Gentiles would not be required to be circumcised, but rather would be asked to follow laws that were very close to later Rabbinic Noahadic Laws.[43] James's reason for these requirements was because "The law of Moses has been preached in every city from the earliest times and is read in the synagogues on every Sabbath" (Acts 15:21), which indicates that the Gentiles were thought to have been adequately exposed to the traditions of Israel and could be held accountable to live in harmony with those traditions.[44] As we saw, there was a precedent for this expectation of righteous Gentiles who were to experience eschatological salvation already, and it is consistent with one trajectory for the relationship of Jews with Gentiles. The best understanding of the letter from the Jerusalem Council is that these requirements were consistent with maintaining the ancient traditions and culture in the Jewish Christian community in continuity with what held in Diaspora Jewish communities. The support for James's motivation was pragmatic: "It is my judgment . . . that we should

---

43. Bock states, "The list seems to reflect an ethos instead of being the invocation of a specific text. In Judaism this ethos is summarized in a text such as [the Babylonian Talmud Šebi'it 7b], where idolatry and the shedding of blood are prohibited and chastity is urged," though Bock insists that the issue is about "having a spirit of sensitivity about that which may cause offense" rather than ethics per se (Bock, *Acts*, 507).

44. Contra both Barrett and Bock who assume that preaching of the Law of Moses is an indication of the Jews' knowledge of the Law (Barrett, *Acts 15–28*, 737; Bock, *Acts*, 507). In this context it is more consistent with the Diaspora discussion to understand that James meant that the proclamation of the Law in these public areas resulted in Gentiles hearing it and knowing it.

not make it difficult for the Gentiles who are turning to God" (Acts 15:19).[45] Therefore, the letter does not require circumcision, but it does not rule it out as an option for a Gentile who would choose to be more closely incorporated into the civic bodies, households, and friendships of Judaism.

James's statements that Gentiles are exposed to the Law of Moses in every city and synagogue and Gentiles should not be hindered from turning to God is consistent with the language of other Jews such as Josephus and Philo in that he appears to expect Gentiles to be exposed to Judaism and attracted to Christianity as they are to Judaism as a matter of course. He is willing to make circumcision optional for Gentiles, but he allows the essential nature of the Jewish community and culture as it has existed in Judea, Galilee, and the Diaspora to be maintained. It is clear from Acts 21:20–25, that James and the Jerusalem leadership still expected all Jewish Christians to keep the Law of Moses, while they reiterated that Gentile believers might keep the lesser requirements for righteous Gentiles.[46]

What distinguished Paul's role as the apostle to the Gentiles from Peter's role as the apostle to the Jews? Paul deliberately attempted to plant indigenous churches that were embedded in the Gentile culture rather than a sub-culture that was an export or product of Judaism.[47] In 1 Cor 9:20–23, Paul indicated this commitment when he said that he became like the people to whom he was ministering. But in the case of circumcision, more was at stake than mission strategy. Paul appeared to forbid the Gentiles in his churches to be circumcised. The problem was created by the Judean believers who came from James and said that the Gentiles needed to be circumcised to be *saved*, and if that was how circumcision was understood, it

---

45. As Barrett summarizes, "The Gentile converts must not be pestered; the context makes clear that this means that demands of full legal observance must not be made" (Barrett, *Acts 15-28*, 730).

46. James expected Paul to keep the Law of Moses. It is not as clear to commentators whether Paul had the same expectation of himself. However, Paul had Timothy circumcised before he would take him on the Second Missionary Journey "because of the Jews who lived in that area, for they all knew that his father was a Greek" (Acts 16:3). Of course, this account has the same ambiguity: Was Paul complying when in the presence of Jews to keep the peace?

47. As Lemke writes, "distinct social groups (classes, genders, religious sects, etc.) often speak distinct discourses which they take, metadiscursively, to be allied with or opposed to the discourses of other groups. Social identity, the relations among social positions and roles, and social alliances and conflicts are maintained and in part constituted by the relations construed between usual ways of speaking about various subjects" (Lemke, "Intertextuality and Text Semantics," 97).

had to be rejected. His criticism of salvation by works is better understood as directed at the Jewish Christians' combination of Jewish practice and the Christian focus on salvation rather than directed towards Judaism as a whole. He claimed that if anyone in his churches was circumcised to be made righteous, it would alienate them from Christ and result in a fall from grace (Gal 5:4).[48] Paul furthermore determined that Gentiles did not have to be integrated into the Jewish culture or community to live a life of faith. In fact, he became antagonistic towards any attempts to persuade his churches to adopt aspects of Jewish culture (or other competing cultures) concerning food and holy days (Col 2:16).[49] Consequently, Paul was committed to establishing indigenous churches throughout the Roman Empire rather than integrating Gentiles into the Diaspora Jewish Christian communities. This was a clear innovation on the patterns of conversion in Judaism, but it is not inconsistent with the views about the status of ethical monotheism and the righteous Gentile, particularly given the added element of salvation through Christ alone. Paul was not as radical as he seems, once the context of the Diaspora discussion and practices about conversion of the Gentiles are considered. According to many Jewish readings of the Old Testament, Gentiles were going to be included in eschatological salvation. For Christian Jews, Jesus' life and death signaled the arrival of the last days. Therefore, in Paul's view, Gentile converts should remain Gentiles culturally to fulfill the prophecies, and the church community should be suited to the local culture and led by local Christians. God would not speak in Paul's churches exclusively with a Judean accent. But Paul stayed connected with the Jerusalem church and complied with the Jerusalem leadership.

---

48. As Longenecker summarizes, "The Judaizers must have assured the Galatians that in accepting supervision for their lives from the prescriptions of the Mosaic Law they were not forsaking Christ or renouncing grace, but rather were completing their commitment to both. Paul, however, tells them just the opposite: commitment to Christ and commitment to legal prescriptions for righteousness, whether that righteousness is understood in forensic terms (i.e., 'justification') or ethical terms (i.e., 'lifestyle' and expression), are mutually exclusive; experientially, the one destroys the other" (Longenecker, *Galatians*, 228). Note that the goal of circumcision is different than with Izates. Izates specifically wanted to become a Jew.

49. Barth and Blanke state that Paul "now turns against the 'teachers' who seek to differentiate the non-chosen from the chosen and who seek to make visible the exclusivity of the latter" (Barth and Blanke, *Colossians*, 339). O'Brien cautions, "Paul is not condemning the use of sacred days or seasons as such; it is the wrong motive involved" (O'Brien, *Colossians, Philemon*, 139).

In contrast, Peter and the rest of the apostles conducted a mission to the Jews that looked more like the mission patterns that Jesus established in the Gospels and those practiced by the Diaspora communities than Paul's mission did.[50] It is clear that the rest of the apostles engaged in missionary journeys that were comparable to Paul's missionary journeys. Paul complained that the Jewish Christians leadership (Peter, the other apostles, and Jesus' brothers) got to take their wives with them on mission trips (1 Cor 9:5).[51] When Paul wrote to the Romans, he said "there is no more place for me to work in these regions" (Rom 15:23), since he was trying to preach the gospel where Christ was not known, and he wanted to avoid "building on someone else's foundation" (Rom 15:20).[52] Apparently he had to go to all the way to Spain to find a place where the gospel was not preached. It is not plausible that Paul's mission team alone had saturated all other areas or that Paul's sense of territory and purpose was so restricted that he considered his job done in all but the extreme west. The conduct of mission by the apostles and the apparent "saturation" implies that the gospel was being preached aggressively by the group of apostles that Jesus commissioned (except Judas

---

50. Schnabel argues: "The first challenge for the early Christian missionaries was the lack of models for an international religious operation that seeks to win new converts in new regions and establish new religious communities in new cities and towns" (Schnabel, *Early Christian Mission*, 1:536). However, this assertion is based on a narrow definition of mission, and misses the applicability of Jesus' example. Ultimately, it does not sufficiently take into account the contribution of the Hellenistic Jews and the Diaspora experience.

51. The brothers of Jesus would include James, Joses (Joseph), Judas, and Simon (Mark 6:3). Eusebius states that Jesus' relatives were associated with the leadership in Jerusalem and specifically mentions James (Eusebius, *Hist. eccl.*, 2.1.10–17; 3.11). As Thiselton observes, this is the only mention in the New Testament about Jesus' brothers going on mission trips or receiving support from the churches, so "we know nothing more about the reasons or the role which they may have performed in this context" (Thiselton, *1 Corinthians*, 682).

52. Jewett states, "In Paul's formulation, building only on his own foundation implies avoidance of areas where either Gentile congregations or Jewish Christian congregations were already in existence, as in Rome," and "the scope for founding new congregations in crucial urban areas on the circle for which Paul feels called to minister is exhausted" (Jewett, *Romans*, 916, 923). On the other hand, according to Dunn, Paul's claim that there is no longer room for him is a reference "to the strategic vision and policy sketched out in vv. 19–20. The word should certainly not be read as a claim to have done all that could be done, even in terms of foundation-laying, in the East. Paul limited his mission to the arc 'from Jerusalem to Illyricum' (v. 19) and his claim to be 'apostle to the Gentiles' evidently did not involve, in his perspective, a commission to such important regions as Mesopotamia and Egypt. Others had no doubt been commissioned to cover these regions" (Dunn, *Romans 9–16*, 871).

Rejection

Iscariot, and James who was already martyred)—possibly they had divided territories among them as tradition indicates.[53] This also indicates that Gentiles were being attracted to both the gospel and Jewish traditions and culture, as Jewish literature claimed. They would be integrated as righteous Gentiles into a community that was Jewish in culture and both Jewish and Christian in worship format and content. It is doubtful that these churches would have a problem with a Gentile who decided to be circumcised in order to be fully integrated into the community. These communities had a primary association with Israel, so that there may have been some form of adoption into Israel for believing Gentiles who would be seen as genealogical orphans, giving them a genealogy that represented their new identity. This may have been the background behind the "endless genealogies" that were criticized in the Pastoral Epistles (1 Tim 1:4; Tit 3:9).[54] The placement of Gentile believers into the family of God and the commonwealth of Israel as is described by Peter (1 Pet 2:4–10) may have generated a thriving practice for scribes to produce new genealogies that would have the effect of providing Gentiles with new documents of identification and citizenship, consistent with their new fictive kinship relationships, similar in practice to how in Catholicism a woman adopts a religious name when she enters a convent.

The Jewish Christian corpus (Matthew, Mark, John, Hebrews, James, 1 and 2 Peter, 1, 2 and 3 John, Jude, and Revelation) reflects the mission and concerns of the Jewish Christian community consistent with its function as cities of refuge, and the mission of the Jewish Christian community

---

53. See Schnabel, *Early Christian Mission*, 1:527–33 for a survey of later traditions, often independent accounts, ranging from the late first century to the sixth century, that indicate that the apostles left Jerusalem and concentrated on different regions that divided the known world into areas of missionary responsibility. While these accounts have been challenged, they fit Paul's description of missionary activity by others in Romans.

54. As Towner observes, the term "genealogy" (γενεαλογία) has a long history of use, describing lists of family names (family trees), and the process of constructing them, that served various purposes. Within Judaism, genealogies played the key role of establishing a person's bloodline and link to a particular family and tribe: rights by birth determined in this way allowed, for example, entrance into the priesthood" (Towner, *Timothy and Titus*, 110). In other words, in the ancient world, genealogies were roughly comparable to one's identification (i.e., passport). Sometimes a person in the Middle East would purchase a genealogy, which was equivalent to trying to falsify one's papers (Mernissi, *Veil*, 47). However, Towner suggests that this may involve speculation on stories about the early biblical characters, saying "Speculation fitting roughly into this category was known to have been practiced in Jewish communities." See 1QapGen; Pseudo-Philo; and Kittel, "Genealogia."

can be described as the formation of identity, vision, values, and strategy.[55] They were concerned with the identification of Jesus as the Messiah—the development of Christology in the Johannine literature and Hebrews is the greatest theological contribution of the corpus. First Peter particularly develops the identity of the people of God as the true Israel in relationship to Jesus the Messiah. The vision of moving forward as a community and the apocalyptic visions of hope are the special contributions of Hebrews and Revelation. James, Jude and 2 Peter are devoted to developing and maintaining the values that characterize the community. The strategy involved radical commitments to proclaim the gospel to the Jews, build discipleship, and form communities of true Israel, with the conviction that God would draw unbelievers and convert them. Revelation, 1 Peter, and Hebrews make the major contributions in the New Testament to the experience and response to living as exiles with rejection and suffering, and the entire corpus is characterized by a keen sense of social justice and solidarity with the poor and oppressed, particularly James and 1 John. These characteristics emerged largely out of the Diaspora experience, and were sharpened by the particularly difficult experience of Jewish Christianity.[56]

The Jewish Christian approach to relationships with the Gentiles was the dominant model of Christianity during the time that the New Testament was written, rooted in the Old Testament Scriptures and in continuity with flexible patterns informed by the Diaspora experience and in obedience to both Jesus' model and his instructions in the Gospels. They were to reach out to the lost sheep of Israel in all nations of the Diaspora, whose Messiah had come, and the Gentiles in those nations would be attracted, come to faith, and share Israel's blessings. The idea was: build it and they will come, and do not make it hard for them.[57] The Pauline practice of creating indig-

---

55. See Westfall, "Hebrew Mission," for a fuller description. See particularly 196–203 for a more detailed description of the relationship of the aspects of the mission to the Jewish Christian corpus.

56. The aspects that made the existence of the Jewish Christian community difficult included its formation of a high Christology that placed it in conflict with unbelieving Jews, the loss of the temple and its cult, official and unofficial retaliation for the Jewish revolt (including the War Reparation Tax), the criminalization of Christianity by the Roman Empire, and the disassociation of unbelieving Jews from believers (see Westfall, "Running the Gamut"; Westfall, "Church and the Synagogue," 88–94; Westfall, "Continue to Remember the Poor").

57. This is therefore a variation on Schnabel's claim that the apostles were aware of "the assignment to preach the good news among the Gentiles" (Schnabel, *Early Christian Mission*, 1:521).

enous communities of righteous Gentiles based on the biblical theme of the eschatological salvation of Gentiles who are grafted into Israel was innovative, disturbing, and completely deconstructive of the nature of the people of God in application. In the Pauline corpus and Luke-Acts, Paul and Luke were making every effort to validate this form of the gospel. We have some of Paul's arguments against any efforts to integrate his Gentile churches into the Jewish culture, as well as his vehement criticisms of the theological implications of anything that would imply that circumcision or any other work of the Law could save a believer, very much like the historical debates on baptism in Protestantism. You can see Paul's deep disappointment in the pillars of the church when they seem to undermine or compromise one of the many tenets that he feels are vital for theological consistency and coherence in his mission and the establishment of community in his churches. Nevertheless, according to Luke, when James asked Paul for a show of faith to indicate that he himself was still "living in obedience to the law," as a Jew, Paul complied (Acts 21:24), as he did without compulsion in the case of Timothy's circumcision (Acts 16:1–3).[58] Luke, on the other hand, has been accused of smoothing over the differences between the apostles and Paul. However, if Luke was writing an apologetic for the Pauline mission by showing its continuity with Jesus' mission and the apostolic mission, and by making a case that it was on a trajectory with the Scriptures and work of the Holy Spirit, then we may see Luke as affirming and confirming the Jewish Christian models, but making a plea or an argument for the inclusion of Paul's new model for mission.

IMPLICATIONS FOR RELATIONS WITH JUDAISM AND MISSION MODELS

The church should continue its re-evaluation of the nature of Second Temple Judaism and early Christianity's relationship to it, Christianity's subsequent relationship to Judaism, and our theories about the biblical models for mission. The narratives we tell about the first- and second-century church have an important role in how we understand and interpret the New Testament

---

58. As Barrett claims, opinions differ as to whether Paul actually taught Jews not to keep the Law (Barrett, *Acts 15–28*, 1008). However, Barrett writes, "Luke appears to assume that Paul did not do what he was alleged to do; the charge was not believed by the elders, it was false, and Paul will proceed by his actions to demonstrate his innocence" (ibid., 1009). Bock concludes, "the likelihood is that Paul does not teach non-observance, but neither does he insist on observance where Gentiles are involved" (Bock, *Acts*, 647).

texts. The church needs to radically change its stories about Jewish Christianity and the apostolic leadership of the church. The narrative with which we have traditionally understood the New Testament has been to declare Paul right and the Jews wrong. This includes the Jerusalem apostles and Jewish Christian communities, who are seen as bumblers because of their failure to obey the teachings of Jesus or follow the leading of the Holy Spirit. Their supposed reneging on the agreement of the Jerusalem Council by not engaging in a mission to the Gentiles further contributes to such a negative historical picture of early Christian mission.

Paul's teachings and practices for his churches were forged on the cutting edge of missions, but rather than being seen as innovative, they were seen as normative for both Jews and Gentiles by later Gentile interpreters, so that it came to be seen as wrong to practice Judaism in any form. All Jews became the opposition. Emphasis was placed on the fact that the Jews were the ones who took an oath that their children should bear the guilt for the crucifixion of Jesus (Matt 27:25), and they were also made to be the sole enemies who persecuted Paul wherever he went. They were the synagogue of Satan who joined Rome in persecuting the early church. Eventually, in order to follow Jesus, the church determined that a Jew had to become a Gentile—which is tangled and incoherent, because Jesus was a practicing Jew. Yet this distortion of Jesus was possible because he had become an abstract construction, or an icon, who was divorced from his historic context and certainly from the work of his closest followers: the twelve apostles that he commissioned.[59] Jerome encountered a group called Nazarenes who were found "in all of the synagogues of the East among the Jews" (*per totas orientis synagogas inter Iudaeos heresis est*) who considered themselves both Christians and Jews, but Jerome said they were neither Jew nor Christian.[60] One might ask what Jerome's criteria for Jew and Christian would be. When Christians gained political power, Jews were persecuted, tortured, and killed. Jews have subsequently been persecuted by the Inquisition, the Holocaust, and countless other political as well as vigilante campaigns. We need to continue to be aggressive in revising the

---

59. As Dunn states, "The Jewish complexion of his ministry could be stripped off and thrown away as irrelevant and of no lasting significance or worth. Jesus, the timeless ideal, whether seen in terms of Jesus himself or in terms of his message, transcended his social historical context. What is of continuing value in his message is quite unaffected by his Jewishness. In effect a kind of Docetism emerged—a Jesus himself, or his message, independent of history" (Dunn, "Introduction," 7).

60. Jerome, *Correspondence*, 55.381–382.

Christian narrative concerning Judaism, Jewish Christianity, and Pauline Christianity because of how they frame our interpretation of Scripture and our practice. We also need to take responsibility for the messages that our historic narratives have conveyed. We as individuals and as the church have to consciously change our stories.

As far as our theories about mission are concerned, we ought to have room for different models for conducting mission and resist the search for *the* biblical model. There are at least two transferable models for mission in the New Testament: the centripetal attraction of the Diaspora city of refuge and the centrifugal Pauline model that strives to preach the gospel where Christ is not known (Rom 15:20). This, of course, legitimizes, at least in theory, the Messianic Jewish congregations that follow the pattern of the dominant first-century church. The "build it and they will come" approach corresponds to a number of models for mission that have been successful, not the least of which was the monastic model. Orders such as the Benedictines, the Jesuits, and the Franciscans were the means through which much of Europe and the Americas were converted to Roman Catholicism using an "outpost" mentality where the culture was exported to indigenous populations. We can add to that the Anabaptists, Quakers, Pilgrims, and Shakers, who attracted people by the formation of communities of refuge that were distinct from the surrounding culture, and offered them an alternate way to live a godly life. It is the attraction of the American church abroad that draws all nationalities together for various reasons. It is the function of international churches such as St. George's Anglican in Tunis, as well as countless "international" churches in major centers around the world.

We all probably relate to the Jewish Christian model with varying degrees of comfort or discomfort, in part due to the post-modern re-evaluation of Western cultural imperialism, some of which was implemented through the Christian missionary movement. However, there is power in developing cities of refuge as cultural outposts of intentional living in which the orphans, widows, prisoners, disabled, and oppressed can find a home apart from the dominant culture that oppressed and abused them. We need healing communities in which the sick can thrive. There is power in forming "civic bodies and households and friendships" that show that God makes a difference in the details of our lives—which was at least part of the message of the Law of Moses. The model of the city of refuge is more biblical and compelling than the imperial one of conquest, force, or compulsion through the exercise of political power, and it is in continuity with biblical patterns and traditions. Paul's model of outreach with indigenous churches was innovative, but justified by Scripture, not as a correction or criticism of apostolic Christianity, but as a prophetic option.

CONCLUSION

The Jewish Christian community in the Diaspora made essential contributions to Christianity and provided a model for mission that is equally as valid as the Pauline model. This paper has argued that Jewish Christians in the Diaspora evangelized Gentiles and incorporated them into believing Jewish communities and culture consistent with philosophies and practices in the Second Temple Diaspora, in contrast with Paul, who established indigenous churches within the Gentile culture, through the innovative influence of different trajectories in the Second Temple Diaspora. Jewish Christianity established cities of refuge throughout the Diaspora that attracted Gentiles whom they incorporated into the community. The Jewish Christian communities experienced significant rejection and suffering because they experienced pressure from their situation, the Roman Empire, other Jews, and eventually Gentile Christianity. Jewish Christianity has also been marginalized in biblical scholarship, church history, and ecclesiology. The church needs to commit to telling the correct story about the role of Jewish Christianity in order to understand the New Testament texts that we confess as authoritative.

BIBLIOGRAPHY

Bamberger, B. J. *Proselytism in the Talmudic Period*. Cincinnati: Hebrew Union College Press, 1939.
Barrett, C. K. *Acts 15–28: A Critical and Exegetical Commentary on the Acts of the Apostles, Vol. 2*. ICC. Edinburgh: T. & T. Clark, 1998.
Barth, Markus, and Helmut Blanke. *Colossians*. AB 34B. New York: Doubleday, 1994.
Bauckham, Richard. "James and the Jerusalem Community." In *Jewish Believers in Jesus: The Early Centuries*, edited by Oskar Skarsaune and Reidar Hvalvik, 55–95. Peabody, MA: Hendrickson, 2007.
Becker, Adam H., and Annette Yoshiko Reed, eds. *The Ways that Never Parted: Jews and Christians in Late Antiquity and the Early Middle Ages*. Minneapolis: Fortress, 2007.
Boccaccini, Gabriele. *Middle Judaism: Jewish Thought, 300 B.C.E. to 200 C.E.* Minneapolis: Fortress, 1991.
Bock, Darrell L. *Acts*. Grand Rapids: Baker, 2007.
Boda, Mark J. "'Declare His Glory among the Nations': The Psalter as Missional Collection." In *Christian Mission: Old Testament Foundations and New Testament Developments*, edited by Stanley E. Porter and Cynthia Long Westfall, 13–41. MNTS 9. Eugene, OR: Wipf & Stock, 2010.

Boyarin, Daniel. "Semantic Differences or, 'Judaism'/'Christianity.'" In *The Ways that Never Parted: Jews and Christians in Late Antiquity and the Early Middle Ages*, edited by Adam H. Becker and Annette Yoshiko Reed, 65–85. Minneapolis: Fortress, 2007.

Braude, W. E. *Jewish Proselyting in the First Five Centuries of the Common Era*. Providence, RI: Brown University Press, 1940.

Broadhead, Edwin K. *Jewish Ways of Following Jesus: Redrawing the Religious Map of Antiquity*. WUNT 266. Tübingen: Mohr Siebeck, 2010.

Cohen, Shaye. *The Beginnings of Jewishness: Boundaries, Varieties, Uncertainties*. Los Angeles: University of California Press, 1999.

Dix, George. "The Ministry in the Early Church." In *The Apostolic Ministry: Essays on the History and Doctrine of Episcopacy*, edited by K. E. N. Kirk, 183–304. London: Hodder & Stoughton, 1946.

Donaldson, Terence L. *Judaism and the Gentiles: Jewish Patterns of Universalism (to 135 CE)*. Waco, TX: Baylor University Press, 2007.

Dunn, James D. G. "Introduction: From Baur to Saunders." In *The Partings of the Ways: Between Christianity and Judaism and Their Significance for the Character of Christianity*, edited by James D. G. Dunn, 1–23. 2nd ed. London: SCM, 2006.

———. "The New Perspective on Paul." *Bulletin of the John Rylands Library* 65 (1983) 95–122.

———. *The New Perspective on Paul: Collected Essays*. WUNT 185. Tübingen: Mohr/Siebeck, 2005.

———. *Romans 9–16*. WBC 38B. Waco, TX: Word, 1988.

Feldman, Louis H. *Jew and Gentile in the Ancient World: Attitudes and Interactions from Alexander to Justinian*. Princeton, NJ: Princeton University Press, 1993.

———. "Was Judaism a Missionary Religion in Ancient Times?" In *Jewish Assimilation, Acculturation and Accommodation: Past Traditions, Current Issues and Future Prospects*, edited by Menachem Mor, 24–37. Studies in Jewish Civilization 2. Lanham, MD: University Press of America, 1992.

Frankfurter, David. "Beyond 'Jewish Christianity.'" In *The Ways that Never Parted: Jews and Christians in Late Antiquity and the Early Middle Ages*, edited by Adam H. Becker and Annette Yoshiko Reed, 131–43. Minneapolis: Fortress, 2007.

Frederiksen, Paula. "What 'Parting of the Ways'? Jews, Gentiles, and the Ancient Mediterranean City." In *The Ways that Never Parted: Jews and Christians in Late Antiquity and the Early Middle Ages*, edited by Adam H. Becker and Annette Yoshiko Reed, 35–63. Minneapolis: Fortress, 2007.

Georgi, Dieter. *The Opponents of Paul in Second Corinthians*. Philadelphia: Fortress, 1986.

Gerdmar, Anders. *Roots of Theological Anti-Semitism: German Biblical Interpretation and the Jews from Herder and Semler to Kittel and Bultmann*. Studies in Jewish History and Culture 20. Leiden: Brill, 2008.

Goodman, Martin. "Jewish Proselytizing in the First Century." In *The Jews among Pagans and Christians in the Roman Empire*, edited by Judith Lieu, John North, and Tessa Rajak, 53–78. London: Routledge, 1992.

———. *Mission and Conversion: Proselytizing in the Religious History of the Roman Empire*. Oxford: Clarendon, 1994.

———. "Modeling the 'Parting of the Ways.'" In *The Ways that Never Parted: Jews and Christians in Late Antiquity and the Early Middle Ages*, edited by Adam H. Becker and Annette Yoshiko Reed, 119–29. Minneapolis: Fortress, 2007.

Harnack, Adolf von. *The Mission and Expansion of Christianity in the First Three Centuries.* London: Williams & Norgate, 1908.
Hvalvik, Reidar. "Jewish Believers and Jewish Influence in the Roman Church until the Early Second Century." In *Jewish Believers in Jesus: The Early Centuries*, edited by Oskar Skarsaune and Reidar Hvalvik, 179–216. Peabody, MA: Hendrickson, 2007.
Jackson-McCabe, Matt, ed. *Jewish Christianity Reconsidered: Rethinking Ancient Groups and Texts.* Minneapolis: Fortress, 2007.
Jerome. *Correspondence.* Edited by Isidorus Hilberg. Corpus Scriptorum Ecclesiasticorum Latinorum. Vienna: Verlag der osterreichischen Akademie der Wissenschaftern, 1996.
Jewett, Robert. *Romans.* Hermeneia. Minneapolis: Fortress, 2007.
Kittel, G. "Genealogia des Pastoralbriefe." *ZNW* 20 (1921) 49–69.
Köstenberger, Andreas, and P. T. O'Brien. *Salvation to the Ends of the Earth: A Biblical Theology of Mission.* New Studies in Biblical Theology 11. Downers Grove, IL: InterVarsity, 2001.
Kraabel, A. Thomas. "The Roman Diaspora: Six Questionable Assumptions." *Journal of Jewish Studies* 33 (1982) 445–64.
Lemke, J. L. "Intertextuality and Text Semantics." In *Discourse in Society: Systemic Functional Perspectives*, edited by Peter Howard Fries, Michael Gregory, and M. A. K. Halliday, 85–114. Norwood, NJ: Ablex, 1995.
Longenecker, Richard. *Galatians.* WBC 41. Waco, TX: Word, 1990.
McKnight, Scott. *A Light among the Gentiles: Jewish Missionary Activity in the Second Temple Period.* Minneapolis: Fortress, 1991.
Mernissi, Fatima. *The Veil and the Male Elite: A Feminist Interpretation of Women's Rights in Islam.* Translated by Mary Jo Lakeland. New York: Basic, 1987.
Meyer-Ortmanns, Hildegard. "Immigration, Integration and Ghetto Formation." *International Journal of Modern Physics, Computational Physics and Physical Computation* 14 (2003) 311–20.
Moore, George Foot. *Judaism in the First Centuries of the Christian Era.* 3 vols. Cambridge, MA: Harvard University Press, 1927–30.
Munck, Johannes. *Paul and the Salvation of Mankind.* London: SCM, 1959.
O'Brien, Peter T. *Colossians, Philemon.* WBC 44. Waco, TX: Word, 1982.
Reed, Annette Yoshiko. "'Jewish Christianity' after the 'Parting of the Ways.'" In *The Ways that Never Parted: Jews and Christians in Late Antiquity and the Early Middle Ages*, edited by Adam H. Becker and Annette Yoshiko Reed, 189–231. Minneapolis: Fortress, 2007.
Sanders, E. P. *Paul and Palestinian Judaism: A Comparison in Patterns of Religion.* London: SCM, 1977.
Schnabel, E. J. *Early Christian Mission.* 2 vols. Downers Grove, IL: InterVarsity, 2004.
Schürer, Emil. *The History of the Jewish People in the Age of Jesus Christ (175 B.C.—A.D. 135).* Revised by Matthew Black, Martin Goodman, Fergus Millar, and Geza Vermes. 3 vols. Edinburgh: T. & T. Clark, 1987.
Skarsaune, Oskar, and Reidar Hvalvk, eds. *Jewish Believers in Jesus: The Early Centuries.* Peabody, MA: Hendrickson, 2007.
Thiselton, Anthony C. *The First Epistle to the Corinthians: A Commentary on the Greek Text.* NIGTC. Grand Rapids: Eerdmans, 2000.
Thompson, Michael B. *The New Perspective on Paul.* Cambridge: Grove, 2002.

Towner, Philip H. *The Letters to Timothy and Titus*. NICNT. Grand Rapids: Eerdmans, 2006.

Westfall, Cynthia Long. "The Church and Synagogue: Continuity and Discontinuity." In *The Church Then and Now*, edited by Stanley E. Porter and Cynthia Long Westfall, 68–96. MNTS. Eugene, OR: Pickwick, 2011.

———. "Continue to Remember the Poor: Social Justice within the Poor and Powerless Jewish Christian Communities." In *The Bible and Social Justice*, edited by Cynthia Long Westfall and Bryan R. Dyer. MNTS. Eugene, OR: Pickwick, forthcoming.

———. "The Hebrew Mission: Voices from the Margin?" In *Christian Mission: Old Testament Foundations and New Testament Developments*, edited by Stanley E. Porter and Cynthia Long Westfall, 187–207. MNTS 9. Eugene, OR: Wipf & Stock, 2010.

———. "Running the Gamut: The Varied Responses to Empire in Jewish Christianity." In *Empire in the New Testament*, edited by Stanley E. Porter and Cynthia Long Westfall, 230–58. MNTS. Eugene, OR: Pickwick, 2011.

Wright, N. T. *Paul: In Fresh Perspective*. Minneapolis: Fortress, 2005.

6

Jewish and Gentile Refugees in the Second Temple Period

A Response to Loren T. Stuckenbruck and Cynthia Long Westfall

BENJAMIN E. REYNOLDS

INTRODUCTION

LOREN T. STUCKENBRUCK AND Cynthia Long Westfall's papers offer two separate perspectives on the question of alienation and refuge in the Second Temple period. Both authors strive to come to terms with the way in which the Jewish people connected to the wider Hellenistic world with its cultural, political, and socioeconomic pressures. Did they feel rejected, and, if so, how did they address their rejection? If Gentiles were attracted to Judaism, how were they to be incorporated into the Jewish communities and what did it mean that they wanted to be included? The answers are varied.

A RESPONSE TO STUCKENBRUCK

Introduction

Professor Stuckenbruck has presented us with a look at four Jewish texts from the Second Temple period that offer insights into four ways in which Second Temple Jews faced and addressed rejection and oppression by political powers (Tobit, cf. *4 Ezra*), cultural and religious pressure (Book of Watchers), or religious and economic alienation by other Jews (Epistle of Enoch). He rightly notes the way in which crises may have been the driving

REJECTION

force behind numerous Jewish writings during the Second Temple period.[1] These various crises alienated Jewish communities, and recent studies of Second Temple Jewish literature, particularly Jewish apocalyptic literature, have begun considering more seriously the sociological contexts of this literature.[2] Professor Stuckenbruck's paper is a contribution to this examination of sociological contexts.

Of the four texts that Stuckenbruck engages, the Book of Watchers is most likely the oldest. He notes that the authors of this text are likely to have been part of a priestly or scribal community located in northern Galilee that felt alienation from the growing Hellenistic influence following Alexander the Great's conquest of the East and the subsequent rise of the Ptolemaic and Seleucid empires after the dissolution of Alexander's empire. The strategy of the Book of Watchers is to describe the enemies as rejected by God and to expect a reordering of the world that will take place in a future along the lines of God's destruction of the world in the Noahic flood. Tobit, on the other hand, presents an expectation that Jerusalem will be rebuilt and the exiles can return, but this does not involve an eschatological reordering. The faithful are to pray, give alms, and remain faithful to the land. In a sense, they are to embrace their status as refugees and endure the exile. The temple may be destroyed and Jerusalem distant, but those who are faithful can rightfully worship through the present heavenly Jerusalem. The Epistle of Enoch addressed alienation not by imperial powers but by fellow Jews who had a differing opinion of the law. Stuckenbruck argues that the Epistle presents a future that is discontinuous with the present order, one that requires eschatological resolution and not merely a reordering of the present reality. In *4 Ezra*, which was written later than these previous three texts, God is implicated in the rejection of his people and Jerusalem. Ezra's critique is directed to God, yet Ezra's questions are never directly answered (cf. Job 38–40). Stuckenbruck argues that the strategy for addressing rejection in *4 Ezra* is to honestly lament the loss and sin and to console others in their lamentation.

Apocalyptic and Non-Apocalyptic Literature

What I would like to offer in response to Stuckenbruck's paper are some insights and features that his probing of these alienated Second Temple

---

1. Collins, "Early Christian Apocalypticism," 6–7; Hellholm, "Problem of Apocalyptic Genre," 27; Aune, *Apocalypticism*, 62–64.
2. See Portier-Young, *Apocalypse against Empire*, for an excellent study.

Jewish groups brings to light. First, Stuckenbruck's comparison of three Jewish apocalypses—Book of Watchers, the Epistle of Enoch, and *4 Ezra*—and the book of Tobit highlights a striking difference in the way apocalyptic writers tend to look toward the resolution of time for vindication. As Stuckenbruck argues, this resolution may take place through continuity (Book of Watchers) or discontinuity (Epistle) with the created order. The Jewish apocalyptic perspective can draw attention to the revelation of resolved time through a revealed cosmology. As Stuckenbruck notes, the Book of Watchers describes the heavenly temple where God's glorious presence and power dwell.[3] *Fourth Ezra* contains not so much a revealed cosmology as a revealed wisdom in tandem or synonymous with the Law, which indicates the resolving of time.[4] The Jewish apocalypses present a cosmological and eschatological hope, although their manner of doing so differs.

In contrast, Stuckenbruck notes that Tobit lacks the cosmological perspective or future hope for a resolved time. Instead, the challenge for the readers and hearers of Tobit is to remain faithful, pray, give alms, and come to terms with their rejection and alienation (cf. Daniel 1–6). Even though they are in exile and separated from the land, God is present with the people and answers their prayers. The heavenly Jerusalem exists in the present and allows worship of God to take place now, even with their alienation from the land. Stuckenbruck states: "those who embrace piety can engage authentically in the worship of God by focusing on Jerusalem in its heavenly dimension" (p. 67). Unlike the Jewish apocalypses, Tobit presents no clear expectation of a future resolution of time when the Jewish people's enemies will be held to account by God.

Variety of Alienation

Second, the four texts Stuckenbruck examines also indicate that alienation may derive from different sectors. Tobit provides an example of socio-political alienation. The imperially forced exile creates distance from the homeland and proper Torah-directed worship in the temple. Location is not a choice but one imposed by outside forces, and thus, it functions as both physical and psychological alienation. Similarly, *4 Ezra* portrays a socio-political alienation in the destruction of Jerusalem and the temple (cf. *2 Baruch*). However, as Stuckenbruck notes, the rejection in *4 Ezra* is presented as rejection by God and not as rejection by outside political

---

3. See Himmelfarb, *Ascent to Heaven*, 9–28.
4. Cf. Stone, *Fourth Ezra*, 33–35.

forces (e.g., the Babylonians/Romans). Sinners have been allowed to conquer God's chosen people.

On the other hand, the Book of Watchers and the Epistle of Enoch depict alienation and rejection on a less international scale. Stuckenbruck argues that within the Book of Watchers we find a scribal community alienated by cultural shifts toward Hellenization and a related "socio- religious accommodation." The alienation may be caused by imperial forces in the resulting cultural shift toward Hellenization, but the alienation is not so much socio-political as it is cultural and religious. Similarly, in the Epistle of Enoch the alienation is also socio-religious; however, in this case it is an intra-Jewish alienation. It appears that a group of those who declare themselves "righteous" view present earthly blessing as a sign of faithfulness (cf. Job and his friends), suggesting that socio-economic alienation occurs simultaneously with the socio-religious alienation. The rich view the poor (the true "righteous") as transgressing the law because they are poor, and thus, the rich reject the poor from participation in their shared socio-religious and socio-economic context.[5]

Stuckenbruck's analysis of these four texts indicates that different types of rejection and alienation existed in Second Temple Judaism. Is it therefore any surprise that these Second Temple Jewish texts present different strategies for coping with their respective crises?

How Many Strategies?

Considering that an examination of four Second Temple Jewish texts has brought to light various ways of addressing rejection and different sources of that rejection of God's people, it does beg the question how many strategies for addressing rejection and alienation we would find if we explored more Second Temple texts. For instance, the Apocalypse of Weeks, which can be placed in the context of the Seleucid oppression under Antiochus IV Epiphanes, is another example of a socio-political alienation of God's people. However, connected to this socio-political alienation is also a socio-religious rejection in the form the Seleucid dynasty's repression of Jewish religious practice. The Apocalypse of Weeks looks to an eschatological redemption by God beginning in the seventh of ten weeks. Like the Epistle of Enoch, this redemption is discontinuous with the present created order. In contrast to the Jewish apocalypses that look to a resolution of time, the Apocalypse of Weeks, as Anathea Portier-Young argues, is resistance

---

5. See Nickelsburg, *1 Enoch 1*, 425–29.

literature that commissions the righteous to take up the sword in the eighth week against those who are oppressing them (*1 En* 91:11–12). She states: "God equips them, but the task of transforming the present world order is theirs to carry out."[6] Unlike the Book of Watchers and the Epistle of Enoch where the reordering of creation takes place through God's hand, it is the righteous resisting their alienators and oppressors that brings about the resolution. An examination of the Apocalypse of Weeks, we could argue, presents violent uprising as a fifth strategy for Second Temple Jews to address their rejection and alienation.

But what about the *Apocalypse of Abraham* or other Second Temple Jewish texts? If we probe more broadly, will we end up with numerous strategies, or have we already addressed the breadth of options? If so, how many strategies are there, and could they be placed in a certain set of categories? Stuckenbruck's study is helpful but some questions remain.

Summary

Stuckenbruck has drawn attention to four strategies for addressing the crises facing Second Temple Jewish communities in Palestine and in the Diaspora. The Book of Watchers, Tobit, the Epistle of Enoch, and *4 Ezra* show the variety of rejection faced by the Jewish people in this period, the different origins of this rejection, and also the ways in which the writers faced alienation. What is consistent across the strategies, as Stuckenbruck concludes, is the way in which the relationship between God and his people is central to facing rejection.

A RESPONSE TO WESTFALL

Introduction

Cynthia Long Westfall has addressed the topic of Gentile inclusion in early Christianity and how this inclusion was connected with the incorporation or conversion of Gentiles within Diaspora Judaism. The scholarly discussion on this topic is wide-ranging and fraught with many unknowns and shifting paradigms concerning what is meant by "Jewish Christianity."[7] Westfall must be applauded for tackling this topic and for particularly

---

6. Portier-Young, *Apocalypse against Empire*, 315.

7. For example, see Boyarin, *Jewish Gospels*, esp. 1–24; Skarsaune, "Jewish Believers in Jesus in Antiquity"; Paget, "Definition"; Jackson-McCabe, "What's in a Name?"; Reed and Becker, "Traditional Models."

highlighting the way in which our understanding of the so-called "parting of the ways" has shaped present-day Christian understandings of the Jewish people in relation to Christianity. The world has shifted from a time in which all believers in Jesus were Jews to a time where it unfortunately seems odd to have "Jewish Christians" and "Jews for Jesus."

The central argument of Westfall's paper is that "Jewish Christians in the Diaspora converted Gentiles and incorporated them into believing Jewish communities and culture consistent with philosophies and practices in the Second Temple Diaspora, in contrast with Paul who established indigenous churches within the Gentile culture, through the influence of other trajectories in the Second Temple Diaspora" (p. 109). Westfall's thesis raises a few questions which, in my opinion, could use some further clarification.

"Cities of Refuge"?

First, Westfall argues that in the same way Gentiles were attracted and became adherents, God-fearers, or converts to Judaism throughout the Jewish Diaspora, so Gentiles were attracted to Jesus-believing Jewish communities.[8] The Jewish communities drew the Gentiles in through attraction and centripetal force and not outright evangelization.[9] Since Jewish communities did not actively recruit Gentiles, Jesus-believing Jews did not either.

Westfall contends that Jesus-believing Jews who remained halakhically-observant and continued in the synagogue welcomed the Gentiles who were attracted to Jesus, but they required these Gentiles to be circumcised and to observe other halakhic requirements (e.g., food, Sabbath, and festivals) in order to be fully incorporated into these Jewish Christian communities. In this light, three of Terrence Donaldson's four categories of Gentile relationship with Judaism during the Second Temple Period—sympathizer, ethical monotheists, and participants in eschatological redemption—were not sufficient for Gentiles to be included into Jesus-believing Jewish communities.[10] Instead, Gentiles had to become full converts to Judaism in order to become part of the Jewish Christian communities (cf. Galatians 1–2; Acts 11:19).

---

8. This argument has close similarity with Bird's argument in *Crossing over Sea and Land*.

9. On non-Jesus-believing Judaism, see the argument of Donaldson, *Judaism and the Gentiles*; Bird, *Crossing over Sea and Land*, esp. his conclusion.

10. Donaldson, *Judaism and the Gentiles*, 471–505.

Westfall describes these Jewish communities that included Gentiles as "cities of refuge." The phrase is part of her title and used on six other occasions (pp. 86, 89, 98, 104, 108, 109). Whether or not these "cities of refuge" functioned in the way that she argues, the terminology appears problematic for a number of reasons. First, the Old Testament referent for the "cities of refuge" is entirely different. In Num 35:9–15 (also Deut 4:41–43; Josh 20:1–6), the Lord directs Israel to establish six cities as cities of refuge for those people who unintentionally kill another person. Deuteronomy 19:5–6 states: "when someone goes into the forest with his neighbor to cut wood, and his hand swings the axe to cut down a tree, and the head slips from the handle and strikes his neighbor so that he dies—he may flee to one of these cities and live, lest the avenger of blood in hot anger pursue the manslayer and overtake him" (ESV). In these cities of refuge, the "manslayers" can await their trial without fear of revenge being carried out against them (cf. Exod 21:12–13). Thus, in the Old Testament, the phrase "cities of refuge" indicates refuge, but it is refuge for those who have transgressed the commandment not to kill. Further, this refuge only lasts until the accused is brought to trial. There is no guaranteed long-term salvific sense or the connotation of citizenship transfer to the phrase "cities of refuge" in the Pentateuch.

Second, Westfall's view that the Jewish communities provided "cities of refuge" for Gentiles seems to derive from Philo's discussion of Gentile proselytes in *On Special Laws* 1.51–52 and also from Terrence Donaldson's interaction with Philo's discussion. Philo states that Gentiles who "make the passage to piety" should be considered equals with those who were born Jewish. The reason for treating these proselyte Gentiles equally is that these Gentiles

> have left . . . their country, their kinsfolk and their friends for the sake of virtue and religion. Let them not be denied another citizenship or other ties of family and friendship, and let them find places of shelter standing ready for refugees to the camp of piety.[11]

In this quotation, we see the idea that conversion to Judaism may imply the denial of a Gentile's original "citizenship or other ties of family and friendship" and that the Jewish community may provide such a convert a "place of shelter" or a "place of refuge" (1.52). Before this citation, Philo describes the Gentile proselytes as those who have left (ἀπολελοιπότες) their country, families, and friends. They join with the Jewish community in

---

11. Philo, *Spec. leg.* 1.51–52 (F. H. Colson, LCL).

piety or reverence to God. Philo says that what binds the Jews and proselyte Gentiles together is honor of God.[12]

Donaldson argues that what Philo is talking about "involves a very real social dislocation" for these Gentiles and that "they have been incorporated into a distinct social entity."[13] Thus, Jewish Diaspora communities may have provided actual refuge for Gentile proselytes who became dislocated from their own family and friends, but in reality Gentile proselytes may have been considered lesser members of these "cities of refuge." Donaldson notes that Philo's exhortation to his readers to treat these Gentile proselytes equally suggests that the "refuge" may not always have included a warm welcome or equality.[14]

By way of contrast, earlier in her essay, Westfall argues that Gentiles who became benefactors of Jewish communities imparted "benefits and protection [for the Jews in the Diaspora] virtually without risk. These were relationships that one could draw on when Jews or Israel were under attack" (p. 95). If Gentile benefactors could provide this kind of protection, what sort of refuge were the Jewish communities offering to these and other Gentiles? Who was actually providing refuge for whom?

Jewish communities may have provided cities of refuge, welcoming those Gentiles who chose to become part of the Jewish community; however, it should be kept in mind that this portrait of the situation is drawn primarily from Philo and does not seem to take into account the scholarly consensus that Philo's views of Gentile conversion have two strands.[15] In addition, what about the views of Josephus, the Qumran community, and other Jews during this time? There were various perspectives on the place of Gentiles in the Jewish community. Considering what we know and do not know, care needs to be taken when generalizing about the way in which Jewish communities functioned in relation to Gentile proselytes. Was there a difference between Jewish cities of refuge and "Jewish *Christian* cities of refuge"?[16] Were all Diaspora Jews part of the same communities, welcoming Gentiles in similar ways, but some of them believed Jesus was the Messiah? Can we assume that the incorporation of Gentile-Jesus-be-

---

12. Donaldson, *Judaism and the Gentiles*, 238.
13. Ibid., 237.
14. Ibid., 237–38.
15. Bird, *Crossing over Sea and Land*, 103–9.
16. Cf. Westfall, "Cities of Refuge," 89, 98.

lievers occurred in the same way Gentile proselytes had been incorporated into Judaism earlier?

We may be able to assume so, but there is much that is not clear. We can only piece the various aspects together as best we can. Westfall has made a good effort in this direction. There may have been something akin to what Westfall has called "cities of refuge" for some Gentiles, but whether this was widespread in the Diaspora and whether this terminology is the best description for what took place, it is difficult to say for sure.[17]

Paul: Innovator or Just Another Second Temple Jew?

A second concern is the way in which Westfall seems to draw a sharp distinction between Jewish Christianity and Paul's Gentile mission. She states that the difference between Paul and Peter's roles as apostles was that "Paul deliberately advocated indigenous churches that were embedded in the Gentile culture rather than an export of Jewish culture". She states later that Paul's practice of "creating indigenous communities of righteous Gentiles . . . was innovative, disturbing, and completely deconstructive of the nature of the people of God in application".[18]

The phrase "indigenous churches embedded in Gentile culture" seems to imply that it was possible for Jewish Christian "churches" not to be embedded in Gentile culture. Martin Hengel contends, "From the middle of the third century BC *all Judaism* must really be designated '*Hellenistic* Judaism' in the strict sense."[19] If Jewish believers in Jesus created "cities of refuge" for Gentile converts, these "cities" existed within Hellenistic culture, with its language, education, and customs. If they did exist, is it possible to demarcate lines between "Jewish," "Christian," "Gentile," etc., and if so, how do we do so? Did they differentiate along the lines scholarship has tended to do? Did their differentiation depend on whom you asked?

Further, Donaldson lays out four categories of Jewish integration of Gentiles: conversion, sympathizer, ethical monotheist, and eschatological redemption. Paul's instructions to his converts clearly do not fit Donaldson's conversion category because he did not require circumcision for Gentile believers in Jesus to become full members of the Jesus-believing

17. See Donaldson's citation of sources for and against Judaism as a missionary religion, *Judaism and the Gentiles*, 5–6; also Bird, *Crossing over Sea and Land*, 8–13.

18. These quotations come from Westfall's original paper presented at the conference. She has rephrased her comments in the revision for this volume.

19. Hengel, *Judaism and Hellenism*, 1:104 (emphasis original).

community. However, Paul does seem to see his converts fitting into two of the three other categories: sympathizer and eschatological redemption,[20] which suggests that Paul may not be completely at odds with certain strands of Diaspora Judaism.[21] If he was not, can we say that he was that innovative and deconstructive?

In Acts, Paul is portrayed as almost always entering a synagogue whenever he comes to a city (Acts 13:5, 14; 14:1; 17:2; 18:4; cf. 16:13). In Thessalonica, "Paul went in [to the synagogue], *as was his custom*, and on three Sabbath days he reasoned with them from the Scriptures" (17:1–2). In Corinth, Paul "reasoned in the synagogue every Sabbath, and tried to persuade Jews and Greeks" (18:4). As Westfall notes, Paul complied when James asked him to purify himself and pay the expenses of some men purifying themselves in accordance with a vow in order to address the rumors that he was teaching "the Jews who are among the Gentiles to forsake Moses" (21:20–26), not to mention that the Jerusalem council in Acts 15 explicitly stated that Gentile observance of the law was not necessary for full conversion.

John Barclay refers to Paul as an "anomalous Diaspora Jew."[22] By this, he means that Paul does seem to forsake Moses by appearing to shrug off various requirements of the law and to indicate that the law is irrelevant. Paul in some sense almost severs ties with Judaism, such that the rumors floating around Jerusalem in Acts 21 could be considered accurate. Paul seems to reject Judaism more than Philo, Josephus, and others were willing to, but, at the same time, Barclay draws attention to the way Paul often speaks negatively of Gentiles. The Gentile believers are not part of something new, but they are part of Israel. They are grafted into the olive tree (Romans 11). The Gentiles can become the righteous children of God, the descendants of Abraham, and the recipients of God's promise to Abraham.

Considering the variation and breadth within Second Temple Judaism and the variety within Paul's writings and how little we actually know, I am hesitant to say that Paul was that innovative or deconstructive. The often-cited example from Josephus of Ananias and Eleazer in the conversion of Izates to Judaism indicates that among Second Temple Jews there were

20. Westfall says that Paul is "not inconsistent" with ethical monotheism, but it would seem that a philosophical and moral perspective consistent with Moses and the Law might not be sufficient for Paul (cf. Romans 1).

21. Cf. Josephus's account of the conversion of Izates (*Ant.* 20.34–48).

22. Barclay, *Jews in the Mediterranean Diaspora*, 381. For the following paragraph, see 381–95.

strict views of what it meant to become Jewish and less strict understandings.[23] Paul and the men from James easily fit within this diversity. What is not to be doubted is that Gentile association with the people of Israel was possible. In agreement with Westfall's overall argument and that of Michael Bird, Diaspora Jewish approaches to Gentile inclusion reflect the broader way in which Gentiles were incorporated into Jesus-believing Judaism, but there is an obvious place for Paul in that diversity.

Summary

Westfall argues that the early Jewish Jesus-believers followed previous patterns of Gentile inclusion into Judaism as they incorporated Gentiles into their communities of belief. Whether this inclusion functioned specifically as "cities of refuge" in the way Westfall contends is not entirely clear. However, in her conclusion, Westfall helpfully points out how Paul's arguments took an anti-Semitic turn in later Christian contexts. She states: "All Jews became the opposition" (p. 107). Eventually, Jews had to become Gentiles in order to become Christians rather than the reverse. This reality poses a challenge for contemporary Christianity to reconsider its Jewish roots and what it means to be a follower of Jesus, whether Jew or Gentile.

CONCLUSION

Both Stuckenbruck and Westfall have expanded our perspective on rejection and alienation within the Second Temple period. Second Temple Jews faced various kinds of alienation and they addressed it with different strategies. When it came to the incorporation of Gentiles into Jesus-believing Jewish communities, it makes sense that this took place in a similar fashion to the incorporation of Gentile proselytes into Judaism. What is noteworthy from this entire discussion is the way in which our knowledge is almost entirely dependent on extant texts. We are left to speculate scenarios for which we really know very little, and we do so through the lenses of previous interpretation and understanding. We should push ahead and attempt to formulate ideas and answer our continuing questions, but we should also remember that we face limitations in this search.

---

23. Josephus, *Ant.* 20.34–48.

BIBLIOGRAPHY

Aune, David E. *Apocalypticism, Prophecy, and Magic in Early Christianity: Collected Essays.* Grand Rapids: Baker Academic, 2008.

Barclay, John M. G. *Jews in the Mediterranean Diaspora: From Alexander to Trajan (323 BCE–117 CE).* Edinburgh: T. & T. Clark, 1996.

Bird, Michael F. *Crossing over Sea and Land: Jewish Missionary Activity in the Second Temple Period.* Peabody, MA: Hendrickson, 2010.

Boyarin, Daniel. *The Jewish Gospels: The Story of the Jewish Christ.* New York: New Press, 2012.

Collins, Adela Yabro. "Introduction: Early Christian Apocalypticism." *Semeia* 36 (1986) 1–11.

Donaldson, Terrence L. *Judaism and the Gentiles: Jewish Patterns of Universalism (to 135 CE).* Waco, TX: Baylor University Press, 2007.

Hellholm, David. "The Problem of Apocalyptic Genre and the Apocalypse of John." *Semeia* 36 (1986) 13–64.

Hengel, Martin. *Judaism and Hellenism: Studies in Their Encounter in Palestine during the Early Hellenistic Period.* 2 vols. Translated by John Bowden. London: SCM Press, 1974.

Himmelfarb, Martha. *Ascent to Heaven in Jewish and Christian Apocalypses.* Oxford: Oxford University Press, 1993.

Jackson-McCabe, Matt. "What's in a Name? The Problem of 'Jewish Christianity.'" In *Jewish Christianity Reconsidered: Rethinking Ancient Groups and Texts*, edited by Matt Jackson-McCabe, 7–38. Minneapolis: Fortress, 2007.

Nickelsburg, George W. E. *1 Enoch 1: A Commentary on the Book of 1 Enoch, Chapters 1–36; 81–108.* Hermeneia. Minneapolis: Fortress, 2001.

Paget, James Carleton. "The Definition of the Terms *Jewish Christian* and *Jewish Christianity* in the History of Research." In *Jewish Believers in Jesus: The Early Centuries*, edited by Oskar Skarsaune and Reidar Hvalvik, 22–52. Peabody, MA: Hendrickson, 2007.

Philo. *On Special Laws.* Translated by F. H. Colson et al. 10 vols. LCL. Cambridge, MA: Harvard University Press, 1929–62.

Portier-Young, Anathea. *Apocalypse against Empire: Theologies of Resistance in Early Judaism.* Grand Rapids: Eerdmans, 2011.

Reed, Annette Yoshiko, and Adam H. Becker. "Introduction: Traditional Models and New Directions." In *The Ways that Never Parted: Jews and Christians in Late Antiquity and the Early Middle Ages*, edited by Annette Yoshiko Reed and Adam H. Becker, 1–33. Minneapolis: Fortress, 2007.

Skarsaune, Oskar. "Jewish Believers in Jesus in Antiquity—Problems of Definition, Method, and Sources." In *Jewish Believers in Jesus: The Early Centuries*, edited by Oskar Skarsaune and Reidar Hvalvik, 3–21. Peabody, MA: Hendrickson, 2007.

Stone, Michael Edward. *Fourth Ezra: A Commentary on the Book of Fourth Ezra.* Hermeneia. Minneapolis: Fortress, 1990.

7

From Diaspora to Diaspora
Paul Writes to Fellow Refugees

Stanley E. Porter

INTRODUCTION

THE FOCUS OF THIS volume is upon God's refugees—his people throughout time who have lived as refugees, that is, those rejected by their surrounding or even their own cultures, and who have been forced to find refuge elsewhere.[1] We typically think of refugees as those who are physically displaced, and there certainly is a long history of God's people being physically displaced—such as his people Israel living in Egypt or Babylon or throughout the rest of the Mediterranean world. However, there is also a very tangible sense of spiritual displacement—the kind of displacement that people feel when they are alienated from their ambient culture. This culture may be one that they believe they are part of or even have some kind of right to be fully integrated within, but from which they then find themselves estranged. In either instance, as a result of displacement there is an inevitable sense of alienation, in which God's people must find refuge outside of the normal boundaries of physical security and even outside the bounds of expected or anticipated spiritual security. The result often is discomfort, alienation, and estrangement—

1. I recognize that there is a range of terminology used in the various essays of this volume regarding "displaced persons" and the acts and movements that have displaced them. These terms include diaspora, exile, and refugee, among others. These terms clearly do not have the same senses, but—at least in the appropriate contexts—have partial synonymy. I trust that my use in context will disambiguate and conflate senses as appropriate.

Rejection

but also possibly dispersion. This dispersion can include (and too often has included) being physically ejected from places of comfort and into strange and alien places; this dispersion may also include spiritual separation from places of tranquility and into challenging locations, confines where there is apparently little comfort and rest. Such a situation does not necessarily mean, however, that God has abandoned his people. In some instances it may mean this, but in others it may mean that God has called his people to another type or level of existence, whether physically or spiritually. The sense of calling to another sphere of existence is what I wish to explore in this chapter. I have been given the task of treating the topic of what it means to be one of God's dispersed and alien people within the world in which we live, especially as seen through the letters of the Apostle Paul to various churches and their people within the ambit of early Christianity.

In this paper, I will begin by setting the stage within Paul's own life and experience as a man of the Diaspora. My contention is that Paul, as a Diaspora Jew, grew to cognitive and spiritual maturity with the deeply ingrained realization of personal and ethnic alienation, possibly an acute alienation that he hoped to remedy by his "return" to Palestine and Jerusalem. I will then turn to his letters, and explore within them the notion of diaspora. Paul's letters are, for the most part, addressed to churches predominantly Gentile in character, although there were no doubt Jews in them as well.[2] Rather than their being at home within the Greco-Roman context, Paul challenges his readers to recognize that, because of their unity in Christ, they are now members of a new dispersion, a people alienated from their surrounding culture and members of a new spiritual order of inclusion. Their dispersion or displacement from the Greco-Roman world means their welcome to the spiritual world of citizenship in Christ.

PAUL, THE DIASPORA APOSTLE

We do not know when Paul's ancestors settled in Tarsus of Cilicia, one of the major intellectual centers of the Greco-Roman world.[3] Because they

---

2. The composition of the Pauline churches is a subject of recent high contention. Particularly highly debated is the book of Romans, where various scholars contend for the full range of views, from a Gentile to a mixed to a Jewish church.

3. The major ancient source on Tarsus is Strabo, *Geography* 14.5. For discussion of Paul, his life, his upbringing, and his background, see McDonald and Porter, *Early Christianity*, 325–32. The information on his education is brought up to date by Porter and

had probably been in the area for a sufficient period of time for one of Paul's ancestors to have earned Roman citizenship—at this time still a difficult thing for a non-Roman to achieve—it is entirely possible that Paul's relatives had moved to Tarsus at the time of the Jewish dispersion after the exile, when Jews migrated to various corners of the known Western world. It is also possible that his ancestors had first returned to Palestine and then moved into self-imposed exile by dispersing themselves into the Greco-Roman world (note Paul had relatives in Jerusalem, as seen in Acts 23:16). In any case, settling in Tarsus probably occurred many generations before Paul was born somewhere between 1 and 10 CE. Nevertheless, this family apparently lived the life of Diaspora Jews. Paul was fully acculturated as a Roman citizen and member of the Greco-Roman cultural milieu—his first language was Greek and he probably was educated through grammar school in Tarsus.[4] However, Paul was also an alien in this culture—his family maintained the Jewish traditions of use of Hebrew as a religious language and of Aramaic probably as a domestic language, worshipped Yahweh, knew their ancestral lineage through the tribe of Benjamin, and fulfilled the mandates of the written and oral Torah, so that Paul was circumcised on the prescribed eighth day and followed the law faithfully (Phil 3:4–6).

We do not know the motivation for Paul to leave Tarsus and to move to Jerusalem, apart from the fact that he ended up, according to the book of Acts, as a student of Gamaliel, the leading Jewish teacher of his time (Acts 22:3). However, from what we do know about Paul's family and his claims to having led a life of legalistic exactitude, he may well have desired to fulfill what may have been a sense of spiritual calling to the "holy" land itself.[5] Paul may well have wished to remedy the effects of life in the Diaspora and perhaps what he sensed as distance or alienation from the center of Judaism, and by an act of physical relocation—in itself a type of double dispersion, in which he dispersed himself from his habitation, which was itself a place of dispersion, and by a new act of alienation attempted to overcome the original dispersion—he attempted to move forward by going back to Palestine. In any case, he certainly appears to do so. Paul became a student of Gamaliel in order to learn the law more thoroughly, and became a

---

Pitts, "Paul's Bible," 11–21.

4. See Pitts, "Hellenistic Schools," 27–33.

5. I realize that reference to the "holy land" is a relatively recent phenomenon. Nevertheless, the "land" was seen as having a special place in Judaism. See Davies, *Gospel and the Land*.

Pharisee, one of the small group of men who knew the law thoroughly and attempted to translate its mandates into the activities of daily life. In this he reached the point of calling himself faultless with regard to its fulfillment, and demonstrated the zeal of his faith by persecuting those who did not uphold it as he did. In all of this, from every indication that we have of his life in the Judaism of Palestine, Paul was, at last, apparently perfectly content. As he describes it in Phil 3:5–6, he had confidence in what he was doing as a fulfillment of what it meant to be one who was now no longer a part of the Diaspora, no longer dispersed from God's presence, and no longer alienated from his cognitive and theological self.

On the day in which Paul experienced his "fortunate fall,"[6] Paul confronted the risen Jesus on the way to Damascus to persecute Christians. The Lord, who identified himself as Jesus, called out to him in a way that Paul seems to have recognized all too well—whether he recognized the voice instinctively or identified its message from things he had heard from those he had persecuted is unclear—and, during this brief moment of confrontation, the risen Jesus taught Paul several crucial lessons. The first was, to use the title of the book by Thomas Wolfe, "you can't go home again."[7] The trip from Tarsus to Jerusalem had been not a restorative trip home, but in fact a journey into increased alienation from God, a double diaspora of an unanticipated sort, if you will. As a result, Paul was now alienated from God both physically and spiritually—having left home to pursue God, he now realized that he was instead further distanced from God. Paul had thought, with all of his intellectual knowledge, that doing was a substitute for being, when in fact God through Christ was not just calling him to a new type and form of knowledge—though this was an important element of it, in which he recognized and accepted Jesus as the Christ, God's one and only Son—but was also transforming him into an entirely new type of being that resulted in doing of a completely different kind. Paul was to become a follower of the very one whose followers he had been actively persecuting. Alienation is the fundamental fallen human condition until one is restored to God through Jesus Christ.

---

6. The notion of the fortunate fall, patterned after the biblical fall of Adam and Eve in the Garden of Eden, involves the protagonist's gaining enlightenment through experiencing unfortunate and often self-induced circumstances. There is the further irony, of course, of Paul's "falling to the ground" (Acts 9:4) when confronted by the risen Christ.

7. The contention of the novel is that one cannot return to a physical place and expect life there to be the same as it was before one left.

The second thing that Paul realized, part of both his cognitive and spiritual awakening, was that home is not a physical space but a spiritual relationship. Paul overtly claims to have been very self-satisfied in his religious convictions and practices as a disciple of Gamaliel, to the point of overt counter-evangelism for his cause—that is, persecution of those who did not believe as he did (Phil 3:5–6). However, his confrontation with the risen Jesus Christ made explicit that these efforts of human achievement, no matter how zealous or religiously motivated they may have been, were fundamentally misguided. The simple reason was that Paul had, among other things, come to believe that things were more important than people, one Person in particular, and that doing was more important than being. His fundamental alienation from God existed no matter where he was and what he was doing—until he met the risen Jesus Christ. His traversing the eastern Mediterranean, no matter how noble he considered the cause or enthusiastically he pursued it, was profoundly wrong in both motivation and goal. The Acts account makes it clear—Paul was transformed from one who was impatiently hurrying to the next task to one who, blinded by the experience, was forced to wait, for three days until meeting Ananias, before he could fully experience his own resurrection to new life, when the scales fell from his eyes (Acts 9:1–19; cf. Acts 22, 26). The third insight is that the notion of alienation must itself be reconfigured. For Paul, diaspora alienation meant living within an alien culture while a member of God's chosen people, the Jews. Paul came to learn that alienation from God in Christ meant that wherever he lived—including in Palestine—he was an alien until he came to be "in Christ."[8] This fundamental notion, Paul realized, applies to both Jew and Gentile alike. It is only as a follower of Christ that one can find genuine peace and be at home, not a continual refugee within one's own self and experience. This home is not here on this earth nor is it built with human hands, but it is a home nevertheless—a place where, indeed, one's heart is, a heart not of flesh but of spirit. The fourth insight is that the Christian condition—the condition of one who is truly allegiant to the risen Jesus Christ—is one of constant and continual alienation, exile, and dispersion from the world in which we live. In one sense, Paul's mission as

---

8. This language (ἐν Χριστῷ and related forms) is repeatedly used by Paul in his letters to speak of the spiritual relationship that exists from being within the sphere of Christ's control. See Porter, *Idioms*, 159; contra Campbell, *Paul and Union with Christ*, 67–199, who, besides seemingly treating prepositions as content rather than function words, follows a principle of splitting rather than lumping, resulting in a variety of nuances hard to differentiate within the given texts.

apostle to the Gentiles meant that he had been divinely appointed to bring alienation to Gentiles, so that they too—like the Jews before them—could be alienated from their ambient culture in order to be reconciled to God in Jesus Christ. Both Jew and Gentile are now refugees, whose only hope and rest is in Jesus Christ.

Paul learned much on that one small trip to Damascus. God performed a mighty act of transformation of Saul the persecutor into Paul the apostle. He transformed him from being a man of misguided ambition and with a mistaken notion of what it means to be God's diaspora people into a man of focused ambition and a genuine sense of what it means to be God's true diaspora people—aliens looking forward to their new home in Christ. This is the same message that Paul conveys in his letters.

PAUL'S LETTERS AND DIASPORA

Within the New Testament, Paul wrote thirteen letters, nine of them to churches and four of them to individuals.[9] In these thirteen letters, he does no systematic exposition of the notion of diaspora for his newly alienated converts or fellow believers. Instead, he embeds within them firm indicators of what it means for alienation from God to be overcome by God's love expressed through Jesus Christ and for such transformation to result in life as an alien within this world.

There are two ways that this topic of diaspora in Paul's letters can be discussed. The first approach is to proceed serially through the individual letters, and the other is to discuss as a whole individual ideas that Paul interweaves into one or more of his letters. There are advantages and disadvantages to each method—and each runs the risk of missing some important overall conceptual patterns or neglecting particular details. Using the integrated approach, I wish to organize my comments in two parts. The first concerns Paul's salvific progression, and the second, the larger, his direct address of the situation of the human as alienated in the world. As I will attempt to demonstrate in what follows, Paul fundamentally believes in a three-stage ideational conception that moves from human sinfulness that results in alienation from God to divine action to remedy the human condition to eschatological homecoming

---

9. On these letters, including discussion of matters of authorship, see McDonald and Porter, *Early Christianity*, 409–516. I endorse the Pauline authorship of all of the thirteen canonical letters attributed to him, as well as a Pauline imprisonment. On matters of dating the letters, especially the Pastoral letters, see Porter, "Pauline Chronology," and on implications of authorship for wider issues regarding Scripture, see Porter, "Implications."

that overcomes temporary earthly displacement with eternal rest and refuge. While we are on this progression towards eternity, we are inevitably—or at least should be—alienated from the world.

SALVIFIC PROGRESSION

I begin with Paul's discussion of the human progression from alienation from God to divine and eternal habitation. There is so much more that can be said here about this, and I know that I run the risk of too much brevity. I take that risk in an attempt to offer an overall perspective on Paul's thought.

Paul's belief in salvific progression—found elsewhere in his letters, though perhaps not to the same extent—is encapsulated in the structural flow of his letter to the Romans, especially Romans 1–8.[10] Paul states that God has made himself known to humanity, who has suppressed this awareness by means of its own wickedness and evil (Rom 1:18). In fact, humans have compounded the difficulty, to the point of denigrating themselves below common animals by their worship of them. As a result, God gave humanity over to its own desires, and the result was physical and mental depravation, all too commonly displayed in various ways (Rom 1:28–31). The result is the verdict of death, both physical and spiritual. This is the common human condition, for both Jews and especially non-Jews. God would be warranted in bringing the full force of his anger upon humanity (Rom 3:3–4). Therefore, Paul can boldly state that "all have sinned and lack the glory of God" (3:23).[11] Humans have violated God's explicit and implicit laws (which, in any case, were never designed to bring the human into right relationship with God by their fulfillment), have degraded themselves with impurity, and have severed any relationship with him. In other words, humans are alienated from God, estranged from their fellow humans with whom they are involved in such perverse behavior, and even alienated from themselves.

At the nadir of the human condition, God acted for human benefit. Paul uses three distinct ways of talking about God's remedy of the human condition, ways that he utilizes elsewhere in his letters as well. The first is justification. Justification is the means by which God addresses the human's

---

10. See Porter, "Newer Perspective," esp. 372–86, where this outline is laid out and explicated. In modified fashion, this forms the basis of the organization of my forthcoming commentary on Romans.

11. See Enderlein, "To Fall Short," but with corrections in Porter and Cirafesi, "ὑστερέω."

legal situation of being a law-breaker. There is now a way of being put in right legal standing with God apart from (because it was impossible to do so) doing of the human law (often referred to as works of the law). This right standing with God comes about through faith in Jesus Christ to those who believe (3:22), on the basis of the sacrificial death of Jesus Christ. I realize that there is much more that can be said about justification, but I must leave it at this.[12] The result of justification is that forensic alienation—that is, the fact that humans are divine lawbreakers—is overcome by God's accepting the sacrifice of Jesus Christ.[13] Similar justification language is used by Paul in 2 Corinthians, Galatians, Ephesians, and Philippians. The second way in which Paul speaks about God acting on behalf of humans is reconciliation. At least in Paul's argument in Romans, reconciliation is a separately identifiable means by which God addresses the human condition, in this case personal alienation from God (to be differentiated from the forensic alienation overcome by justification). The sacrifice of Christ was similarly sufficient so that, even though we as humans were God's enemies, we were reconciled to God through Jesus Christ. Reconciliation language is language of relationship, in which enmity and estrangement are replaced with right relationship. Like justification, reconciliation is also an act of God performed through the death of Jesus Christ. Second Corinthians 5:18–21 states similarly that God was reconciling the world (of humanity) to himself by means of the work of Christ, which then makes us God's ambassadors to others. Our restored relationship with God enables us to be his representatives to alienated others.[14] As Ephesians 2:16 says, this enabled God to break down the barrier of hostility that existed between Jews and Gentiles, thus creating one humanity. Colossians 1:22 says we can then be presented to God without accusation against us. The third way that Paul puts this change in relationship effected by God is in terms of salvation, or even by means of what it means to be baptized into Christ's death. We are not only buried with Christ, but we are raised with him so that we may live a new life (Rom 6:4), united with him in both this life and in his

---

12. Discussion of Paul's relationship to Judaism, including justification, continues at an astronomical pace, although too much of it appears simply to be unsubstantiated politically correct speculation. For two good treatments of the issue, see Seifrid, *Justification by Faith*, and Westerholm, *Perspectives Old and New on Paul*.

13. For discussion of some of the contemporary issues, see Husbands and Treier, *Justification*.

14. See Porter, Καταλλάσσω, 140. The following passages on reconciliation are also discussed in this volume.

resurrection, freed from the power of sin and corruption, so that they have no further control over us. This is the language that Romans uses, but elsewhere Paul speaks of this transformed human condition with language of holiness, as in 1 Thess 4:3–8, where he speaks of our being holy and leading holy lives, on the basis of the power of his Holy Spirit. In that sense, we are no longer alienated from God on the basis of our impurity, but are to live lives that are freed from the control of the world around us.

The third and final stage that Paul speaks of is eschatological homecoming, when our earthly alienation, though spiritually satisfied in the interim, is fulfilled in both spirit and form in our being united with Christ for eternity. In 1 Thess 4:13–18, Paul says that humans, whether they are dead or not at the moment of the coming of the Lord, will meet him and be with him forever. First Corinthians 15 goes into more detail on this eschatological transformation. Paul there speaks of the resurrection of the dead as based upon the resurrection of Jesus Christ. Jesus Christ's resurrection is the token or guarantee of the coming resurrection of all of those who are in him, of those who are resurrected to what Paul calls an imperishable body (1 Cor 15:42) or spiritual body, one reserved only for those whose alienation from God has been overcome by being clothed in imperishable and immortal bodies through the victorious death of Jesus Christ (1 Cor 15:57).

As we see from this brief exposition based upon the flow of Romans 1–8, Paul outlines a pattern by which alienation is overcome through God acting in Christ to effect repatriation and eternal homecoming and refuge.

ALIENS IN AN ALIEN LAND: THE CHRISTIAN CALLING

To this point, most of what I have said may sound (at least in some ways) much like a fairly standard exposition of Paul's soteriology, recast in the language of alienation, in this case, alienation from God overcome by the work of Jesus Christ. This is no doubt true, but that is because anything else that Paul may have to say about the notion of how we are estranged from our environments must be seen within Paul's wider perspective of how we are first and foremost estranged from God. It is only after we have come to terms with this fundamental spiritual alienation that we can address the question of our earthly alienation, and overcoming our spiritual alienation puts this earthly alienation in its proper perspective.

In this section, I want to tease out the notion of double diaspora in Paul's thinking. What I mean by that is that Paul himself was a Diaspora Jew who knew what it meant to live as a refugee from Palestine, the land of his forefathers. This was in one sense a physical diaspora, but it also was, more importantly, a spiritual diaspora, in that Paul himself had never been to the land before going there to become a student of Gamaliel and hence he probably believed that he was alienated from his spiritual home. However, Paul was wrong about this diaspora. His alienation was not from the land, but it was nevertheless a very real spiritual diaspora. It was a diaspora in relation to God. Paul was living a life alienated and estranged from God, regardless of where he was physically living. Thus, his diaspora was not a physical diaspora at all, but a spiritual one that could be overcome only through faith in Jesus Christ, who was sent by God to overcome human dispersion and exclusion. This spiritual condition was remedied for Paul on the road to Damascus, when he was confronted by the risen Jesus Christ.

What does such a notion of diaspora as overcome by Jesus Christ mean for life in this world? For Paul, I think that it means that we continue in a very tangible sense to be a dispersed people. However, we are now a dispersed people in relation to the world around us, in anticipation of finding our home and final rest with God. Paul makes this clear in a number of ways in his letters.

Before I discuss several of the key passages regarding this earthly alienation in anticipation of eschatological inclusion, I want to make a point about some recent research on Paul and empire. The world that Paul is addressing in his letters is the Greco-Roman world. As a result, by logical extension, it is the Greco-Roman world from which the Christians that he addresses will be alienated. There have been a number of scholars who have interpreted this to mean that Paul is frequently, whether implicitly or explicitly, engaging in anti-imperial Roman rhetoric throughout his letters.[15] Some have even argued that this is one of the major formative constructs for Paul's thinking.[16] I do not wish to dismiss completely the idea that Paul was against Roman imperialism. I think that Paul was strongly against many of the things that Roman imperialism stood for. Paul opposed Roman belief that Caesar was the son of God and the savior of the world who came to bring good news to the world (as the Priene inscription says of Caesar Augustus). Paul also opposed Roman oppression by imposition of unjust laws (Rom 13:1) and did not believe that Christians had an obligation to obey unjust laws imposed by secular authorities. When writing his

---

15. For a recent, perhaps overly sympathetic, evaluation of such imperialistic work in New Testament studies, see McKnight and Modica, *Jesus Is Lord*.

16. An example is Wright, "Paul's Gospel and Caesar's Empire."

letter to the Romans, in other words when writing his major letter to the Christian churches located at the center of the empire in its very capital, Paul does directly posit Jesus as the true son of God, who is the Savior of the world, and who has indeed brought good news. This would certainly have been inflammatory to the Roman authorities if they read the letter in that light.[17]

This does not mean, however, that everything that Paul wrote or did was anti-Roman. Paul was a Roman citizen who took full advantage of the rights that this provided, including exemption from certain types of punishment, the right to a hearing before punishment, and the right of appeal to Caesar, among others. He also took full advantage of the luxuries that the Roman world provided, such as safe travel by foot or by sea, an able military presence to ensure the peace, the reasonable expectation of a fair trial before punishment, and the ability to send correspondence by various messengers throughout this world, again among other things.

In other words, Paul was what we might today call a principled pragmatist or a realist. He had principles inspired by his interpretation of God's word, but his goal was not to call for overt overthrow of the Roman government, because that government provided a number of societal constructs that aided his larger agenda of the spread of the gospel of Jesus Christ. However, he held no brief for the Roman government, and in the course of his teaching set into motion plans that would have devastated the very structures of such a society by calling for new standards of human relationship that transformed societal structures (standards for human governance), family structures (e.g., husbands, wives, and children), and socio-economic structures (e.g., slavery).[18]

Therefore, I do not think that it is surprising to find within Paul's letters clear indications that he believed that Christians occupied the unique position of being those who were alienated from their true home, those who lived as refugees without a secure abode, and those who were estranged from the culture in which they lived.

I see that complex notion expressed in three ways.

First, the church is seen as an alternative microcosm created as a bulwark against the world at large and as a foretaste of the life beyond. The church is described in a number of different ways by Paul.[19] In many of

17. See Porter, "Paul Confronts Caesar," 168–89, on Romans.
18. I argue for these at greater length in Porter, "Reframing Social Justice."
19. See Porter, "The Church in Romans and Galatians," for my perspective on the

these, he sees the church as an organism, comparing it to the human body (1 Cor 12:12–30; Eph 5:23–32; Col 1:24). Just as the body has various parts to it, so the church has various members. The church, as a body, is a complex organism, rather than a unitary one. Hence it needs all of its members to survive, not just one or a select few. Even those parts that are often considered lowly are of inestimable value to the larger organism, so that there are none that are expendable or to be overlooked or neglected. This entity, because of its organic nature, has various roles that must be played within it, and hence it has structure and organization, such as is served by various people in various ways on the basis of their gifts.

In Ephesians and Colossians when Paul speaks of the church as a body, he adds the important detail that Christ is the head of the church. This addition is important for several reasons. One of these is that this indicates that for the church, whatever role and function it may play in the earthly sphere—and its function is primarily earthly—its ultimate authority and origin come from Christ himself, not from any earthly sphere or realm or power. In that sense, the church is an institution whose organizational structure transcends its earthly limitations and functions. The second area of importance is that this line of dependence and connection isolates the church in significant ways from the surrounding world. Whereas its lines of authority transcend the earthly sphere, its function is, as the organic metaphor conveys, to encompass its parts into a whole. The church is not depicted as part of or dependent upon or in any other way intertwined with other earthly structures, such as the political powers, economic powers, or other institutional powers of the earth. That kind of unfortunate entwining came later with Constantine, but is not part of its original mandate or description.[20] The third way the headship of Christ is important is that the church is answerable only to Christ and not to any earthly authorities. Christ is the head of the church, and his position of pre-eminence is not compromised by or mediated through any earthly power, such as those al-

---

Pauline church.

20. I indeed believe that the institutionalization of Christianity, in conjunction with its being made not only a "legal religion" but *the* legal religion of the Roman Empire, was an event with catastrophic consequences, from which we have not yet today recovered. I realize that such an action (and I believe that Constantine was genuine in his belief and sincere in what he did), although it may have spared many Christians from persecution, helped to transform Christianity from an alien religion into an established religion in which it was far too easy to become "Christian" to advance within society, and this led to the identification of Christianity with culture.

ready mentioned above. This of course has the result of placing Christians who are members of the church—which membership they gain through incorporation into Christ—into the difficult position of being members of two realms, the spiritual realm of the church and the realm of earthly habitation and responsibility. This directly leads to the next point.

Second, true citizenship is seen to be spiritual not earthly. Lest there be confusion regarding whether our allegiances as Christians are to the earthly realm or to the spiritual realm of Christ, Paul makes this clear in a number of places. I have already mentioned a very important passage, Rom 13:1–7.[21] This passage does not call for unqualified obedience to earthly authorities. The word that is often translated "governing" is better glossed as "qualitatively superior." What Paul is calling for is obedience to those authorities that are qualitatively superior, that is, those that are morally upright, that do not demand that their citizens perform morally wrong acts, and that reward those who do right and punish those who do wrong. Those authorities that are not qualitatively superior, that is, those that do reward evil and not good, are not to be obeyed. Paul leaves it to the individual conscience of the believer to decide which is which—although perhaps membership within the church is the means by which such decisions are to be made. The church, as we observed above, is in some senses a substitute for—not an equal to or adjunct of—the earthly state. The church is the earthly organization that has direct connections through its headship of Christ with the spiritual realm, the realm of ultimate citizenship. The earthly state is a tool used by God to do good, and therefore to help the church and its members when it does good and to punish those who do wrong.

The second important passage is Phil 3:20, where Paul says that our citizenship is in heaven. The entire context of Philippians must be taken into account. This is a book written to a church located within a city that was settled by retired Roman soldiers (hence more inscriptions are in Latin than Greek—the only major Roman city in the eastern part of the empire where this is the case), and hence a church that was very familiar with matters political.[22] Paul writes to the Philippians most likely from Rome, as reference to the Praetorian Guard (Phil 1:13) and Caesar's household (Phil 4:22) indicate.[23] Thus the context of both writing and reception of this letter

---

21. I first made the following argument in Porter, "Romans 13:1–7." I have not seen what I consider to be any serious refutation of my argument, only ignoring of it.

22. McDonald and Porter, *Early Christianity*, 461–63.

23. Ibid., 470.

is found within the structures of Roman political life. Nevertheless, when Paul speaks to the Philippians, probably because there was some confusion on their part, he tells them that they should conduct themselves (the word here is cognate with our word politics, πολιτεύομαι) in a manner worthy of the gospel of Christ (Phil 1:27). He does not say that they should act in a way that is pleasing to the Romans, pleasing to the powers that be, or pleasing to any other earthly force. Instead, when he arrives he wants to know that they have stood firm in one spirit and have contended with one spirit for the faith of the gospel, and that they have not been frightened by those who oppose them (Phil 1:27–29). Why would this be important? Paul offers a number of reasons, not least the example of Christ. However, he also says that there are many who are enemies of Christ. They are destined for destruction, because their mind is on earthly things. By contrast, for those of us who follow Christ, our citizenship is in heaven, whence we can expect to receive our Savior, the Lord Jesus Christ, who will transform our humble body into the body of his glory, by the power that enables him and brings everything under his control (Phil 3:19–21).

The third important expression is language that discusses the inhabited world and the place of the believer within it. To do full justice to this topic would extend this paper beyond the limits prescribed. Instead of attempting to trace all of these lines of thought, I will confine myself to several important areas of discussion. The first is that Paul envisions the world as a fallen and hostile place. Though God created the world, because of its fallenness he is going to judge it (Rom 3:6), because the world is guilty before him (Rom 3:19). After all, it is because of the sin of one person that sin entered the world (Rom 5:12), which corrupted the entire world, and gave it over to the god or controlling powers of this world (2 Cor 4:4; Gal 4:3; Eph 6:12; Col 2:8, 20). As a result, the wisdom of the world is foolish (1 Cor 1:20; 3:19) to the point of making those who think they are wise confounded by it (1 Cor 1:27). The world is filled with those who are evil (1 Cor 5:10 among many) and it is to be judged by those who are holy (1 Cor 6:2). Paul says that it is through Christ's cross that he has been crucified to the world and the world crucified to him (Gal 6:14). Instead, we brought nothing into this world (1 Tim 6:7), and though we must live within it (Col 2:20) and are to be lights within it (Phil 2:15), we are ultimately to be delivered from it (Gal 1:4). Even such a passage as Rom 8:18–25 is probably better interpreted not as indicating an ultimate redemption of the created order but signifying the redemption of the human being.[24] In other words, this world is one in which we live as aliens, and we are those who are dispersed throughout it to be light within a hostile environment, until that time when we are rescued from it and find final refuge in God.

CONCLUSION

Paul was a person who moved from one diaspora to another—from being a Diaspora Israelite to being a diaspora Christian. The Pauline model of life in this world is of one who is in a continual condition of alienation from the world in which he or she lives. For the follower of Christ, the world is alien, a foreign country in which one does not have citizenship if you will, because it is filled with the unredeemed. The creation itself is not to be redeemed, but individuals within it can be. Those redeemed through justification, reconciliation, and sanctification become members of the body of Christ, the church, God's mediating institution between the fallen human world and the believer's ultimate place of security in the presence of Christ forever. As a result, it is entirely appropriate that Pauline Christians living in this world feel estranged from it, as if this is not their ultimate or final home—because it is not. If Christians do find the wisdom of this world too appealing, it is a warning that perhaps they have not fully grasped the nature of the two worlds that they inhabit. They are caught between earth and heaven, between the here and the hereafter, between the already and the not yet. This is a difficult place to live. Christians can rightly be said to be aliens in a foreign land—at least I think that that is what Paul would have said.

BIBLIOGRAPHY

Campbell, Constantine R. *Paul and Union with Christ: An Exegetical and Theological Study*. Grand Rapids: Zondervan, 2012.
Davies, W. D. *The Gospel and the Land: Early Christianity and Jewish Territorial Doctrine*. The Biblical Seminar. Repr., Sheffield: Sheffield Academic, 1994.
Enderlein, Steven E. "To Fall Short or Lack the Glory of God? The Translation and Implications of Romans 3:23." *Journal for the Study of Paul and His Letters* 1 (2012) 213–24.
Fewster, Gregory P. *Creation Language in Romans 8: A Study in Monosemy*. Linguistic Biblical Studies 8. Leiden: Brill, 2013.
Husbands, Mark, and Daniel J. Treier, eds. *Justification: What's at Stake in the Current Debates*. Downers Grove, IL: InterVarsity, 2004.

---

24. See Fewster, *Creation Language*, esp. 168–69.

Rejection

McDonald, Lee Martin, and Stanley E. Porter. *Early Christianity and Its Sacred Literature*. Peabody, MA: Hendrickson, 2000.

McKnight, Scot, and Joseph B. Modica, eds. *Jesus Is Lord, Caesar Is Not: Evaluating Empire in New Testament Studies*. Downers Grove, IL: InterVarsity, 2013.

Pitts, Andrew W. "Hellenistic Schools in Jerusalem and Paul's Rhetorical Education." In *Paul's World*, edited by Stanley E. Porter, 19–50. Pauline Studies 4. Leiden: Brill, 2008.

Porter, Stanley E. "The Church in Romans and Galatians." In *The New Testament Church: The Challenge of Developing Ecclesiologies*, edited by John Harrison and James D. Dvorak, 85–102. Eugene, OR: Pickwick, 2012.

———. *Idioms of the Greek New Testament*. 2nd ed. Biblical Languages: Greek 2. Sheffield: Sheffield Academic, 1994.

———. "The Implications of New Testament Pseudonymy for a Doctrine of Scripture." In *Interdisciplinary Perspectives on the Authority of Scripture: Historical, Biblical, and Theoretical Perspectives*, edited by Carlos R. Bovell, 236–56. Eugene, OR: Pickwick, 2011.

———. *Καταλλάσσω in Ancient Greek Literature, with Reference to the Pauline Writings*. Córdoba: Ediciones El Almendro, 1994.

———. "A Newer Perspective on Paul: Romans 1–8 through the Eyes of Literary Analysis." In *The Bible in Human Society: Essays in Honour of John Rogerson*, edited by M. Daniel Carroll R., David J. A. Clines, and Philip R. Davies, 366–92. JSOTSup 200. Sheffield: Sheffield Academic, 1995.

———. "Paul Confronts Caesar with the Good News." In *Empire in the New Testament*, edited by Stanley E. Porter and Cynthia Long Westfall, 164–96. MNTS. Eugene, OR: Pickwick, 2011.

———. "Pauline Chronology and the Question of Pseudonymity of the Pastoral Epistles." In *Paul and Pseudepigraphy*, edited by Stanley E. Porter and Gregory P. Fewster, 65–88. Pauline Studies 8. Leiden: Brill, 2013.

———. "Reframing Social Justice in the Pauline Letters." In *The Bible and Social Justice*, edited by Cynthia Long Westfall and Bryan R. Dyer. MNTS. Eugene, OR: Pickwick, forthcoming.

———. "Romans 13:1–7 as Pauline Political Rhetoric." *Filología Neotestamentaria* 3 (1990) 115–39.

Porter, Stanley E., and Andrew W. Pitts. "Paul's Bible, His Education and His Access to the Scriptures of Israel." *JGRChJ* 5 (2008) 9–40.

Porter, Stanley E., and Wally V. Cirafesi. "ὑστερέω and πίστις Χριστοῦ in Romans 3:23: A Response to Steven Enderlein." *Journal for the Study of Paul and His Letters* 3, no. 1 (2013) 1–9.

Seifrid, Mark A. *Justification by Faith: The Origin and Development of a Central Pauline Theme*. NovTSup 68. Leiden: Brill, 1992.

Westerholm, Stephen. *Perspectives Old and New on Paul: The "Lutheran" Paul and His Critics*. Grand Rapids: Eerdmans, 2004.

Wolfe, Thomas. *You Can't Go Home Again*. New York: Scribners, 1940.

Wright, N. T. "Paul's Gospel and Caesar's Empire." In *Paul and Politics: Ekklesia, Israel, Imperium, Interpretation*, edited by Richard A. Horsley, 160–83. Harrisburg, PA: Trinity, 2000.

8

Persecution in the Early Christian Mission according to the Book of Acts

ECKHARD J. SCHNABEL

THERE IS NO COMPREHENSIVE historical analysis of persecution of Christians in the first century, nor a comprehensive study of persecution in the book of Acts. This is surprising, given the importance that is repeatedly accorded to the reality of persecution in and for the early church. Scott Cunningham provides a theological analysis of the functions of persecution.[1] Renzo Lavatori and Luciano Sole present a fuller study of persecution, evangelization, and the church in the book of Acts, investigating in particular the significance of persecution for the growth of the church, the existence of the church, the implementation of God's saving plan, and the revelation of the church.[2] A comprehensive monograph on the significance of persecution of Christians in the first century was only written recently, by James Kelhoffer, who, however, is more interested in assertions of standing, authority, and power, which are made on the basis of persecution.[3] His thesis and conclusion are, like Cunningham's, theological: he argues that "a prominent emphasis in Acts is to question, confirm, and derive legitimacy because of persecution": the

---

1. Cunningham, *'Through Many Tribulations.'*
2. Lavatori and Sole, *Persecuzione.*
3. Kelhoffer, *Persecution*; his central thesis is that "corroboration stemming from persecution plays a prominent and heretofore underappreciated role in NT constructions of legitimacy" (361).

author "questions the legitimacy of the depicted persecutors, who are usually Jewish" and "he confirms the standing of the persecuted Christians."[4]

I understand the term "persecution" to be more than a hostile attitude concerning the followers of Jesus: it is aggressive harassment, deliberate ill-treatment, ranging from initiating court proceedings to beatings, flogging, and banishment from a city to execution or lynch killings. The Greek term διωγμός can be defined as "a program or process designed to harass and oppress someone."[5] We will discuss, first, the scope of persecution in the book of Acts, in particular the initiators of persecution, the geographical scope of persecution, targets of persecution, and actions of the persecutors. Second, we will investigate the reasons for persecution. The third section will examine the reaction of the early Christians to persecution. The focus will be on the presentation of the evidence and on an analysis in the various historical contexts.

THE SCOPE OF PERSECUTION ACCORDING TO ACTS

A survey of the persecution passages in the book of Acts demonstrates the pervasiveness of aggressive hostility towards the early followers of Jesus. Luke details nineteen occurrences or "events" of persecution.

1. 30 CE (April?). Acts 4:1–22

    The priests, the captain of the temple, and the Sadducees arrest Peter and John in one of the halls surrounding the outer court of the Jerusalem temple, probably Solomon's Portico (cf. 5:12). The two apostles are imprisoned and brought before the Sanhedrin court where the leaders, elders, and scribes conduct a legal hearing. After threatening further action, they release Peter and John.

2. 30 CE (April?). Acts 5:17–41

    The high priest and the Sadducees arrest the apostles in Jerusalem. After a night in prison, they are brought before the Sanhedrin, some of whose members want to kill them. After Gamaliel's intervention they are merely flogged and released.

---

4. Ibid., 360.

5. BDAG, s.v. διωγμός. Kelhoffer, *Persecution*, 8, defines "persecution" and "unjust suffering" interchangeably to designate "any undeserved penalty or punishment—whether real, imagined, anticipated, or exaggerated."

3. 31/32 CE. Acts 6:9—7:60

   Greek-speaking Jews in Jerusalem accuse Stephen of blasphemy. They arrest him, incite the people of Jerusalem, the elders, and the scribes, and initiate legal proceedings before the Sanhedrin. The high priest leads the interrogation that results in Stephen's execution, in which the members of the Sanhedrin are involved.

4. 31/32 CE. Acts 8:1; 11:19

   The high priest and the members of the Sanhedrin (cf. 7:1, 54–60) seek to suppress the church in Jerusalem, taking actions that force the followers of Jesus to flee the city and go to Samaria, Phoenicia, Cyprus, and Antioch. Saul/Paul is involved in the persecution that moves from house to house (8:3).

5. 31/32 CE. Acts 9:1–14

   Saul/Paul obtains from the high priest (Joseph Caiaphas) letters to the synagogues at Damascus giving him authority to arrest followers of Jesus in Damascus and bring them to Jerusalem for trial.

6. 33/34 CE. Acts 9:23–24

   Jews in Damascus plot to kill Paul; they watch the gates in order to arrest him, but Paul manages to escape.

7. 33/34 CE. Acts 9:29–30

   Greek-speaking Jews in Jerusalem plot to kill Paul when he proclaims the gospel in the city. Paul has to leave Jerusalem and moves to Tarsus in Cilicia.

8. 41 CE (April?). Acts 12:1–19

   Herod Agrippa I arrests several followers of Jesus, among them James and Peter. James is executed. Peter is evidently sentenced to be executed as well, but manages to escape. James's execution demonstrates that Agrippa's measures against the church are severe and violent, ending the period of tranquility of about ten years since the persecution that ensued after Stephen's execution.

9. 46 CE. Acts 13:50–51

    The Jews of Pisidian Antioch enlist women of high social standing among the Godfearers and the leading men of the city to expel Paul and Barnabas from the city.

10. 46 CE. Acts 14:5–6

    Local Jewish and non-Jewish residents of Iconium, including the magistrates, plan to attack and stone Paul and Barnabas, which forces the latter to flee and move to Lycaonia.

11. 46 CE. Acts 14:19

    Jews from Pisidian Antioch and from Iconium manipulate the residents of Lystra who proceed to stone Paul in an attempt to kill him. Paul survives and goes with Barnabas to Derbe.

12. 49 CE (August/October?). Acts 16:16–40

    The owners of a fortune-telling slave girl seize Paul and Silas and accuse them before the magistrates in the forum of Philippi, who order them flogged and imprisoned. They are released the next day.

13. 49 CE (October/November?). Acts 17:5–10

    Jews in Thessalonica who object to Paul's preaching manage to organize a mob that causes an uproar in the city. They search for Paul and Silas, and when they fail to find them they attack the house of Jason, who is taken to the magistrates together with other followers of Jesus. After bail is posted, Jason and the other Christians are released. Paul and Silas leave the city and go to Berea.

14. 49 CE (December?). Acts 17:13–14

    Jews from Thessalonica find Paul and Silas in Berea. When they manage to incite the crowds, Paul is immediately taken to the coast.

15. 51 CE. Acts 18:12–16

    Jews in Corinth initiate legal proceedings against Paul before Gallio, the governor of the province of Achaia, who, however, dismisses the charges. Paul stays in Corinth.

16. 55 CE. Acts 19:23–41

    The leader of the guild of the silversmiths incites the citizens of Ephesus to protest in defense of the preeminence of Artemis Ephesia against the growing Christian movement. The situation seems to be dangerous, especially for Paul, who is prevented by Christians and by the Asiarchs from going into the theater (19:30–31).[6]

17. 57 CE (April). Acts 20:3

    Jews in Corinth make a plot against Paul, to be carried out, perhaps, during the sea voyage to Jerusalem for the Passover festival.

18. 57 CE (May). Acts 21:27–36

    Jews from the province of Asia seize Paul in one of the inner courts of the Jerusalem temple and accuse him of having profaned the temple. Jewish residents of Jerusalem rush to the temple mount, seize Paul and try to kill him. Paul is rescued by the tribune of the Roman cohort stationed in the Antonia fortress. When the tribune becomes aware of a plot of local Jews to kill Paul, he transfers him to Caesarea (23:12–33).

19. 57 CE (May). Acts 24:1—25:12

    The high priest Ananias and some of the elders (24:1, 5–6) initiate legal proceedings against Paul before the Felix, the Roman prefect of Judea, in Caesarea, with the goal of obtaining a death sentence. When Festus arrives in the province as the new prefect, they plan an ambush to kill Paul during a requested transfer of the case to Jerusalem (25:2–3). Paul appeals to the emperor and is transferred to Rome.

Initiators of Persecution

As regards Jerusalem, Luke mentions twelve different entities as initiating repressive measures against the followers of Jesus. Other entities initiate persecution outside Jerusalem. They are listed here in chronological sequence.

---

6. The opposition in the synagogue of Ephesus, and the action that Paul took, moving his activities to the hall of Tyrannus (19:9), is not an instance of persecution, but seems to reflect a decision as to the advisability of insisting on meeting in a venue in which he was not welcome by many of the members of the synagogue.

Rejection

1. The "priests" (οἱ ἱερεῖς; 4:1),[7] i.e., the officials who are responsible for the temple, particularly for the sacrifices and matters such as the temple tax.

2. The "captain of the temple" (ὁ στρατηγὸς τοῦ ἱεροῦ; 4:1 Hebr. סָגָן), i.e., the official in charge of all temple affairs, the second in authority in the temple after the incumbent high priest, the head of the temple guard (often called temple police), which consisted of 200 priests and Levites. According to Josephus and the New Testament, he was the official who was responsible for maintaining order in and around the temple.[8] The rabbinic tradition uses the phrase "prefect of the priests" (סְגַן הַכֹּהֲנִים) for the official who was regarded as next to the high priest in rank[9] and who stood next to the high priest when the daily sacrifice was offered.[10]

3. The Sadducees (οἱ Σαδδουκαῖοι; Acts 4:1; 5:17), i.e., the members of the priestly families who constituted the aristocracy in Jerusalem.[11]

4. The "leaders" (οἱ ἄρχοντες) who were involved in the hostile interrogation of Peter and John (Acts 4:5) are probably identical with the names given in 4:6: Annas the high priest, Caiaphas, John and Alexander, who all belonged to the high-priestly class. Annas served as high priest (ἀρχιερεύς, Hebr. הַכֹּהֵן הַגָּדֹל) from 6 to 15 CE.[12] John (Ἰωάννης) may be Jonathan, son of Annas, who was high priest after Caiaphas[13]

---

7. Manuscripts B and C read ἀρχιερεῖς ("chief priests"), probably a harmonization with v. 6 (and with Luke 22:4, 52; Acts 5:24, 26, where the "captain of the temple" is linked with the chief priests).

8. Cf. Josephus, *Ant.* 20:131, 208; *J.W.* 2:409; 6:294; Acts 4:1; 5:24, 26; cf. Luke 22:4, 52, where the plural στρατηγοί is used. Josephus, *Ant.* 20.131, mentions the *strategos* Ananus, the son of the high priest Ananias (*J.W.* 2.243); he was στρατηγός as late as 48–52 CE, when Ventidius Cumanus was Roman governor of Judea. Cf. Gussmann, *Priesterverständnis*, 100.

9. According to *y. Yoma* 41a, the high priest held the rank of the סָגָן (prefect) before he acceded to the office of high priest. Cf. Schürer, *History of the Jewish People*, 2:278; Jeremias, *Jerusalem in the Time of Jesus*, 161, 163.

10. Cf. *m. Tamid* 7:3; cf. *m. Yoma* 3:9 and 4:1 for his role on the Day of Atonement.

11. Cf. Goodman, "Sadducees and Essenes"; Stemberger, "Sadducees"; Nodet, "Pharisees, Sadducees, Essenes, Herodians."

12. Josephus, *Ant.* 18:26. Annas was appointed high priest by Quirinius, the Roman governor in Syria. On Annas cf. VanderKam, *From Joshua to Caiaphas*, 420–24; Metzner, *Die Prominenten im Neuen Testament*, 234–37, 342–43.

13. Josephus, *Ant.* 18:95, 123; 19:313; 20:163; *J.W.* 2:240–243, 256.

from 36 to 37 CE, and who may have been the captain of the temple.[14] Caiaphas (Καϊάφας, Hebrew קַיָפָא, Qaifa), whose full name was Joseph Caiaphas,[15] Annas's son-in-law, was high priest from 15 to 36 CE.[16]

5. The "elders" (πρεσβύτεροι) are involved in the interrogation of Peter and John (Acts 4:5). They accept the charge of blasphemy brought against Stephen and are involved in initiating legal proceedings against Stephen before the Sanhedrin (6:12). The "elders" were senior officials, members of the Jewish elite, both priests and laymen, among the latter presumably the rich landowners. While it is plausible to assume that many of the "elders" were members of the Sanhedrin, there is no evidence that all "elders" belonged to the Sanhedrin.[17]

6. The Jewish people (ὁ λαός; Acts 6:12) of Jerusalem are involved in the confrontation with Stephen that leads to his arrest, trial, and execution. The Jewish residents of Jerusalem (ἡ πόλις ὅλη καὶ ... συνδρομὴ τοῦ λαοῦ; Acts 21:30) are involved in seizing Paul in one of the inner courts of the Jerusalem temple.

7. Members of the Sanhedrin (τὸ συνέδριον; 6:12) confront and arrest Stephen, and they are involved in his trial and execution (7:54, 57–60). The Sanhedrin was the highest assembly in Jerusalem, the supreme legislative, judicial, and executive body of leading citizens meeting in a council chamber at the center of the city, near the temple.[18]

8. The "scribes" (οἱ γραμματεῖς) of Jerusalem are also involved in the interrogation of Peter and John in a Sanhedrin hearing (Acts 4:5), and they are involved in initiating legal proceedings against Stephen (Acts

---

14. Jeremias, *Jerusalem in the Time of Jesus*, 197, who relies on *y. Yoma* 3.41a (5), a late tradition, which states that a high priest was not nominated unless he had first been captain of the temple. Barrett, *Acts*, 225, remains skeptical.

15. Josephus, *Ant.* 18:35. For the name cf. Ilan, *Lexicon of Jewish Names*, 408.

16. On Caiaphas, cf. VanderKam, *From Joshua to Caiaphas*, 426–36; Bond, *Caiaphas*; Gussmann, *Priesterverständnis*, 419–20; Metzner, *Die Prominenten im Neuen Testament*, 76–84, 343.

17. Rohde, "πρεσβύτερος."

18. Cf. Lohse, "συνέδριον"; Schnabel, "Sanhedrin"; Schürer, *History of the Jewish People*, 2:199–226; Sanders, *Judaism*, 472–88; Mason, "Chief Priests"; Kee, "Central Authority." One needs to take care not to rely on the older discussions of J. Jeremias and others who used the later rabbinic evidence concerning the "Great Sanhedrin" uncritically (cf. Jeremias, *Jerusalem in the Time of Jesus*, 222–32).

6:12). They were specialists in the Law, scholars who are sometimes mentioned together with the priests,[19] sometimes with the Pharisees.[20]

9. The high priest (ἀρχιερεύς; 5:17) who initiates the arrest of the apostles in Jerusalem is probably the incumbent high priest Caiaphas. He is the high priest in 7:1 who conducts the interrogation of Stephen that leads to the latter's execution. And he is the high priest in 9:1 who provides Saul/Paul with letters authorizing him to arrest followers of Jesus in the synagogues of Damascus. In 24:1 the high priest Ananias initiates legal proceedings against Paul.

10. Greek-speaking Jews of Jerusalem (Ἑλληνισταί; cf. Acts 6:9-11 with 9:29) who belonged to the synagogue of the Cyrenians, Alexandrians, Cilicians, and Asians accuse Stephen of blasphemy and initiate legal proceedings. It is probably the same Greek-speaking Jews who attempt to kill Saul/Paul (Acts 9:29) when he returns to Jerusalem after his conversion and missionary work in Nabatea.

11. Saul of Tarsus, (former) rabbinical student of Gamaliel, is involved in the execution of Stephen (8:1) and in the ensuing persecution of other followers of Jesus (8:3), and initiates the plan to arrest Christians in Damascus (9:1-2).[21]

12. Jews from the province of Asia (οἱ ἀπὸ τῆς Ἀσίας Ἰουδαῖοι; Acts 21:27) seize Paul in one of the inner courts of the temple. They may be identical with the people who spread the rumors concerning Paul's annulment of the Mosaic Law (21:21), although Luke does not explicitly identify the two groups.

As regards cities outside of Jerusalem, Luke mentions sixteen groups that instigate persecution:

13. Greek-speaking Jews (Ἑλληνισταί) in Damascus make a "plot" (ἐπιβουλή)[22] to kill Saul/Paul (9:29-30). The apostle's comment in 2

---

19. Luke 9:22; 19:47; 20:1, 19; 22:2, 66; 23:10.

20. Luke 5:21, 30; 6:7; 11:53; 15:2.

21. On Paul's life before his conversion, see Hengel and Schwemer, *Paul between Damascus and Antioch*; Hengel and Schwemer, *Paulus zwischen Damaskus und Antiochien*.

22. The term ἐπιβουλή denotes "a secret plan to do something evil or cause harm" (BDAG, s.v.; cf. 2 Macc 5:7; 3 Macc 1:2, 6); it is used with regard to organized conspiracies against Paul in Acts 9:24; 20:3, 19; 23:30.

Cor 11:32 suggests that the Jews of Damascus evidently had the support of the ethnarch of the Nabatean king Aretas, whose agents were supposed to make the arrest.

14. Herod Agrippa I (12:1–19) initiates a persecution of the followers of Jesus in Jerusalem, in the course of which James is killed and Peter faces death. Agrippa I was born in 10 BCE as the son of Aristobulus IV and his wife Bernice, brother of Herodias (Mark 6:15–28), and grandson of Herod I and Mariamne I (through Aristobulus). He was given the name Marcus Julius Agrippa in honor of Marcus Vipsanius Agrippa, the general and friend of the Emperor Augustus and of Herod I.[23] He grew up in Rome, where he had been sent with his mother in early childhood. He had close relationships with Claudius, the later emperor, and Drusus, the son of the Emperor Tiberius. He spent large sums of money in his attempt to cultivate friendships with these and other members of the imperial family. When Drusus died in 23 CE, he returned to Judea penniless and contemplating suicide. In the 20s he married Cypros, the granddaughter of Herod's brother Phasael. He returned to Rome in 36 CE where Antonia, Tiberius's sister-in-law, paid off of his debts. He cultivated the friendship of Gaius Caligula, but was jailed when Tiberius accused him of sedition. When Gaius became emperor in 37 CE, he was released from prison and given the tetrarchy of Philip (Gaulanitis, Trachonitis, Batanaea, and Panias, with Caesarea Philippi) and the title "king." He initiated the persecution against the leaders of Jesus' followers in Jerusalem early in his reign, presumably in order to win the favor of the Saducean leadership in Jerusalem.

15. The Jews (οἱ Ἰουδαῖοι) of Pisidian Antioch stir up opposition against Paul and Barnabas (Acts 13:50), which leads to their expulsion from the city. Together with Jews from Iconium, the Pisidian Jews manipulate the residents of Lystra into attempting to kill Paul by stoning (14:19). Luke does not specify who "the Jews" (οἱ Ἰουδαῖοι) included; they were certainly Jews who had contacts with the local elites, perhaps the officials of the synagogue.

---

23. See Braund, "Agrippa"; Bond, "Agrippa"; Schürer, *History of the Jewish People*, 1:442–54; Schwartz, *Agrippa I*; Kokkinos, *Herodian Dynasty*, 271–304; Hengel and Schwemer, *Jesus und das Judentum*, 83–92; Metzner, *Die Prominenten im Neuen Testament*, 393–405. Josephus gives an account of his reign in *Ant.* 19:292–316.

16. Gentile women of high social standing (αἱ γυναῖκες αἱ εὐσχήμοναι; 13:50) who belong to the Godfearers, i.e., who attend the synagogue services in Pisidian Antioch, are involved in the opposition against Paul and Barnabas. The prominent Gentile women may have been benefactors of the local synagogue.

17. The "leading men of the city" (οἱ πρῶτοι τῆς πόλεως; 13:50), i.e., influential members of the local aristocracy, perhaps including the *duoviri*, the highest municipal magistrates, force Paul and Barnabas to leave Antioch.

18. Jews (οἱ Ἰουδαῖοι) of Iconium (14:5) plan an attack against Paul and Barnabas, whom they want to stone. They are also involved, together with Jews from Pisidian Antioch, in encouraging the residents of Lystra to attack and stone Paul (14:19).

19. The non-Jewish residents (τὰ ἔθνη) of Iconium (14:5) join the local Jews in their plan to attack and eliminate Paul and Barnabas.

20. The city officials (οἱ ἄρχοντες; 14:5)[24] who are involved in the plot to attack Paul and Barnabas in Iconium should probably be seen as including descendants of the Roman colonists, as Iconium had been refounded as a Roman colony.

21. The owners of a fortune-telling slave girl in Philippi (16:19) seize Paul and Barnabas and take them to the magistrates.

22. The city officials (οἱ ἄρχοντες; 16:19) of Philippi, i.e., the magistrates who have administrative authority in Philippi, among whom are the "chief magistrates" mentioned in 16:16, 20, order Paul and Silas to be flogged and imprisoned.

23. Jews (οἱ Ἰουδαῖοι) of Thessalonica (17:5) organize a mob with a view to attacking Paul and Silas, who are forced to leave the city. When they find the two missionaries in Berea, they incite the population there, forcing them to leave.

24. Bad characters (ἄνδρας πονηρούς) in the agora of Thessalonica who are organized by the local Jews to "form a mob" (ὀχλοποιήσαντες; 17:5).

---

24. Inscriptions attest a "first leader" (πρῶτος ἄρχων) for the city of Iconium; see CIG 4001; IGR III 262.

When they cannot find Paul and Silas, they attack and arrest newly converted Christians.

25. The city officials (οἱ πολιτάρχαι; 17:6, 8) of Thessalonica who are involved in the action against the local Christians, consisted of five or six senior magistrate officials. They were responsible for convening both the assembly of the people (ἐκκλησία) and the city council (βουλή), introducing motions, and confirming its decisions. They were responsible to act for the people (δῆμος), carrying out the wishes of the assembly of the citizens. They possessed judicial authority, and they were responsible to maintain peace and order to ensure that the Roman authorities would not be forced to intervene in the affairs of the city.[25]

26. Jews (οἱ Ἰουδαῖοι) of Corinth (18:12) initiate legal proceedings against Paul before Gallio, the governor of the province of Achaia.

27. Demetrius (Δημήτριος; 19:24), the leader of the guild of silversmiths in Ephesus (19:25), incites a protest against the presence of Paul and his coworkers in the city.

28. Jews (οἱ Ἰουδαῖοι) of Corinth (20:3) make a "plot" (ἐπιβουλή) against Paul. Perhaps the Jews who had unsuccessfully tried to obtain Paul's punishment in the legal case they brought before Gallio, the Roman governor (18:12–17), recognized the significance of Paul's activities not only for Corinth but for other Jewish communities, causing them to take the desperate action of trying to eliminate Paul outside of the Roman court system. It has been plausibly suggested that Jews who planned to travel to Jerusalem as pilgrims for the Passover festival, taking the same ship as Paul, hoped to kill him en route to Judea.[26]

This long list of initiators of persecution demonstrates the near universal scope of persecution, which was initiated by various segments of society. Of the twenty-eight entities mentioned, nineteen are Jewish and nine are non-Jewish. The Jewish initiators of persecution range from their

---

25. Horsley, "Politarchs," 425, 430. The politarchs were not officials of the Roman provincial administration, although in the first century many holders of the annual office (which could be held more than once) would have had Roman citizenship.

26. Ramsay, *Paul the Traveller*, 220; cf. Bruce, *Book of the Acts*, 382 n. 15; Barrett, *Acts*, 946; cf. Bornkamm, *Gesammelte Aufsätze*, 4:136.

high priests in Jerusalem (Annas, Caiaphas, Ananias) and Herod Agrippa I, and members of the elite (leaders, elders, Sadducees, members of the Sanhedrin) to priests, scribes, native Jewish residents, Greek-speaking Jewish residents, and individual perpetrators such as Saul/Paul, who was probably not the only individual taking the initiative. As regards persecutions outside of Jerusalem, the description is more general: Luke speaks of the Jews of Damascus, Pisidian Antioch, Iconium, Thessalonica, and Corinth. The non-Jewish initiators of persecution are mostly city officials (Pisidian Antioch, Iconium, Philippi, Thessalonica); once, a mob is mentioned (Thessalonica); individual instigators of hostile attacks are the owners of the fortune-telling slave girl in Philippi and Demetrius in Ephesus.

There are three clusters of instigators of persecution: (1) The arrest of Peter and John and the subsequent hearing before the Sanhedrin (Acts 4:1–22) is linked with the priests, the captain of the temple, the Sadducees, the leaders, the elders, and the scribes. (2) The arrest, trial, and execution of Stephen (Acts 6:9—7:60) is linked with the Greek-speaking Jews of Jerusalem, the people of Jerusalem, the elders, the scribes, the high priest, and the members of the Sanhedrin. (3) The expulsion of Paul and Barnabas from Pisidian Antioch (Acts 13:50–51) is connected with the Jews of Antioch, women of high social standing among the God-fearers, and the leading men of the city.

Geographical Scope

Eight instances of persecution are related for Jerusalem (events 1–4, 7, 8, 18–19), two for the province of Syria (Damascus; events 5, 6), three for the province of Galatia (Pisidian Antioch, Iconium, Lystra; events 9–11), three for the province of Macedonia (Philippi, Thessalonica, Berea; events 12–14), two for the province of Achaia (Corinth; events 15, 17), and one for the province of Asia (Ephesus; event 16; cf. event 18). The fact that the ethnarch of the Nabatean king Aretas in Damascus wants to arrest Paul (2 Cor 11:32) suggests not only missionary activity in Nabatea/Arabia (cf. Gal 1:17), but also persecution in this still autonomous region south of Damascus. No persecution is related for the mission of Paul and Barnabas to Cyprus, nor for their missionary work in the province of Pamphylia (Perga; Acts 14:25). Thus, the apostles are persecuted in Jerusalem, and Paul is persecuted both in Jerusalem and in essentially all the provinces and regions in which he proclaims the gospel.

Targets of Persecution

The first person for whom Luke reports "persecution," not mentioned so far, is Jesus of Nazareth. Luke relates in his account of Peter's sermon on the feast of Pentecost that Peter explained to his Jewish listeners, "this man, handed over to you according to the definite plan and foreknowledge of God, you crucified and killed by the hands of those outside the law" (Acts 2:23), accusing both the Jewish leaders of Jerusalem and the Roman prefect of being complicit in the execution of Jesus.

As regards the nineteen events of persecution listed above, Luke mentions seven different individuals who were targets: Peter (events 1, 8), John (event 1), Stephen (event 3), James (event 8), Paul (events 6, 7, 9–15, 17–19), Barnabas (events 9, 10), and Silas, Paul's coworker (events 12–14). Peter, Silas, and Paul are linked with multiple events of persecution: Peter twice, Silas three times, Paul thirteen times. Groups that are targets of persecution are the Jerusalem apostles (event 2), and Jesus' followers in Jerusalem (events 4, 8), Damascus (event 5), and Ephesus (event 16). Luke mentions the personal names of Christians who are persecuted only in the case of leaders. His references to entire local churches being persecuted demonstrate, however, that there were situations in which few if any Christians of a local congregation escaped the aggressive hostility of opponents.

Actions of the Persecutors

The following sixteen types of specific actions against followers of Jesus are related by Luke:

1. Opponents in Jerusalem "approach" (ἐφίστημι) followers of Jesus with hostile intent (event 1).[27] The same verb is used for the attack on the house of Jason in Thessalonica (event 13).

2. Persecutors in Jerusalem enter "house after house" (κατὰ τοὺς οἴκους εἰσπορευόμενος; event 4), apparently in order to arrest followers of Jesus.

3. Opponents "arrest" (ἐπιβάλλω τὰς χεῖρας)[28] the apostles, first Peter and John, then other disciples, as well as other believers in Jerusa-

---

27. Cf. BDAG, s.v. ἐφίστημι 1, "to stand at or near a specific place, *stand at/near*," often with connotation of suddenness; 3, "to come near with intention of harming, *attack*;" BDAG assumes the first meaning for Acts 4:1.

28. Cf. Radl, "χείρ."

lem (events 1, 2, 8). Stephen is "seized" (συναρπάζω) with force, i.e., arrested (event 3). There are plans to arrest believers in Damascus (event 5). Paul is arrested (ἐπιλαμβάνομαι) in Philippi (event 12) and in Jerusalem (ἐπιβάλλω τὰς χεῖρας; event 18).

4. Believers in Jerusalem are "bound" (δέω) in connection with their arrest (event 4), presumably with ropes.

5. Paul and Silas are "stripped of their clothes" (περιρήξαντες αὐτῶν τὰ ἱμάτια; event 12) as preparation for the flogging that was administered on the bare skin.

6. The twelve apostles are "flogged" (δείραντες; event 2). Paul and Silas are "beaten with rods" (ῥαβδίζω; event 12). Flogging and beating (Lat. *verbera*) occurred in the Roman legal system as concomitant punishment combined with other penalties, e.g., the death penalty or the removal of citizenship. During the imperial period, beatings were also administered as independent penalty. Flogging was also used during interrogation to extort a confession.

7. Gentile and Jewish residents of Iconium intend to "mistreat" (ὑβρίζω) and "stone" (λιθοβολέω) Paul and Barnabas (event 10). It appears that some Jewish, Greek, and Roman citizens of Iconium wanted to harass the missionaries and pelted them with stones as a deterrent to further activities, probably accepting the possibility that they would be seriously injured or even killed. Paul is nearly killed by stoning (λιθάζω) in Lystra (event 11).

8. Peter and John are "put in custody" (ἔθεντο εἰς τήρησιν), probably a reference to the prison of the Sanhedrin (event 1),[29] the Twelve are "put in the public prison" (ἔθεντο αὐτοὺς ἐν τηρήσει δημοσίᾳ),[30] perhaps a reference to the Jewish "state prison" that was in Herod's old

---

29. The term translated as "prison" (τήρησις) is a *nomen actionis* that describes the "act of holding in custody" and can also be used to describe the place where someone is held under guard. Cf. BDAG, s.v. τήρησις; for meaning 2, "a place for custody, *prison*" reference is made to BGU 388 III 7; Thucydides 7.86.1; Josephus, *Ant.* 18:235. Barrett, *Acts*, 221, insists on the meaning of the *nomen actionis*; however, when people are "in custody" over night, they are "in prison," unless a lockup in temporary facilities is assumed.

30. Cf. BDAG, s.v. δημόσιος 1, "to belonging to the state, *public*." In the papyri, a public road is called ὁδὸς δημόσιος; cf. P.Köln VII 322; P.Oslo II 31; P.Oxy VI 918; SB I 4661, 5168, 5320.

palace, the praetorium on the west side of the city[31] (event 2). Paul and Silas are "thrown into prison" (ἔβαλον εἰς φυλακὴν), specifically "in the innermost cell" (εἰς τὴν ἐσωτέραν φυλακὴν), i.e., in an inner maximum security cell, where the jailer secures (ἠσφαλίσατο) their feet in the stocks made of wood (εἰς τὸ ξύλον; event 12).[32] The magistrates employed incarceration as a police measure for the short-term penalty of misbehaving individuals in the context of their *coercitio*, i.e., "the authority of Roman magistrates to intervene when they judged the public order had been violated by citizens and non-citizens, restricting their rights and exercising sovereign power."[33]

9. The Greek-speaking Jews in Jerusalem "stir up" (συγκινέω) the people of Jerusalem as well as the elders and the scribes (event 3).[34] Jews in Pisidian Antioch "incite" (παροτρύνω) women of high standing among the Godfearers and the leading men of the city (event 9). Jews in Thessalonica form a mob (ὀχλοποιέω) and start a riot (θορυβέω; event 13). In Berea they "stir up" (σαλεύω) and "incite" (ταράσσω) the crowds (event 14). Demetrius stirs up the silversmiths and eventually the residents of Ephesus (event 16).

10. Jews in Pisidian Antioch "slander" (βλασφημοῦντες) Paul (13:45). The "slander" may have involved the utterance of blasphemies, probably against Jesus, presumably pronouncing the curse of the Torah (Deut 21:22–23) upon the crucified Jesus.[35]

---

31. Lake, *Additional Notes*, 478; Rapske, *Paul in Roman Custody*, 137. Others assume that the public prison was in the lower level of the palace of the high priest, cf. Stählin, *Apostelgeschichte*, 89; Zmijewski, *Apostelgeschichte*, 263, which is less likely.

32. Cf. BDAG, s.v. ξύλον 2b, "a device for confining the extremities of a prisoner, *stocks*." These contraptions often consisted of "wood pierced at regular intervals with notches or holes and split along the length so that the feet of the prisoner could be set in and secured" (Rapske, *Paul in Roman Custody*, 127). In the gladiator's barracks of Pompeii such stocks made of metal were discovered, holding the leg bones of two skeletons of people who had perished in the eruption of Mt. Vesuvius while being imprisoned. In the papyri, the verb (ἀσφαλίζω) often denotes the capture and securing of a suspect; cf. Spicq, "ἀσφάλεια κτλ."

33. Gizewski, "Coercitio."

34. Cf. BDAG, s.v. συγκινέω "arouse/excite someone."

35. Cf. Pesch, *Apostelgeschichte*, 2:45, with reference to Gal 3:13; 1 Cor 12:3.

Rejection

11. Legal proceedings are related for Peter and John (event 1) and the twelve apostles (event 2) in Jerusalem, and for Paul in Philippi (event 12), Corinth (event 14), and Caesarea (event 19).

12. Threats after legal proceedings are related for Peter and John (event 1). The chief priests, elders, and scribes threaten Peter and John with consequences if they do not stop proclaiming a message that involves Jesus.

13. The magistrates of Thessalonica force Jason and other local Christians, to pay bail (λαβόντες τὸ ἱκανόν; translating the Latin expression *satis accipere*, "to receive bail, bond, security;" 17:9). He is either forced, or he volunteers, to give security for Paul and Silas, guaranteeing their good behavior and/or their departure.[36]

14. City magistrates "expel" (ἐκβάλλω) Paul and Barnabas from Pisidian Antioch and the territory controlled by the city (event 9). In earlier and later cases of persecution, the flight of Christians from the city in which they were residents does not seem to be a decision of magistrates but the result of the intense pressure resulting from aggressive actions threatening Christians with imprisonment and punishment. Christians are forced to flee from Jerusalem in the persecution after Stephen's execution (event 4); Paul is forced to leave both Damascus and Jerusalem (events 6, 7); Peter is forced to leave Jerusalem (event 8); Paul and Barnabas are forced to leave Iconium and Lystra (events 10, 11); Paul and Silas are ordered to leave Philippi (event 12), and they have to leave Thessalonica and Berea in a hurry (events 13, 14).

15. On several occasions opponents communicate plans to kill Jesus' followers. Some members of the Sanhedrin want to kill the apostles (event 2). Herod Agrippa wants to kill Peter (event 8). Jews in Damascus want to kill Paul (event 6), as do Jews in Jerusalem (event 7), Jews in Corinth (event 17), and again Jews of Jerusalem (events 18, 19).

---

36. Sherwin-White, *Roman Society*, 95–97; followed by most commentators, cf. Barrett, *Acts*, 816; Bock, *Acts*, 553; also Dunn, *Beginning from Jerusalem*, 680. The passive voice of the verb "we were made orphans" in 1 Thess 2:17 confirms that Paul's departure from Thessalonica was forced upon him; cf. Malherbe, *Thessalonians*, 61. In 1 Thess 2:18 Paul attributes his inability to return to Thessalonica to the supernatural force of Satan, which may be an allusion to the actions of the politarchs.

16. There are killings and executions: Stephen is killed by stoning (λιθοβολέω; event 3). James is executed by the sword (event 8).

REASONS FOR PERSECUTION

The persecution passages detail twelve types of reasons why Jews and Gentiles aggressively oppose Jesus' followers.

1. Unauthorized teaching. The priests, the captain of the temple, and the Sadducees arrest Peter and John since they are "annoyed" (διαπονούμενοι) because (διά) they were teaching (Acts 4:2). They are "teaching the people" (διδάσκειν τὸν λαόν) in the Solomon's Portico complex without authorization, which annoys the priests who are responsible for the affairs of the temple.

2. Proclamation of a link between Jesus and the resurrection of the dead. In Jerusalem, Peter and John are arrested because they are "proclaiming that in Jesus there is the resurrection of the dead" (4:2). Peter argues that Jesus' resurrection from the dead (ἐν τῷ Ἰησοῦ)[37] is an event that has taken place recently, and thus before the day of resurrection of the dead, which must annoy not only the Sadducees but also the Pharisees.

3. Teaching in the name of Jesus. Peter and John are teaching in the name of Jesus, proclaiming (καταγγέλλειν) him publicly (4:2)[38] to be the promised Messiah, whose crucifixion was engineered by the chief priests, implying that the Jewish authorities have made a serious mistake.

4. Accusation of blasphemy. When Stephen begins to explain Jesus' significance as messianic Son of Man standing at the right hand of God (7:55–56), the members of the Sanhedrin "cover their ears" (συνέσχον τὰ ὦτα αὐτῶν; 7:57) and "rush" (ὥρμησαν) at him. The blasphemous

---

37. The phrase ἐν τῷ Ἰησοῦ can be interpreted as (1) "in the case of Jesus," i.e., the apostles proclaim that "in the case of Jesus, *the* (ultimate) resurrection—the resurrection expected by Pharisaic faith at the end of history—had taken place" (Moule, *Origin of Christology*, 167; Bock, *Acts*, 187); (2) "by means of," i.e., the apostles proclaim the resurrection of the dead by means of the story of Jesus (Barrett, *Acts*, 220). These are not mutually exclusive alternatives, cf. Zmijewski, *Apostelgeschichte*, 211.

38. Cf. BDAG, s.v. καταγγέλλω, "to make known in public, with implication of broad dissemination, *proclaim, announce.*"

utterance, in their view, is Stephen's declaration that he sees Jesus, the Son of Man of Daniel's prophecy, standing at the right hand of God: no one has the right to share the glory of God at God's right hand.[39]

5. Zeal for the Law. Luke relates that when Jews of Pisidian Antioch see the crowds who want to hear Paul and Barnabas speak, they are "filled with zeal" (ἐπλήσθησαν ζήλου; 13:45). The term translated as "zeal" (ζῆλος) has been interpreted in terms of the Jews' zeal for the law[40] or in terms of their envy or "jealousy" (NET, NIV, NLT, NRSV) regarding the missionary success of Paul and Barnabas.[41] Some interpreters combine the theological and the psychological explanations.[42] The social situation of the Jewish Diaspora communities in the historical context of the first century must have played a role as well. The Jews of Pisidian Antioch certainly opposed Paul and Barnabas because they disagreed with their teaching. However, there are reasons to believe that the significance of maintaining their religious and ethnic identity also played an important role in their forceful and sometimes violent reaction. The Jews of Asia Minor were surely concerned to preserve the social and political rights and privileges that they had enjoyed since Julius Caesar, which had come under pressure in different places at different times,[43] rights and privileges that might be jeopardized if the movement of the followers of Jesus was ignored. Jesus was a man who, after all, had been executed by the Roman governor of Judea (v. 28). Also, the Jews of Asia Minor might have been motivated by concerns regarding the financial strength of their community, and they were probably also concerned to avoid actions and resist developments that

---

39. Cf. Bock, *Acts*, 312; Segal, *Two Powers*, 94-95. See Bock, *Blasphemy and Exaltation*, 113-83, for a discussion of the Old Testament and Jewish sources on blasphemy.

40. Cf. Pesch, *Apostelgeschichte*, 2:45; cf. Zmijewski, *Apostelgeschichte*, 518, who argues that the term describes a theological position of the Jews in Antioch who are convinced that the purity of Israel is at stake: they regard the new teaching about salvation as an offense against the Mosaic Law, particularly against circumcision and the cultic commandments.

41. Jervell, *Apostelgeschichte*, 362; Barrett, *Acts*, 655; Witherington, *Acts*, 414-15, who suggests that the Jews' reaction involved jealousy "presumably because Paul and Barnabas were attracting a large Gentile audience while apparently the local Jews themselves had been less successful in attracting Gentiles."

42. Cf. Marshall, *Acts*, 229-30.

43. Cf. Pucci Ben Zeev, *Jewish Rights*; for details see Schnabel, "Jewish Opposition."

contravened decisions made by the leadership of the Jewish commonwealth in Judea.[44]

The motivation of the Jews in Thessalonica who opposed Paul and his coworkers is also described with reference to jealousy (ζηλώσαντες οἱ Ἰουδαῖοι; 17:5), a term that refers probably not simply to the jealousy over the conversion of Jews and of a large number of Gentiles including Godfearers, but to their "zeal" for the traditional understanding of the Mosaic Law, for the maintenance of Jewish identity and its religious distinctives in the capital city of the province of Macedonia, and for the preservation of the rights and privileges that the Jewish communities enjoyed in the cities of the Roman provinces (see on 13:45).[45] As several women of high social status, who apparently had been attending the synagogue, were converted to faith in Jesus, unbelieving Jews would have feared the loss of influential patrons in the city. These Jews from the synagogue had heard Paul expound his convictions about Jesus as Israel's Messiah. They were not convinced, and they decided to take steps to silence Paul and his associates.

6. Political expediency. The wave of persecution under Herod Agrippa I in 41 CE seems to have been grounded in political expediency. Agrippa, who grew up in Rome, and had played a role in the accession of Claudius to the imperial throne, was awarded consular rank in 41 CE and given the Roman province of Judea, including Idumea and Samaria. Agrippa thus ruled over the restored kingdom of his grandfather Herod. On coins minted under Claudius and also in inscriptions he calls himself "the Great," a title that the senate in Rome had conferred on him. In inscriptions of his son Agrippa II, he is called "friend of the emperor" and "friend of the Romans."[46] When he arrived in Jerusalem in the spring of 41 CE, he organized a triumphal entry into the city and offered sacrifices. He presented himself as a pious king who loved the Jewish people, and demonstrated this in the lowering of taxes and the improvement of the fortification of Jerusalem with a third wall. He championed the sanctity of the temple. His actions against the leaders of the Jerusalem congregation of Jesus'

---

44. Schnabel, "Jewish Opposition," 70. Similarly Dunn, *Beginning from Jerusalem*, 426.

45. Cf. Schnabel, "Jewish Opposition," 234–35, 239–43, 270.

46. Cf. OGIS 419; cf. Boffo, *Iscrizioni greche e latine*, 336.

followers seem to have been part of these measures that were initiated to demonstrate his promotion of traditional Jewish concerns.

7. Financial loss. The syndicate in Philippi who own a psychic slave girl "see" (ἰδόντες) that their prospects for financial gain have vanished after Paul drives out the girl's spirit (16:19). When the spirit of divination leaves (ἐξῆλθεν; 16:18), their "hope" (ἐλπίς) for continued financial gain from their psychic slave leaves (ἐξῆλθεν) as well. When Demetrius, the president of the guild of the silversmiths in Ephesus, initiates action against Paul and his coworkers, he also is motivated by the prospect of financial loss. The first sentence of his speech before the artisans reminds the men of the fact that their prosperity derives from "this business" (ἐκ ταύτης τῆς ἐργασίας; 19:25), i.e., from the manufacture and sale of devotional Artemis objects.

8. Accusation of attacking the patron deity of the city. Demetrius accuses Paul of discrediting the cult and the temple of Artemis (19:27). He suggests that there is the risk that the temple of Artemis "may be looked upon as nothing" (εἰς οὐθὲν λογισθῆναι). If the people who are "deceived" by Paul accept his teaching that gods made with hands are not gods, the temple of Artemis will no longer be looked upon as one of the main reasons for the fame of Ephesus—the grand structure in which the famous image of "the great goddess Artemis" (ἡ μεγάλη θεὰ Ἄρτεμις)[47] awes the thousands of visitors to the temple, the sanctuary famous for its size and antiquity, for its beauty and the works of art in its precinct, the "common bank of Asia" and the "refuge of necessity"[48] granting asylum to people unjustly accused of murder or facing imprisonment.[49] And Demetrius warns of the damage that the success of Paul's activities will inflict on the cult of Artemis Ephesia: there is the risk that the great goddess Artemis will "suffer the loss of her grandeur" (καθαιρεῖσθαι τῆς μεγαλειότητος αὐτῆς). The grandeur of Artemis was connected with her numerous palpable manifestations (*epiphaneia*)—physical appearances reported in myth, novels,

---

47. Xenophon, *Ephesiaca* 1.11:5 speaks of "our ancestral goddess, the great Artemis of the Ephesians" (τὴν πάτριον ἡμῖν θεόν, τὴν μεγάλην Ἐφεσίων Ἄρτεμιν). Both the second declension form (θεός) and the first declension form (θεά) are used for Artemis; in v. 37 the town clerk speaks of τὴν θεὸν ἡμῶν.

48. Aelius Aristides, *Or.* 23.24.

49. Thomas, "At Home in the City of Artemis," 98–100.

and mentioned in inscriptions, and revelations in response to prayers for safety and healing.⁵⁰ The grandeur of Artemis is also reflected in the fact that she is worshiped not only in Ephesus, but by "the entire province of Asia" (ὅλη ἡ Ἀσία) and indeed by "the entire world" (ἡ οἰκουμένη).

9. The syndicate who control the slave girl who has a spirit of divination accuse Paul and Silas before the "chief magistrates" (οἱ στρατηγοί) of Philippi of introducing new customs (ἔθη) that are "unlawful" (ἃ οὐκ ἔξεστιν) for Roman citizens (16:21). They evidently argue that the two Jewish men are seeking to alter the ancestral customs (*mores*) of the Roman colony of Philippi, altering the way of life of the Romans living in Philippi, as these visitors teach the Philippians to live like Jews (e.g., by refusing to worship in pagan temples), which in Roman eyes amounts to revolution.⁵¹ Roman custom (*mos*), understood as *mos maiorum* ("custom of the fathers"), "is the core concept of Roman traditionalism. As little in Rome was regulated by positive law, in all areas of life people in many respects followed custom (*mos*; sometimes connected with *disciplina*) and traditional practice (*instituta*). It was generally assumed that usage was exemplary and binding, because of its age and the *auctoritas maiorum*."⁵² Public teaching about a Jewish Savior, and a public exorcism performed by invoking the Messiah of the Jewish people (16:18) can easily be construed as undermining the Roman identity and the civic distinctiveness of Philippi and its citizens. If the Roman citizens in Philippi are aware of recent developments in the city of Rome, the charges of Paul's accusers may be linked with the fact that this is a critical time for the Jews in Rome: Seneca, the anti-Jewish adviser of the imperial court, has returned from exile, and Claudius is intensifying his program of restoring the ancient Roman religion while

---

50. Cf. Oster, "Holy Days," 80–81. Note the epithet ἐπιφανεστάτη used for Artemis (I. Eph Ia 27, 385).

51. Cf. Van Unnik, "Anklage," (whose theory that the expulsion of Jews from Rome by the praetor Peregrinus Cn. Cornelius Hispalus in 139 BCE is connected with the veneration of the god Sabazios as Highest God in Phrygia, referred to in the cries of the slave girl in v. 17, is not plausible; cf. Pilhofer, *Die erste christliche Gemeinde Europas*, 192). Jews were exempt from serving in the military, and they were allowed to observe the sabbath, keep special food laws, and send money to Jerusalem—all customs that were unacceptable for Romans.

52. Kierdorf, "Mos maiorum," cf. Van Unnik, "Anklage," 382–83. The *auctoritas maiorum* refers to the affirmation of the consuls and praetors.

at the same time (but for other reasons) expelling the Jews from the city of Rome because "men of foreign birth" have caused disturbances at the instigation of a certain Chrestus.[53] In such a political climate, the public teaching of "Jewish customs," from the Roman perspective, is an example of promoting what the emperor is restricting.

In Corinth, Jews accuse Paul that he is "persuading people to worship God in ways that are contrary to the law" (18:13). The vaguely formulated charge of the Corinthian Jews who accuse Paul makes sense if we take 18:13 to be the beginning of the pre-trial hearing in which the charges are summarized, with the prospect that the actual trial will bring the fuller charges to light.[54] From a narrative and historical perspective, a reference to Roman law makes most sense: Roman governors were not responsible for coercing Jews to keep Jewish laws. A breach of Roman law is precisely the point where the highest administrator of a province can be expected to intervene. Paul is accused of violating the laws of the Roman Empire—not the laws of the city of Corinth, for which the local magistrates would be responsible. The charge includes a comment on the problematic nature of Paul's teaching activity. Paul's teaching is regarded as dangerous because it is "against the law," i.e., its very content is dangerous.

Demetrius accuses Paul of having misled a considerable number of people in Ephesus and in almost the entire province of Asia "by saying that gods made with hands are not gods" (19:26). According to Demetrius, Paul's activity consists in his efforts to convince the people to give up worshiping the traditional gods. Once people refrain from worshiping the gods, they will also refrain from buying replicas of a deity such as Artemis and replicas of her temple—efforts that are surprisingly and enormously successful.

---

53. Suetonius, *Claud.* 25:3-4. Cf. Riesner, *Paul's Early Period*, 194. On Claudius's policies against the Jews, see Botermann, *Judenedikt*.

54. Omerzu, *Prozeß*, 257. Winter, "Gallio's Ruling," 220, suggests the following outline of the legal petition that initiated the proceedings: 1. *exordium*, with a summary of the case and an emphasis on Gallio's competence to hear the case (18:13 can be taken as such a summary); 2. *narratio*, with an outline of the evidence that proves that Paul is a law breaker and a Jewish political dissident; 3. *confirmatio*, with the proofs that Paul indeed violated the laws of the empire; 4. *peroratio*, with an emphasis on Paul being a troublemaker who promotes an un-Roman cult and on the need to deal with Paul decisively.

10. Accusation of sedition. The syndicate in Philippi accuses Paul and Silas of causing an uproar in the city (16:20). The Greek verb (ἐκταράσσουσιν) denotes the action of causing an uproar. Causing a disturbance in the city would have to be punished by the authorities, whose main responsibility—particularly in a Roman colony—was the maintenance of order. The punishment depended on the kind of disturbance that had been provoked. Roman law distinguished different kinds of disturbances sanctioned as *crimen*. There was the *tumultus*, the disturbance of the peace, the public brawl or assault, which was closely related to the charge of *turba*, both punished by the payment of damages. More serious was the charge of *seditio*, understood as a serious disturbance of public order, a breach of the public peace, particularly in connection with larger groups banding together, in other words a rebellion, punished by exile (*exilium*), with loss of citizenship and all assets, and even death, and mere participation resulting in more lenient punishment such as banishment (*relegatio*) for up to ten years, or in perpetuity, to live in another city or on an island (*relegatio ad insulam*).[55]

The people of Thessalonica accuse Paul and Silas (in absentia) as well as Jason and the other believers, of being agitators who have upset the stability (ἀναστατώσαντες)[56] of the world (τὴν οἰκουμένην) in other regions of the Roman Empire and who have now "come here" (καὶ ἐνθάδε πάρεισιν; 17:6).[57] The charge was not completely invented if the Jews of Thessalonica had heard of Paul's activities in other provinces

---

55. The crime of *seditio* was addressed in the *lex Iulia de vi* by Caesar and the *lex Iulia de vi* by Augustus. See Von Ungern-Sternberg, "Seditio"; Gamauf, "Exilium"; Végh, "Relegatio"; Omerzu, *Prozeß*, 126. Luke distinguishes different kinds of disturbances: he speaks of rebellion (στάσις, Luke 23:19, 25; Acts 19:40; 24:5; ἀναστατόω, Acts 17:6; 21:38; this corresponds to Lat. *seditio*) and tumults (θόρυβος, 20:1; 21:34; 24:18; θορυβέω, 17:5; 20:10); the terms τάραχος and (ἐκ)ταράσσω (12:18; 15:24; 17:8; 19:23) designate tumults as well (Lat. *tumultus*), but could overlap with *turba*; cf. Stegemann, *Zwischen Synagoge und Obrigkeit*, 216 n. 102; Stegemann links the accusation in Acts 16:20–21with the later situation under Domitian and the obligation placed on diaspora Jews to pay the *fiscus Judaicus* (Stegemann, *Zwischen Synagoge und Obrigkeit*, 220–25); this interpretation has been duly criticized for overreaching historical criticism; cf. Omerzu, *Prozeß*, 137.

56. Cf. BDAG, s.v. ἀναστατόω, "to upset the stability of a person or group, *disturb, trouble, upset;*" LSJ: "unsettle, upset, destroy." In 21:38 the verb is used for the Egyptian revolutionary who led an armed revolt against Rome.

57. This charge is much more serious than translations such as "these men have upset the world" (NASB) or even "these men have turned the world upside down" (RSV, ESV, cf. NRSV) suggest.

through contacts with the Jewish communities in Palestine and Syria, or through contacts with the Jewish community in Philippi, a few days travel north of Thessalonica. Wherever Paul proclaimed his message, trouble ensued both in the local Jewish communities and among the citizens of the cities in which he was active—as a result of the disputes that arose in the Jewish communities, as a result of the conversion of Jews and Gentiles, as the result of the emergence of a new group whose members adopted new practices in worship and in personal behavior. The fact that Paul and his associates more often than not were forced by magistrates to leave the city in which they had been teaching indicates, certainly, that they caused disturbances that the officials in these cities were not willing to tolerate. The accusation of threatening the stability of the world, designed to portray Paul and Silas as criminals, uses allegations from the traditional arsenal of polemics, slander, and defamation,[58] while being rooted to some degree in the reality of the effects of Paul's missionary ministry.

Ananias and the Jewish elite, through their advocate Tertullus, accuse Paul of sedition (24:5). They assert that Paul is a "public enemy" (λοιμός).[59] The term is explained by the statement that Paul is a man who causes riots among all (πᾶσιν) the Jews throughout the world (κατὰ τὴν οἰκουμένην). The term used for Paul's activities—"riots" (στάσεις)—denotes uprisings, revolts, and rebellions that threaten the civil harmony and peaceful conduct (ἡσυχία) that Roman governors are responsible for maintaining. The transposition of the religious charges (21:28; also 23:29 in Lysias's letter) into political charges is not necessarily a clever tactical move or an intentional distortion of the facts. The religious accusations are present in the background, as the charge of temple profanation (24:5) demonstrates. Moreover, Paul's missionary work had regularly provoked controversies that disturbed the harmony and peace not only of the various local Jewish com-

---

58. Cf. Dunn, *Beginning from Jerusalem*, 679, who speaks of "exaggerated populist rhetoric so readily drawn upon in all ages on such occasions of public confrontation." He suggests that Paul's eschatological teaching with its "veiled allusion to the removal of the imperial power" (Bruce, *Acts of the Apostles*, 371) allows us to see "how the accusation may arise."

59. Cf. BDAG, s.v. λοιμός II. The Greek term means "being diseased" or "pestilential" when used for birds of prey; when used of human beings, the term means "public menace" or "public enemy." The author of 1 Maccabees (10:61; 15:21) uses the term for wanted criminals, and Demosthenes for people who are dangerous to the welfare of the public (*Or.* 25.80).

munities but also of the cities themselves. The comparison of a riot (στάσις; Lat. *tumultus*) with a disease is a common theme of Greek and Roman legal language.[60] The charge of *seditio* diminishes the possibility that the Jews can influence the course of the trial, since causing riots is a crime that only the governor can examine. At the same time, the charge of *seditio* puts Paul in the awkward situation of having to defend himself against a charge that on the surface is plausible. The charge of *seditio* cannot simply be dismissed by Felix. It is has been suggested that the language of the first charge against Paul deliberately echoes a letter that the Emperor Claudius wrote in 41 CE to Aemilius Rectus, the Roman prefect in Alexandria,[61] dealing among other matters with the Jews who had been involved in "disturbances and rioting" (ταραχῆς καὶ στάσεως) and whom he threatens if they disobey his injunctions. He warns them not to "bring in or invite Jews coming from Syria or Egypt," otherwise he will be "forced to conceive graver suspicions" and says that he "shall proceed against them in every way as fomenting a common plague for the whole world (κοινήν τινα τῆς οἰκουμένης νόσον)."[62] Whether or not Tertullus's charge of *seditio* intentionally echoes Claudius's letter to his governor in Egypt written seventeen years earlier, the emperor's intervention demonstrates Rome's sensitivity to the danger posed by foreign cults and religions to the peace and stability of the cities in the provinces.[63] Paul is also accused of being a "ringleader" (πρωτοστάτης) of the sect of the Nazarenes. In Tertullus's summary of legal charges against Paul, the term is used *in malam partem* in the sense of "ringleader."[64] Paul is accused of leading a faction from which the religious and political leadership

---

60. Cf. Lösch, *Epistula Claudiana*, 24–33. The suggestion of Jervell, *Apostelgeschichte*, 568, that Luke wants to describe the dispute between Judaism and Pauline Christianity and is thus not interested in a political charge against Paul, suggesting that στάσις here means "strife, discord" (as also suggested by BDAG, s.v. στάσις 3), is unconvincing. The fact that Paul remained in Roman prisons for at least four years, and the fact of his appeal to the emperor, show that matters of Roman law were indeed at stake; see Omerzu, *Prozeß*, 433 n. 60.

61. P. Lond. VI 1912 = CPJ II 153, Jewish matters are addressed in lines 73–104 (quotations from lines 73 and 100). For an English translation see Feldman and Meyer, *Jewish Life*, 91–92 (No. 4.19). See the discussion in Kasher, *Jews in Egypt*, 310–26; Omerzu, *Prozeß*, 193–98; Schnabel, "Jewish Opposition," 248–49.

62. Cf. Sherwin-White, *Roman Society*, 51–52.

63. Omerzu, *Prozeß*, 198.

64. Cf. BDAG, s.v.; thus most English translations.

Rejection

of the Jews distance themselves. While establishing local assemblies with regular meetings was a potential problem given the suspicious attitude of some emperors concerning voluntary associations,[65] the connection between Paul's group, labeled "Nazarenes" (Ναζωραῖοι) by the Jews,[66] and Jesus of Nazareth, who was crucified by the Roman governor twenty-seven years earlier, explains the seriousness of this charge. Paul leads a party that pledges devotion to a man who was executed by the Roman authorities as a teacher who (allegedly) seduced the people and who falsely claimed to be the king of the Jews.[67]

11. Accusation of acting contrary to the decrees of the emperor. In Thessalonica, Paul and Silas, together with Jason and the other believers, are accused of acting (πράσσουσιν) contrary to the decrees of the emperor (17:6). This is an explicit political charge. The term τὰ δόγματα denotes formal statements "concerning rules or regulations that are to be observed," here, more specifically, the imperial declarations of the emperor. At the time, the emperor was Tiberius Claudius (41–54 CE).[68] This specific accusation is substantiated by a reference to the beliefs and teachings of the accused: they say (λέγοντες) that there is a rival king (ἕτερος βασιλεύς εἶναι) whose name is Jesus (Ἰησοῦν); the term translated as "king" is used in Greek texts to denote the Roman emperors.[69] In other words, Paul and his associates are charged with advocating loyalty to a certain Jesus rather than to the emperor in Rome. Paul's proclamation that Jesus is Israel's Messiah (v. 3) is construed in a political sense: Paul speaks of Jesus as king—not only as king of the

---

65. While Hardin, "Decrees and Drachmas," suggests that the Christian assemblies could be accused of violating the laws against voluntary associations, Arnaoutoglou, "Roman Law and *collegia* in Asia Minor," argues that there was no general ban on associations.

66. The designation of the Christians as "Nazarenes" was probably coined by opposing Jews, as a derogatory term reflecting the insignificance of the town (village) of Nazareth.

67. Note the *titulus* on the cross that included the designation Ναζωραῖος: "Jesus of Nazareth, the King of the Jews" (Ἰησοῦς ὁ Ναζωραῖος ὁ βασιλεὺς τῶν Ἰουδαίων), John 19:19; cf. Luke 23:1, 38 (without the term Ναζωραῖος).

68. Cf. Balsdon and Levick, "Claudius"; Eck, "Claudius"; Levick, *Claudius*, passim.

69. LSJ, s.v. βασιλεύς, III.3. English versions have generally translated "king" in 17:7, although the translation "saying that there is another emperor, named Jesus" is also possible. Cf. Barrett, *Acts*, 816: "they act against the decrees of Caesar by proclaiming a rival emperor" (although Barrett also translates βασιλεύς here as "king"); cf. Johnson, *Acts*, 307; Fitzmyer, *Acts*, 596, cautions that the title "emperor" was not yet used in Rome then.

Jews (which would suffice to constitute sedition, since Claudius had appointed Agrippa as king of Judea in 41 CE), but also of the Greeks and Romans in Thessalonica whom he invites to become followers of Jesus. Luke's reference to the decrees (plural) of Caesar that Paul and Silas and the Thessalonian believers are accused of violating have been interpreted in two ways. Either they are accused of committing the crime of treason, i.e., of violating the Roman law of treason (*maiestas*, short for *maiestas populi romani minuta*, "diminishing the majesty of the Roman people"),[70] or they are accused of violating the legislation of Augustus and Tiberius prohibiting astrology and predictions of the change of rulers,[71] and more specifically, of rejecting the oath of allegiance to the emperor that provinces and cities swore, pledging reverence and obedience to the emperor, with the local magistrates being responsible for administering the oath.[72]

12. Accusation of having profaned the Jerusalem temple. Jews from Asia accuse Paul, who is visiting Jerusalem, of having profaned the temple by bringing a Gentile into the inner courts (21:27–30). The high priest Ananias and the Jewish elite, through their advocate Tertullus, who accuse Paul of sedition, offer as proof that Paul tried to profane the temple (24:6).[73] A defilement of the temple would necessitate purification rites and a rededication of the temple by means of legitimate sacrifices, per-

---

70. Cf. Blass, *Acta Apostolorum*, 187; Tajra, *Trial of St. Paul*, 36–42; Omerzu, *Prozeß*, 190, 200–207. For objections, see Judge, "Decrees of Caesar," 456–57; Hardin, "Decrees and Drachmas," 30–33. The law concerning the crime of treason (*crimen maiestatis*) was formulated with regard to offenses of Roman noblemen. It was established by public law rather than by imperial decree, and it would hardly have been the foundation of an accusation in the local courts of a free city.

71. Note Paul's proclamation concerning the returning Lord Jesus, the Messiah (cf. 1 Thess 4:16; 5:2–3; 2 Thess 2:3–12), which could be construed to refer to a prediction of a change of ruler. Cf. Judge, "Decrees of Caesar," 457–61.

72. Mitford, "Cypriot Oath"; Bömer, "Der Eid beim Genius des Kaisers"; Herrmann, *Der römische Kaisereid*, 125–26 (No. 6); Donfried, "Cults of Thessalonica," 32–34. For a critique of Judge's explanation see Hardin, "Decrees and Drachmas," 34–38.

73. In the summary of Tertullus's speech, Acts 24:6 seems to function as *confirmatio*. Cf. Lombardi, "Motivi giuridici," 10; Winter, "Importance of the *captatio benevolentiae*," 515, 519; Winter, "Official Proceedings," 320; Rapske, *Paul in Roman Custody*, 162; Padilla, *Speeches of Outsiders*, 220. Other scholars interpret 24:6 as the second charge and thus have to assume that Tertullus's speech has no *confirmatio*; cf. Omerzu, *Prozeß*, 429; Neyrey, "Forensic Defense Speech," 216–17; Soards, *Speeches in Acts*, 117–18; Witherington, *Acts*, 704–5; Parsons, *Acts*, 325; Pervo, *Acts*, 594–95. This analysis is unlikely, given the formal features of Tertullus's speech, and unwarranted, given the substance of 24:6.

haps similar to the rededication of the temple by Judas the Maccabee on the 25th of Kislev in the year 164 BCE, three years after Antiochus IV had defiled the temple by offering pagan sacrifices.[74] Tertullus argues that Paul has brought his activities from the Jewish communities "throughout the world" to Jerusalem. If this is accepted as fact, Felix will have to take the Jewish demand for Paul's summary execution seriously, particularly if he fears Claudius's wrath that was communicated to the governor in Egypt. Tertullus does not assert that Paul actually defiled the temple (cf. 21:28), but, rather, that he tried (ἐπείρασεν) to desecrate the temple. While this seems a "milder form of the accusation,"[75] it does not improve Paul's legal position since the Jews can present their intervention as a preventive measure that has taken place just in time.[76] Also, he now has to prove not only that he did not actually desecrate the temple but that he harbored no intentions of profaning the temple, a subjective charge that is difficult to rebut.

THE REACTION OF THE EARLY CHRISTIANS TO PERSECUTION

The reaction of the earliest followers of Jesus to persecution, as reported by Luke, can be classified in terms of twelve types of reactions.

1. Courageous defense of actions. When Peter and John are interrogated by the Sanhedrin in Jerusalem, their very life being potentially at stake, they defend themselves with what we might call aggressive confidence (Acts 4:8-12).

2. Fearless defense of faith in Jesus. When Peter defends himself before the Sanhedrin after his first arrest, he argues that the healing miracle took place through the power of Jesus of Nazareth, whom he believes to be the Messiah. He asserts that the Jewish leaders are responsible for Jesus' crucifixion (ὃν ὑμεῖς ἐσταυρώσατε; 4:11). When Peter is ordered "never" (τὸ καθόλου) to speak (μὴ φθέγγεσθαι) to people about Jesus, nor to teach (μηδὲ διδάσκειν), under any circumstances, by the highest Jewish court (4:18), he immediately protests against this ban

---

74. Cf. 1 Macc 4:36-59; 2 Macc 10:1-8. The rededication ceremonies could have been based on King Solomon's dedication of the temple (1 Kgs 8:62-65) and on the dedication of the second temple in 515 BCE under Ezra (Ezra 6:16-18). Cf. Dommershausen, "חנך."

75. Witherington, *Acts*, 708.

76. Omerzu, *Prozeß*, 437; cf. Bruce, *Book of Acts*, 441.

(4:19). He challenges the Sanhedrin with a rhetorical question to accept the conclusion that God must be obeyed, that they have been commissioned by God to speak to other people about Jesus, that they cannot possibly accept the ban on speaking that has just been imposed, and that the prohibition of speaking about Jesus opposes the will of God.[77]

When Stephen is interrogated by the Sanhedrin, he does not back down from making comments about the temple that can be interpreted as disparaging, perhaps blasphemous (7:1–53). He shows in his account of Israel's history that the death of Jesus provoked by the Jewish leaders corresponds to the pattern of rejection of God and his messengers that characterizes Israel's history, going beyond this pattern in that the fathers killed God's messengers, whereas the Jewish leaders whom Stephen addresses have killed the One whom God's messengers had predicted (7:52).

3. Explanation of Jesus' significance. As Peter defends himself before the Sanhedrin, he explains Jesus' significance with four statements (Acts 4:10–12): (i) Jesus of Nazareth is the Messiah (χριστός), i.e., he is Israel's Savior, the eschatological agent of God who would come to restore the nation and to bring salvation.[78] (ii) Jesus has been raised from the dead by God (ὃν ὁ θεὸς ἤγειρεν ἐκ νεκρῶν), which means that Jesus has the power to heal the lame man and that he is vindicated and indeed confirmed as God's Messiah. (iii) Jesus has become the "cornerstone" (κεφαλὴ γωνίας) of Ps 118:22: God is erecting a new building, a new (spiritual) temple[79] in which God's presence among his people is based on Jesus' death and resurrection, and thus contingent upon the acceptance of God's revelation in Jesus, Israel's Messiah, and upon faith in the significance of Jesus for God's people.[80] (iv) Jesus

---

77. Cf. 1 Sam 15:22–23; Jer 7:22–23; 2 Macc 7:2; 4 Macc 5:16–21; Josephus, *Ant.* 17:159; 18:268. As regards the Greco-Roman tradition, note the famous response of Socrates to the injunction to stop teaching his philosophy, "Men of Athens, I respect and love you, but I shall obey the god rather than you" (πείσομαι δὲ μᾶλλον τῷ θεῷ ἢ ὑμῖν); this statement had become a well-known dictum, cf. Plutarch, *Sept. sap. conv.* 152C (7); Epictetus, 1.30.1; Livy, 39.37. Barrett, *Acts*, 237.

78. Tannehill, *Narrative Unity of Luke-Acts*, 61; Johnson, *Acts*, 77; Jervell, *Apostelgeschichte*, 178; Hurtado, *Lord Jesus Christ*, 178.

79. Cf. McKelvey, *New Temple*, 195–204.

80. Cf. Peterson, *Acts*, 192: Jesus is described as "the key figure in God's plan for the restoration of Israel and the whole of his creation."

is the only means of salvation.[81] The negative formulation "in no one else" (οὐκ ἔστιν ἐν ἄλλῳ), placed at the beginning of the sentence for emphasis, expresses the exclusive nature of salvation through Jesus, the Messiah who was crucified and whom God raised from the dead.

4. Prayer and singing. When Peter and John are arrested, imprisoned, interrogated, and then released by the Sanhedrin in Jerusalem, the church prays (4:24–31). When James is executed and several believers, including Peter, imprisoned by Herod Agrippa I, the church "prayed fervently" (προσευχὴ δὲ ἦν ἐκτενῶς; 12:5). When Paul and Silas are in prison in Philippi, they pray and sing (16:25).

5. Protest. When Paul and Barnabas leave Pisidian Antioch, they "shake the dust off their feet" (ἐκτιναξάμενοι τὸν κονιορτὸν τῶν ποδῶν; 13:51), an action that expresses protest "against them" (ἐπ' αὐτούς), i.e., against the Jews and the members of the elite who forced them to leave.

When the city officials order Paul and Silas to be released from prison and charge them to leave the city, Paul protests (16:35–39). The protest consists of five points: two accusations, the rejection of the release conditions, and two demands. The two accusations focus on the illegal beating and on the imprisonment. The two demands call on the magistrates that they come themselves to the prison, and that they personally escort him and Silas out of the prison. Paul wants public rehabilitation, presumably not for his own sake but for the sake of the new community of followers of Jesus in the city, whose safety and legal standing he cannot guarantee, but who at least would not be ridiculed on account of their founder who was beaten bloody in public with impunity.

6. Continued proclamation of the gospel. When Peter is ordered by the Sanhedrin not to speak or teach in the name of Jesus, he insists that he and his friends have no other option but to speak about "what we have seen and heard." The double negative, translated literally as "we cannot . . . not speak" (οὐ δυνάμεθα . . . μὴ λαλεῖν) has the force of a strong affirmative: the apostles *must* speak about Jesus (4:20). Luke reports that the Jerusalem believers continue their witness "with boldness" (μετὰ παρρησίας; 4:31).

---

81. The preposition ἐν expresses here the means or instrument.

When all the apostles are arrested, imprisoned, and miraculously rescued, they go to the temple mount and continue to teach the people (Acts 5:21, 25), despite the Sanhedrin's earlier prohibition of teaching the people after Peter's arrest (Acts 4:18). The believers who have to flee from Jerusalem in the severe persecution after Stephen's execution "traveled from place to place and proclaimed the word" (8:4).

Whether there is a causal connection between the persecution in Jerusalem and the expansion of the church through missionary activity seems doubtful. The Twelve preach the gospel of Jesus Christ in Jerusalem, defying an official ban on speaking about Jesus, facing repeated imprisonments and interrogations, and risking their lives, as the fate of Stephen demonstrates. Also, Peter does not need the pressure of a persecution to be active in the cities of the coastal plain (9:32–43; 10:1–48). The apostles and other leading believers such as Stephen, Philip, and Barnabas are not timid disciples who need to be forced by the Lord, through a persecution, to finally embark on missionary journeys in the direction of the ends of the earth.

When Paul and Barnabas are opposed and slandered in Pisidian Antioch, they speak out fearlessly (παρρησιασάμενοι; 13:46), i.e., they reaffirm their message with courage and boldness, and they formulate the conclusion they draw from the opposition of the Jewish community with openness and clarity. They affirm their commitment to the priority of proclaiming the message of Jesus, Israel's Savior, before Jewish audiences (13:46). And they explain that their proclamation of the message about Jesus Messiah before Jewish audiences and their willingness now to focus on Gentile audiences is a reflection of their obedience to God's commission, and that they will turn to the Gentiles among whom they will now proclaim the good news of God's forgiveness of sins and justification of sinners through faith in Jesus as Savior (13:47).

When Paul and Barnabas are forced to leave Iconium, they proclaim the gospel in Lystra and Derbe and other towns in the region (καὶ τὴν περίχωρον; 14:6–7). And when they are forced to leave Lystra, they initiate missionary work in Derbe (14:21).

Paul and Silas, while in prison, explain the gospel to the jailer in Philippi who asks them what he must do in order to be saved, which leads to conversions in the jailer's household (16:30–34). When Paul is forced out of Philippi, he preaches the gospel in Thessalonica

(17:1–4). When he has to leave Thessalonica, he preaches the gospel in Berea (17:10–12). When he has to leave Berea, he preaches in Athens (17:15–17). After the attempted trial proceedings against him fail, Paul continues to preach the gospel in Corinth (18:18).

7. Fear of persecutors. When the Lord instructs Ananias, a believer in Damascus, to visit Saul/Paul, he protests (9:13–14). Despite the fact that Ananias acknowledges the lordship of Jesus in his address (κύριε), he dares object, a fact that highlights the fear that the believers have of Saul.

8. Joy. When the apostles are released after the Sanhedrin has carried out corporal punishment, they "rejoice" (5:41). The present participle (χαίροντες) describes not just a brief emotional reaction but a continuous sense of gladness. The reason for their joy is expressed with an oxymoron: they rejoice because "they have been considered worthy" (κατηξιώθησαν) "to be insulted" (ἀτιμασθῆναι) on account of the name of Jesus.[82] The reason for their joy is the blessing that Jesus pronounced on his followers who are hated, excluded, reviled, and defamed on account of the Son of Man and who thus "rejoice" (χάρητε) and "leap for joy" (σκιρτήσατε) because their reward is great in heaven "for that is what their ancestors did to the prophets" (Luke 6:22–23). The Twelve may have skipped the leaping after their beating, but they rejoice in the fact that they are treated like the prophets, indeed like Jesus, Israel's Messiah and Savior, because they remain faithful to "the Name"—to Jesus and to his cause.[83] When Paul and Barnabas are slandered in Pisidian Antioch and forced to leave the city, "the disciples were filled with joy and with the Holy Spirit" (13:52).

9. Flight into permanent exile. The severe persecution that breaks out after Stephen's execution forces the believers to leave Jerusalem and go into exile (8:1). The term "scattered" (διεσπάρησαν) in 8:1 means that the congregation is broken up as the individual believers are driven out of Jerusalem in all directions in random fashion. The believers

---

82. Elliott, *Faithful Feelings*, 176, emphasizes the "strong cognitive reasons for why there is joy in suffering" (also 1 Pet 1:6–7; 4:13–14; Jas 1:2–4; Heb 10:32–34).

83. Kelhoffer, *Persecution*, 296, claims that the apostles' reaction in 5:41 "highlights the value of their suffering for asserting their legitimacy." The concept of legitimacy is introduced into the text: in Jerusalem the apostles focus on Jesus, not on themselves or their legitimacy, nor do they question the Sanhedrin's legitimacy, at least not explicitly.

from Jerusalem seek refuge in towns and villages in the countryside (χώρα) of Judea and of Samaria,[84] staying with other believers or with relatives.

10. Flight from a dangerous city. When Jews of Damascus plot to kill Saul/Paul, he leaves the city with the help of the local believers (9:23–25). When Jews of Jerusalem plot to kill Saul/Paul, he leaves the city and moves to Tarsus in Cilicia (9:29–30). When Paul learns that Jews and Gentile city officials in Iconium want to mistreat and stone him and Barnabas, he evidently decides that the collaboration of their Jewish and Gentile enemies with city officials has created a situation so dangerous that they must leave the city in a hurry (κατέφυγον; 14:6).[85] When the magistrates in Thessalonica force Jason and the other believers to guarantee the good behavior of Paul and his coworkers by posting bail, Paul and Silas leave the city (17:10). When Jews from Thessalonica incite the people of Berea, Paul again leaves the city in a hurry (17:14).

11. Change of travel plans. When Paul learns of a plot by Corinthian Jews to kill him, presumably on the ship on which he plans to travel to Jerusalem for the feast of Passover (cf. 20:6), he decides to return to Judea via a northerly route overland through Macedonia (20:3), sailing not from Corinth but from Philippi (20:6).

12. Legal defense. Paul's speech on the staircase from the outer court of the Jerusalem temple to the Antonia fortress (22:3–21) is not a formal defense in a trial context, but a defense speech nevertheless. In his speech before Felix, the Roman prefect, in Caesarea (24:10–21), Paul describes his visit to Jerusalem twelve days earlier whose purpose was to worship God (24:11; *narratio*). The *confirmatio* (*probatio*) advances three proofs for Paul's innocence: he was not involved in any disputes, he did not organize crowds, and the charges brought against him have not been proven (24:12–13). The refutation (*refutatio*), the longest section of the speech, specifically answers the charges that Tertullus, the high priest, and the members of the Sanhedrin have brought against

---

84. For towns in the countryside around Jerusalem, see 5:16. Judea, if understood as a political term at the time when Luke writes Acts, may include Galilee.

85. Cf. BDAG, s.v. καταφεύγω, "to get away from an area, with implication of having a destination in mind, *flee*."

him. Paul first counters the second charge, admitting that he belongs to the so-called Nazarenes, but disputes that he is a criminal ringleader by affirming his commitment to the Scriptures and his belief in the resurrection of the dead (24:14–15). He then refutes Tertullus's first charge (sedition) and the proffered "proof" that he desecrated the temple by asserting that he has a clear conscience before God and the people, by his explanation of his visit to Jerusalem (the purpose was to bring alms), and by his explanation of his visit to the temple in terms of its purpose (to present offerings) and in terms of his respect for the sanctity of the temple (he was in a state of purity when he was in the temple, 24:16–18). In his conclusion (*peroratio*), Paul points to the fact that the Jews from the province of Asia who initiated his arrest are absent, he underlines the absence of proofs in the case of his accusers, and he asserts that there is only one possible charge against him: his belief in the resurrection (24:19–21).

While Tertullus brings two political charges against Paul that rest on theological evidence, Paul reduces the charges to a theological one, viz. his affirmation of the resurrection, an issue that divided the members of the Sanhedrin and that the Roman prefect would not want to discuss further.

CONCLUSION

Luke's reports about various phases and places of persecution is neither stereotypical, nor artificially construed, nor focused on one theme.[86] In the nineteen occurrences of persecution we have discovered twenty-eight different initiators of aggressively hostile opposition to the followers of Jesus: twelve entities in Jerusalem and sixteen entities in cities outside of Jerusalem. Nineteen are Jewish and nine are non-Jewish.[87] As regards the geographical scope, there is essentially no city or region in which Christians were not persecuted: no matter where the gospel was proclaimed, there was hostile opposition. Luke mentions seven specific individuals who were persecuted—Peter, John, Stephen, James, Paul, Barnabas, Silas—some of them multiple times, in particular Paul. Reports about entire local congregations

---

86. Such as "standing" or legitimacy, as claimed by Kelhoffer, *Persecution*, 286, 360–61, and passim.

87. Since nearly a third of the instigators of persecution in Acts are non-Jewish, it is problematic to assert that the depicted persecutors in Acts "are usually Jewish" (pace Kelhoffer, *Persecution*, 286).

being persecuted—in Jerusalem, Damascus, and Ephesus—demonstrate that on some occasions few if any of the local Christians escaped the hostility of opponents. As regards the actions of the persecutors, we classified sixteen types of specific actions against followers of Jesus, ranging from opponents who approached Christians with hostile intent to executions.

The nineteen persecution events reveal twelve types of reasons why Jews and Gentiles aggressively oppose Jesus' followers. They are accused of unauthorized teaching, proclamation of a link between Jesus and the resurrection of the dead, teaching in the name of Jesus, blasphemy, attacking the patron deity of the city, violating religious traditions and civic decrees, sedition, acting contrary to the decrees of the emperor, and profaning the Jerusalem temple. Accusers are motivated by zeal for the Law, political expediency, and fear of financial loss. The reasons for persecuting Christians are political and economic, religious and secular, personal and general.

The nineteen persecution events reveal twelve types of reactions to persecution: courageous defense of actions, fearless defense of faith in Jesus, explanation of Jesus' significance, prayer and singing, protest, continued proclamation of the gospel, fear of persecutors, joy, flight into permanent exile, flight from a dangerous city, change of travel plans, and legal defense.

The first two persecution events reported in Acts 4–5 are paradigmatic in terms of their theological significance and their personal meaning. Christians who proclaim the gospel face the possibility of opposition. They share the fate of the One who was rejected, imprisoned, interrogated, and executed. What Jesus said as a general truth applies specifically here as well, "A disciple is not above the teacher, but everyone who is fully qualified will be like the teacher" (Luke 6:40). Being a Christian does not protect from suffering but, on the contrary, is often the cause for suffering, which may be the distress that comes from discrimination and ostracism, or consist in arrest and imprisonment, corporal punishments, or even execution. Often Christian leaders are persecuted repeatedly. There is no simple answer to the question whether Christians should stay in cities and regions in which their lives are in danger: sometimes they flee, sometimes they stay. Christians may experience divine protection in the midst of suffering. The apostles were rescued from prison through an angel of the Lord. Christians will always rely on God who has not promised, however, that he will always deliver his people from harm in persecutions. A few months after this episode Stephen was killed, and ten years or so later James, one of the Twelve, was executed in another wave of persecution, in the course of which Peter escaped through another miracle involving an angel. Opposition and persecution nearly always lead to new opportunities to explain the gospel of Jesus Christ—to the opponents who challenge the believers, to the judges who interrogate them, to the persecutors who torture them. The affliction and the pain are real, but the joy of having the privilege of suffering for Jesus Christ is real also, as the Holy Spirit thus confirms that we are children of God. Attacks should not discourage or dishearten Christians. The response to opposition and persecution is not stoic resignation, but courage that expects God to work in the difficult situation. Believers do not have to be afraid of hostile authorities, of arrest and imprisonment, or of prohibitions, because they are not alone whatever their specific situation may be. Jesus promised his presence and help exactly for such situations when he said, "When they bring you before the synagogues, the rulers, and the authorities, do not worry about how you are to defend yourselves or what you are to say" (Luke 12:11), and, "I will give you words and a wisdom that none of your opponents will be able to withstand or contradict" (Luke 21:15). Believers do not have to feel intimidated when they are accused and when they have to stand trial on account of their faith or on account of the preaching of the gospel because Jesus has promised the powerful help of the Holy Spirit, when he said, "for the Holy Spirit will teach you at that very hour what you ought to say" (Luke 12:12). Opposition and persecution cannot hinder the growth of the church. If there is a conflict between the word of God and a command of governmental authorities, God's people obey God's word rather than the word of human beings (Acts 4:19). While such opposition may result in prolonged imprisonment and even martyrdom, Christians have no choice but to obey the will of God.

BIBLIOGRAPHY

Arnaoutoglou, Ilias N. "Roman Law and *collegia* in Asia Minor." *Revue international des droits de l'antiquité* 49 (2002) 27–44.

Balsdon, J. P., and B. M. Levick. "Claudius." In *Oxford Classical Dictionary*, edited by Simon Hornblower and Andrew Spawforth, 337–38. 3rd ed. Oxford: Oxford University Press, 1996.

Barrett, C. K. *The Acts of the Apostles*. 2 vols. ICC. Edinburgh: T. & T. Clark, 1994–98.

Blass, Friedrich. *Acta Apostolorum, sive, Lucae ad Theophilum liber alter: Editio philologica* Göttingen: Vandenhoeck & Ruprecht, 1895.

Bock, Darrell L. *Acts*. Baker Exegetical Commentary on the New Testament. Grand Rapids: Baker, 2007.

———. *Blasphemy and Exaltation in Judaism: The Charge against Jesus in Mark 14:53–56*. 1998. Reprint, Grand Rapids: Baker, 2000.

Boffo, Laura. *Iscrizioni greche e latine per lo studio della Bibbia*. Biblioteca di storia e storiografia dei tempi biblici 9. Brescia: Paideia, 1994.
Bömer, Franz. "Der Eid beim Genius des Kaisers." *Athenaeum* 44 (1966) 77–133.
Bond, H. K. "Agrippa." In *NIDB*, 1:79.
———. *Caiaphas: Friend of Rome and Judge of Jesus*. Louisville, KY: Westminster John Knox, 2004.
———. "Herod, Family." In *NIDB*, 2:809–10.
Bornkamm, Günther. *Gesammelte Aufsätze*. 4 vols. Munich: Kaiser, 1966–71.
Botermann, Helga. *Das Judenedikt des Kaisers Claudius. Römischer Staat und Christiani im 1. Jahrhundert*. Hermes Einzelschriften 71. Stuttgart: Steiner, 1996.
Braund, D. C. "Agrippa." In *ABD*, 1:98–99.
Bruce, F. F. *The Acts of the Apostles: The Greek Text with Introduction and Commentary*. 3rd revised and enlarged ed. Grand Rapids: Eerdmans, 1990.
———. *The Book of the Acts*. Revised edition. NICNT. Grand Rapids: Eerdmans, 1988.
Cunningham, Scott. *'Through Many Tribulations'. The Theology of Persecution in Luke-Acts*. JNTSup 142. Sheffield: Sheffield Academic, 1997.
Dommershausen, W. "חָנֵף." *TDOT* 5:21.
Donfried, Karl Paul. "The Cults of Thessalonica." In *Paul, Thessalonica, and Early Christianity*, 21–48. Grand Rapids: Eerdmans, 2002.
Dunn, James D. G. *Beginning from Jerusalem*. Christianity in the Making 2. Grand Rapids: Eerdmans, 2009.
Eck, Werner. "Claudius [III 1]." In *BNP*, 3:405–9.
Elliott, Matthew A. *Faithful Feelings: Rethinking Emotion in the New Testament*. Grand Rapids: Kregel, 2006.
Feldman, Louis H., and Reinhold Meyer. *Jewish Life and Thought among Greeks and Romans: Primary Readings*. Minneapolis: Fortress, 1996.
Fitzmyer, Joseph A. *The Acts of the Apostles*. AB 31. New York: Doubleday, 1998.
Gamauf, Richard. "Exilium." In *BNP* 5:268–29.
Gizewski, Christian. "Coercitio." In *BNP* 3:508.
Goodman, Martin. "Sadducees and Essenes after A.D. 70." In *Crossing the Boundaries: Essays in Biblical Interpretation*, edited by S. E. Porter et al., 347–56. Biblical Interpretation 8. Leiden: Brill, 1994.
Gussmann, Oliver. *Das Priesterverständnis des Flavius Josephus*. TSAJ 124. Tübingen: Mohr Siebeck, 2008.
Hardin, Justin K. "Decrees and Drachmas at Thessalonica: Illegal Assembly in Jason's House (Acts 17.1–10a)." *NTS* 52 (2006) 29–49.
Hengel, Martin, and Anna Maria Schwemer. *Jesus und das Judentum*. Geschichte des frühen Christentums 1. Tübingen: Mohr Siebeck, 2007.
———. *Paul between Damascus and Antioch: The Unknown Years*. London: SCM; Louisville, KY: Westminster John Knox, 1997.
———. *Paulus zwischen Damaskus und Antiochien: Die unbekannten Jahre des Apostels*. WUNT 108. Tübingen: Mohr-Siebeck, 1998.
Herrmann, Peter. *Der römische Kaisereid: Untersuchungen zu seiner Herkunft und Entwicklung*. Hypomnemata 20. Göttingen: Vandenhoeck & Ruprecht, 1968.
Horsley, Greg H. R. "The Politarchs." In *The Book of Acts in Its First-Century Setting*. Vol. 2, *The Book of Acts in Its Graeco-Roman Setting*, edited by D. W. J. Gill and C. Gempf, 419–31. Grand Rapids: Eerdmans, 1994.

Hurtado, Larry W. *Lord Jesus Christ: Devotion to Jesus in Earliest Christianity*. Grand Rapids: Eerdmans, 2003.

Ilan, Tal. *Lexicon of Jewish Names in Late Antiquity*. Part I, *Palestine 330 BCE–200 CE*. TSAJ 91. Tübingen: Mohr Siebeck, 2002.

Jeremias, Joachim. *Jerusalem in the Time of Jesus: An Investigation into Economic and Social Conditions during the New Testament Period*. 1969. Reprint, London: SCM, 1979.

Jervell, Jacob. *Die Apostelgeschichte*. Kritisch-exegetischer Kommentar über das Neue Testament 3. Göttingen: Vandenhoeck & Ruprecht, 1998.

Johnson, Luke Timothy. *The Acts of the Apostles*. Sacra Pagina 5. Collegeville: Liturgical, 1992.

Judge, Edwin A. "The Decrees of Caesar at Thessalonica [1971]." In *The First Christians in the Roman World: Augustan and New Testament Essays*, edited by J. R. Harrison, 456–62. WUNT 229. Tübingen: Mohr Siebeck, 2008.

Kasher, Aryeh. *The Jews in Hellenistic and Roman Egypt*. TSAJ 7. Tübingen: Mohr-Siebeck, 1985.

Kee, Howard C. "Central Authority in Second-Temple Judaism and Subsequently: From Synedrion to Sanhedrin." *Annual of Rabbinic Judaism* 2 (1999) 51–63.

Kelhoffer, James A. *Persecution, Persuasion and Power: Readiness to Withstand Hardship as a Corroboration of Legitimacy in the New Testament*. WUNT 270. Tübingen: Mohr Siebeck, 2010.

Kierdorf, Wilhelm. "Mos maiorum." In *BNP*, 9:216–17.

Kokkinos, Nikos. *The Herodian Dynasty: Origins, Role in Society and Eclipse*. JSPSup 26. Sheffield: Sheffield Academic, 1997.

Lake, Kirsopp, and Henry J. Cadbury, eds. *The Beginnings of Christianity, Part. I: The Acts of the Apostles*. Vol. 5, *Additional Notes to the Commentary*. London: Macmillan, 1933.

Lavatori, Renzo, and Luciano Sole. *Persecuzione e Chiesa negli Atti degli Apostoli*. Lettura pastorale della Bibbia. Bibbia e spiritualità 19. Bologna: Dehoniane, 2003.

Levick, Barbara. *Claudius*. New Haven: Yale University Press, 1990.

Lohse, Eduard. "συνέδριον." In *TDNT*, 7:860–71.

Lombardi, Guido. "Motivi giuridici dell' appello di Paolo a Cesare." In *S. Paolo da Cesarea a Roma. Esegesi, Storia, Topografia, Archeologia*, edited by B. Mariani, 1–20. Turin: Marietti, 1963.

Lösch, Stephan. *Epistula Claudiana: Der neuentdeckte Brief des Kaisers Claudius vom Jahre 41 n. Chr. und das Urchristentum. Eine exegetisch-historische Untersuchung*. Rottenburg: Bader, 1930.

Malherbe, Abraham J. *The Letters to the Thessalonians*. AB 32B. New York: Doubleday, 2000.

Marshall, I. Howard. *The Acts of the Apostles. An Introduction and Commentary*. TNTC. Leicester: Inter-Varsity, 1980.

Mason, Steve. "Chief Priests, Sadducees, Pharisees and Sanhedrin in Acts." In *The Book of Acts in Its First-Century Setting*. Vol. 4, *The Book of Acts in its Palestinian Setting*, edited by R. Bauckham, 115–77. Grand Rapids: Eerdmans, 1995.

McKelvey, R. Jack. *The New Temple: The Church in the New Testament*. Oxford: Oxford University Press, 1969.

Metzner, Rainer. *Die Prominenten im Neuen Testament. Ein prosopographischer Kommentar*. Novum Testamentum et Orbis Antiquus 66. Göttingen: Vandenhoeck & Ruprecht, 2008.

Mitford, Terence B. "A Cypriot Oath of Allegiance to Tiberius." *Journal of Roman Studies* 50 (1970) 75–79.

Moule, C. F. D. *The Origin of Christology*. Cambridge: Cambridge University Press, 1977.

Neyrey, Jerome H. "The Forensic Defense Speech and Paul's Trial Speeches in Acts 22–26." In *Luke-Acts: New Perspectives from the Society of Biblical Literature Seminar*, edited by C. H. Talbert, 210–24. New York: Crossroad, 1984.

Nodet, Étienne. "Pharisees, Sadducees, Essenes, Herodians." In *Handbook for the Study of the Historical Jesus*. Vol. 2, *The Study of Jesus*, edited by T. Holmén and S. E. Porter, 1495–1543. Leiden: Brill, 2011.

Omerzu, Heike. *Der Prozeß des Paulus: Eine exegetische und rechtshistorische Untersuchung der Apostelgeschichte*. BZNW 115. Berlin: De Gruyter, 2002.

Oster, R. "Holy Days in Honour of Artemis." In *New Documents Illustrating Early Christianity*. Vol. 4, *A Review of the Greek Inscriptions and Papyri Published in 1979*, edited by Greg H. R. Horsley and Stephen R. Llewelyn, 74–82. Macquarie University: North Ryde, New South Wales, Australia, 1987.

Padilla, Osvaldo. *The Speeches of Outsiders in Acts: Poetics, Theology and Historiography*. SNTSMS 144. Cambridge: Cambridge University Press, 2008.

Parsons, Mikeal C. *Acts*. Paideia. Grand Rapids: Baker, 2008.

Pervo, Richard I. *Acts*. Hermeneia. Philadelphia: Fortress, 2008.

Pesch, Rudolf. *Die Apostelgeschichte*. 2 vols. Evangelisch-katholischer Kommentar zum Neuen Testament 5. Zürich: Benziger; Neukirchen-Vluyn: Neukirchener Verlag, 1986.

Peterson, David G. *The Acts of the Apostles*. Pillar New Testament Commentaries. Grand Rapids: Eerdmans, 2009.

Pilhofer, Peter. *Philippi*. Vol. 1, *Die erste christliche Gemeinde Europas*. 2nd ed. WUNT 87. Tübingen: Mohr-Siebeck, 2009.

Pucci Ben Zeev, Miriam. *Jewish Rights in the Roman World: The Greek and Roman Documents Quoted by Josephus Flavius*. TSAJ 74. Tübingen: Mohr Siebeck, 1998.

Radl, W. "χείρ." In *EDNT*, 3:463.

Ramsay, William M. *St. Paul the Traveller and the Roman Citizen*. Rev. ed. Edited by M. Wilson. Grand Rapids: Baker, 2001.

Rapske, Brian M. *The Book of Acts in Its First-Century Setting*. Vol. 3, *The Book of Acts and Paul in Roman Custody*. Exeter: Paternoster, 1994.

Riesner, Rainer. *Paul's Early Period: Chronology, Mission Strategy, Theology*. Grand Rapids: Eerdmans, 1998.

Rohde, Pace J. "πρεσβύτερος." In *EDNT* 3:148.

Sanders, E. P. *Judaism: Practice and Belief 63 BCE–66 CE*. London: SCM, 1992.

Schnabel, E. J. "Jewish Opposition to Christians in Asia Minor in the First Century." *Bulletin for Biblical Research* 18 (2008) 233–70.

———. "Sanhedrin." In *NIDB*, 5:102–6.

Schürer, Emil. *The History of the Jewish People in the Age of Christ (175 B.C.–A.D. 135)*. 2 vols. Revised by G. Vermes et al. Edinburgh: T. & T. Clark, 1973–87.

Schwartz, Daniel R. *Agrippa I: The Last King of Judaea*. TSAJ 23. Tübingen: Mohr Siebeck, 1990.

Segal, Alan F. *Two Powers in Heaven: Early Rabbinic Reports about Christianity and Gnosticism*. Studies in Judaism in Late Antiquity 25. Leiden: Brill, 1977.
Sherwin-White, Adrian Nicolas. *Roman Society and Roman Law in the New Testament*. The Sarum Lectures 1960–61. Reprint, Grand Rapids: Baker, 1992.
Soards, Marion L. *The Speeches in Acts: Their Content, Context, and Concerns*. Louisville, KY: Westminster John Knox, 1994.
Spicq, Ceslaus. "ἀσφαλεία κτλ." *Theological Lexicon of the New Testament*. 3 vols. Translated and edited by J. D. Ernest, 1:218. Hendrickson: Peabody, MA: 1997.
Stählin, Gustav. *Die Apostelgeschichte*. Neue Testament Deutsch 5. Göttingen: Vandenhoeck & Ruprecht, 1962.
Stegemann, Wolfgang. *Zwischen Synagoge und Obrigkeit: Zur historischen Situation der lukanischen Christen*. FRLANT 152. Göttingen: Vandenhoeck & Ruprecht, 1991.
Stemberger, Günter. "The Sadducees: Their History and Doctrines." In *Cambridge History of Judaism*. Vol. 3, *The Early Roman Period*, edited by W. D. Davies, W. Horbury, and J. Sturdy, 428–43. Cambridge: Cambridge University Press, 1999.
Tajra, Harry W. *The Trial of St. Paul: A Juridical Exegesis of the Second Half of the Acts of the Apostles*. WUNT 2.35. Tübingen: Mohr Siebeck, 1989.
Tannehill, Robert C. *The Narrative Unity of Luke-Acts: A Literary Interpretation*. Vol. 2, *The Acts of the Apostles*. 1990. Reprint, Philadelphia: Fortress, 1994.
Thomas, Christine M. "At Home in the City of Artemis: Religion in Ephesos in the Literary Imagination of the Roman Period." In *Ephesos, Metropolis of Asia: An Interdisciplinary Approach to Its Archaeology, Religion, and Culture*, edited by H. Koester, 81–117. Harvard Theological Studies 41. Valley Forge, PA: Trinity, 1995.
Van Unnik, Willem C. "Die Anklage gegen die Apostel in Philippi. (Apostelgeschichte 16,20f)." In *Sparsa Collecta*, 374–85. NovTSup 29. Leiden: Brill, 1973.
VanderKam, James C. *From Joshua to Caiaphas: High Priests after the Exile*. Minneapolis: Fortress, 2004.
Végh, Zoltán. "Relegatio." In *BNP*, 12:454.
Von Ungern-Sternberg, Jürgen. "Seditio." In *BNP*, 13:195–96.
Winter, Bruce W. "Gallio's Ruling on the Legal Status of Early Christianity (Acts 18:14–15)." *TynBul* 50 (1999) 213–24.
———. "The Importance of the *captatio benevolentiae* in the Speeches of Tertullus and Paul in Acts 24:1–21." *Journal of Theological Studies* 42 (1991) 505–31.
———. "Official Proceedings and the Forensic Speeches in Acts 24–26." In *The Book of Acts in Its First-Century Setting*. Vol. 1, *The Book of Acts in Its Ancient Literary Setting*, edited by B. W. Winter and A. D. Clarke, 305–36. Exeter: Paternoster, 1993.
Witherington, Ben. *The Acts of the Apostles: A Socio-Rhetorical Commentary*. Grand Rapids: Eerdmans, 1998.
Zmijewski, Josef. *Die Apostelgeschichte*. Regensburger Neues Testament. Regensburg: Pustet, 1994.

9

Paul and the Alienation of the Jews
A Response to Stanley E. Porter and Eckhard J. Schnabel

CHRISTOPHER D. LAND

INTRODUCTION

THE TWO PAPERS TO which I am responding here are concerned with the Pauline letters and the Acts of the Apostles, respectively. In the first of these papers, Stanley Porter argues that Paul of Tarsus experienced a profound transformation upon meeting the resurrected Christ, in which (among other things) an old and dormant sense of alienation was both re-awakened and re-configured. More specifically, Porter argues that Paul's prioritizing of the divine-human relationship and his preoccupation with eschatology demand that any discussion of "exile" or "diaspora" or "alienation" in Paul's writings must be concerned first and foremost with humanity's alienation from God and with the church's heavenly citizenship and eschatological homecoming, because Paul's understanding of what it means for the people of God to be at home was entirely re-configured around these central ideas.

In a second paper, Eckhard Schnabel surveys and systematizes the various accounts of persecution that appear in the Acts of the Apostles. Using a helpful rubric, Schnabel describes the geographical scope of persecution in Acts, the material actions that constitute persecution in Acts, the initiators of persecution in Acts and their reasons for persecuting, and finally the targets of persecution in Acts and their responses to persecution.

Most importantly, Schnabel argues that variation along these parameters hinders all attempts to describe the persecution recounted in Acts as a stereotypical or over-simplistic authorial construct.

In general, neither paper is vulnerable to severe criticism, since there is little that can be faulted as regards their central claims. Few, I think, would wish to dispute that Paul's theology is preoccupied with a multifaceted divine-human relationship, or that his idea of "home sweet home" is quite eschatological, or that his ecclesiology entails the creation of an inclusive safe haven for previously marginalized people dispersed within a world opposed to God. And even though there are scholars who detect aggressive anti-imperialist tendencies in Paul's writings, it nevertheless seems to me that Paul was more or less pragmatic in his interactions with the cultural and political institutions of the soon-to-be-defeated kingdoms of this world. Similarly, although it might be debated whether or not Acts is historically trustworthy as regards its accounts of persecution, or whether Luke's persecution stories reveal anything about his authorial agenda, it is hardly possible to dispute the descriptive fact that Acts paints a colorful and diverse portrait of persecution within early Christianity rather than one that is monochrome or over-simplistic.

So then, accepting the broad claims of these two papers as both sensible and helpful, I will proceed with some remarks about a couple of details in Porter's paper and with some reflections concerning the possible implications of Schnabel's paper.

PORTER ON PAUL

One of the more interesting proposals in Porter's paper is the suggestion that the pre-Christian Paul was burdened by a sense of religious dislocation in Tarsus, longing to be geographically closer to the center of Judaism. As Porter writes, "he may well have desired to fulfill what may have been a sense of spiritual calling in the 'holy' land itself" or he "may well have wished to remedy the effects of life in the Diaspora" (p. 127). As interesting as this proposal is, however, it is as difficult to prove as it is to refute. It coheres with what we know about Paul, but as Porter himself observes, "We do not know the motivation for Paul to leave Tarsus and move to Jerusalem" (p. 127). Paul *may* have been unhappy being a dispersed Jew and he *may* have regarded his relocation to Jerusalem as a kind of religious homecoming, but this is only one of many coherent possibilities.

LAND—*Paul and the Alienation of the Jews*

For example, we might alternatively imagine that Paul was a troublemaker in his youth as much as he was in his later life, and that his parents sent him to live with family in Jerusalem in the hopes that his chances for success would be better there.[1] Reconstructing the pre-Christian Paul in this way—as a kind of Fresh Prince of Jerusalem—still coheres with the basic fact that Paul was a Diaspora Jew who somehow developed into a Pharisaic Palestinian Jew. It provides a remarkably different portrait of Paul's psychology at the time of his move to Jerusalem, however, and thus a different psychological backdrop against which to assess his later transformation into a cross-cultural missionary somewhat at odds with the Palestinian Judaism that had previously constituted his second home. If Paul, as a rebellious and troubled Diaspora Jew, was forced to make a home for himself in Jerusalem, and if he did so by developing a sense of social belonging as a zealously law-abiding Pharisee, then his sense of being a Pharisaic Palestinian Jew becomes somewhat more precarious than is the case with Porter's reconstructed Paul, who actively seeks out a Palestinian homecoming as someone discontented with being a Diaspora Jew.

In any case, my point is simply that the available evidence does not indicate that Paul went to Jerusalem eagerly or that he conceived of his relocation in theological terms at all, making it important to keep in mind alternative possibilities when engaging in speculation concerning his pre-Christian thoughts and feelings.

Similar cautions are also in order with regard to an additional aspect of Porter's reconstruction: namely, the idea that Paul felt entirely at home in Palestinian Judaism during the duration of his residency in Jerusalem, such that his encounter with Jesus on the Damascus Road shattered a self-satisfied sense of belonging and taught him that "You can't go home again." Porter believes that, "from every indication that we have, Paul was, perhaps at last, perfectly content," citing as evidence the fact that Paul regarded himself as faultless and thus "had confidence in what he was doing" (p. 128). Porter's reconstruction is, it seems to me, a coherent one. But here again, this does not mean that it is an accurate one, since a dearth of evidence leaves the door open to a wide range of possible scenarios.

Maybe Paul really was content. Maybe he regarded himself as a former alien of the Dispersion now finally at home in the Holy Land. Confidence, however, does not equal contentment, and the idea cannot be rejected out of hand that Paul's pre-Christian behavior was motivated as much by

---

1. Something along these lines is proposed by Zahn, *Apostelgeschichte*, 751.

a desire to *attain* as by a desire to preserve and protect. Perhaps, even as a blameless Pharisee, Paul regarded the attainment of the Promised Land both for himself and for his fellow Jews as something as of yet in the future. As Porter himself observes (p. 129), Paul's pre-Christian behavior reveals a very driven personality, yet this bent towards effort and achievement can be plausibly related either to contentment or to discontentment. Perhaps the actions of Saul the Pharisee reveal a contented man finally at home in the Holy Land—but perhaps they reveal a discontented man who felt alienated or even exiled.

Thus even though Porter is in one sense correct to say that Paul "had confidence in what he was doing as a fulfillment of what it meant to be one who was now no longer a part of the Diaspora" (p. 128), it remains uncertain how the pre-Christian Paul may have applied the scriptural notions of exile and dispersion to contemporary Judaism. In particular, it remains uncertain what Paul, as both a Diaspora Jew and a Palestinian Pharisee, believed about the corporate and eschatological aspects of the alienation(s) experienced by the Jewish people. For this reason, I would be interested to hear Porter discuss whether or not the pre-Christian Paul had a well-defined and scripturally-shaped notion of corporate exile or of eschatological homecoming. And I would like to hear Porter discuss how these corporate and eschatological facets of dispersion and homecoming may have affected Paul's interactions with his fellow Jews, both before and after his conversion.

SCHNABEL ON ACTS

In his paper on persecution in the Acts of the Apostles, Schnabel has gathered together in one place much of the evidence we possess regarding persecution in Acts, and he has provided some useful analytical categories that illuminate the diversity of the persecution recounted in Acts. Since dissecting the details of a project such as this would do little to advance the discussion that is the focus of this colloquium, I will concentrate instead how Schnabel's observations shed light on the function of Acts as an early Christian text, paying particular attention to the ways in which Luke's persecution stories dovetail with Paul's thinking about the world's alienation from God and the church's alienation from the world.

As regards this matter, Schnabel's remarks concerning the work of James Kelhoffer are noteworthy. In the first place, Schnabel contrasts his own conviction that Acts provides a reliable account of history with

Kelhoffer's more agnostic position that Acts contains only allegations of persecution (pp. 141–42). He argues that in Kelhoffer's work, the concept of legitimacy is introduced into the text even when it is not explicit (p. 172).[2] He challenges Kelhoffer's claim that the persecutors in Acts are usually Jewish (p. 175). And, although he does not come out and say so explicitly, it seems fairly obvious that Schnabel disagrees with Kelhoffer's thesis that the narrative of Acts places a great deal of emphasis upon the illegitimacy of its predominantly Jewish persecutors.

Like Schnabel, I am persuaded that Luke provides us with a more or less reliable account of some events that were important to the development of Christianity.[3] Hence I do not regard it as special pleading to insist that certain things about the narrative of Acts will need to be explained with reference to history as much as with reference to literary or rhetorical categories such as authorial intent and social function. For example, the fact that the initial persecutors in Acts are mostly Jewish may reveal very little about Luke's authorial agenda or the social function of Acts, if few of the earliest stories available to Luke involved non-Jewish persecutors. Moreover, if Luke is accurate in saying that Paul regarded Jewish communities in the Diaspora as a strategic starting point for his evangelistic efforts, it is plausible to suppose that Paul's persecutors—even outside of Palestine—were usually Jewish.[4] Like Schnabel, therefore, I am uneasy with the emphasis Kelhoffer places on the fact that the persecutors in Acts are so often Jewish.

Now, obviously, in order to explain the telling of a purportedly historical event as a story, we must consider the social function of the telling and the way that the story has been shaped so as to perform this function. Yet here I find myself in essential agreement with Kelhoffer. I agree that at least one of the functions of Luke's persecution stories is to challenge the legitimacy and power of those (including non-Christian Jews) who persecute

---

2. Here I suspect that Schnabel has simply misunderstood Kelhoffer, since Kelhoffer is not arguing that Acts 5:41 is explicitly *about* legitimacy or that the apostles are *themselves* concerned with legitimacy but that Acts 5:41 *bestows* legitimacy by giving honor to those who are dishonored for the sake of the name of Jesus. The passage merely displays "[Luke's] concern to identify the faithful by their readiness to suffer" (Kelhoffer, *Persecution*, 296).

3. I take it for granted that a well-crafted story about a historical event can be more or less reliable even when the author who is doing the crafting is biased, selective, interpretive, creative, and in some places dependent on second- or perhaps even third-hand information.

4. For a recent discussion of this longstanding issue, see Miller, "Jewish Context."

Christians, while simultaneously affirming those who suffer as Christians. I simply disagree with Kelhoffer's claim that Luke has focused his narrative on a specific sub-set of persecutors in order to devalue a specific group. To the contrary, Luke has included a wide range of stories and produced an overall portrait that is (to quote Schnabel. p. 174) "neither stereotypical, nor artificially construed, nor focused on one theme."

Where does this leave us as regards the accounts of persecution in Acts? Schnabel's work shows that most of Luke's persecution stories involve either the pillars in Jerusalem or the leaders of the Pauline mission, although Luke is also careful to point out that the Christian community as a whole tends to suffer persecution. Also, Schnabel's work shows that Christian leaders are persecuted for a wide range of reasons, in a wide range of places, by both Jewish and non-Jewish people, and by both Jewish and non-Jewish political leaders. Applying these observations to Kelhoffer's hypothesis about the legitimizing function of persecution stories in Acts, I suggest that Kelhoffer's conclusions are not so much wrong as they are incomplete. And they are incomplete because Kelhoffer has too quickly presumed that the social function of Acts must be assessed against the backdrop of a tension at some remove (both temporally and sociologically) from the controversies that plagued the Apostle Paul.[5]

Paul was moved by a force that drove him around the Mediterranean and caused him to plant mixed Jew-Gentile churches—despite all the difficulties entailed by cross-cultural mission work and multi-cultural communities. Yet other Christian leaders were also planting communities throughout the Diaspora, and these communities wanted to feel at home within Judaism. Together with a number of scholars, I believe that many of the controversies visible in Paul's letters swirl around the inevitable tensions that emerged between these two missions.[6] On the one hand, Paul vehemently

---

5. Kelhoffer views Luke-Acts as having an agenda that is both non-Pauline and anti-Jewish (see Kelhoffer, *Persecution*, 287). He also affirms the idea that Acts depicts so many (non-Christian) Jewish characters negatively because of something going on in Luke's own day (see Kelhoffer, *Persecution*, 344 n. 214, citing Sanders, *Jews in Luke-Acts*, 303). My own contrasting view is that Acts is no more anti-Jewish than Paul himself (except that it takes the view of an outsider rather than the view of an insider) and that Acts communicates a very Pauline response to the controversies that plagued Paul during his lifetime (except that its author is a supporter of Paul rather than Paul himself). Whether the phrase *anti-Jewish* applies to Paul and Luke is a complex matter that cannot be discussed here.

6. The literature on this topic is immense, but key sources include Baur, "Die Christuspartei"; Baur, *Paulus*, and more recently, Goulder, *Paul versus Peter*; Goulder,

opposes the planting of new Jewish-sensitive churches in regions he has already evangelized, arguing that his multicultural churches already provide a place for Christian Jews to be at home. On the other hand, Paul's critics seem to have cited his missionary activities as the fundamental reason why alternative church communities needed to be planted, apparently because Paul's provocative and controversial missionary efforts made it difficult for Christian Jews to remain socially integrated within the Jewish Diaspora.[7]

Interestingly, Kelhoffer himself has expressed some penetrating insights into the Pauline letters that most directly address this situation. Discussing Galatians and 2 Corinthians in particular, Kelhoffer observes that Paul "confirms his apostolic status as one who has suffered but also attacks his opponents for avoiding persecution."[8] Then, Kelhoffer proposes that "interpreters today should be reticent to accept uncritically Paul's confidently presented valuations as if they were beyond rejoinder among the

---

Competing Mission. See also Cindy Westfall's paper in the present volume. In assessing the relevance of the tensions that existed between Paul and other Christian leaders, it is important to avoid over-simplistic dichotomies (e.g., Peter vs. Paul; Jewish vs. Gentile Christianity) and to keep in view the unclear, unstable, and ultimately unsustainable nature of the two-mission arrangement. Indeed, the two-mission arrangement should probably be regarded as a temporary agreement that proved unworkable in the long run, at least in part because the key parties involved had different views on the practical outworking of their agreement (i.e., "The story cannot be clear to us because the evidence is not sufficient; for other reasons it was probably less than clear to those who participated in it" [Barrett, "Councils and Controversies," 53]). Moreover, the tensions and disagreements that existed between Paul and other early Christian leaders must not blind us to the unity that bound him together with them—even amidst the unfolding of some bitter controversies (i.e., "In the place where it matters, Peter stands among the pillars rather than the false brothers" [ibid.]).

7. Amid these disagreements, Paul does not oppose the premise that Christians should attempt to be at home in Judaism. Instead, he at times urges sensitivity, asking his readers to avoid causing unnecessary trouble (e.g., Rom 14:1—15:13; see also 1 Cor 9:19–23). This conciliatory approach, I suggest, coheres well with Luke's depiction of Paul as someone who (at least occasionally) maintained such Jewish practices as circumcision, ritual hair-cutting, and temple participation, and who was willing to put his own life at risk in order to publicly display his continuing commitment to his cultural heritage and to the church in Jerusalem. At the same time, however, some of the beliefs to which Paul was committed would have been quite controversial within traditional Judaism, and Paul admits to deliberately provoking his fellow Jews with his preaching (Rom 11:13–14). What is more, it would seem that the Pauline mission developed a negative reputation because of an alleged inability to enforce appropriate moral and purity standards in its mixed Jew-Gentile communities (see Land, "Integrity of 2 Corinthians," 388–89).

8. Kelhoffer, "Suffering as Defense," 127.

Rejection

addressees and especially among Paul's opponents."[9] Paul no doubt regarded his own interpretation of his sufferings as valid, but as Kelhoffer points out, "we must allow for the likelihood that Paul's opponents would have responded to his arguments with their own (de)valuations of the worth of Paul's suffering."[10] In other words, although Paul interpreted his troubles as the result of his faithful proclamation of the gospel, other early Christians interpreted his troubles quite differently. Some of these critics may even have challenged Paul's right to group his own sufferings together with those of the Jerusalem pillars so as to depict himself as an apostolic sufferer very much like the apostles in Jerusalem.[11]

In view of these remarks, I find it quite puzzling that Kelhoffer does not seem to have considered the possibility that a supporter of Paul, such as Luke, might attempt to refute devaluations of Paul's sufferings by depicting in narrative form the continuity that exists between Paul and the pillars of the church in Jerusalem. After all, the line that emerges from the persecution stories in Acts is closely aligned with what we see in Paul's letters.[12] Just as the Jerusalem apostles suffer at the hands of their fellow Jews and at the hands of local political leaders in Judea, so also Paul suffers at the hands of his fellow Jews and at the hands of local political leaders around the Mediterranean. And Paul never suffers because his ministry is defective or anti-Jewish; rather, Paul is unpopular because he fearlessly proclaims that human beings—both Jews and non-Jews—are alienated from God.[13]

---

9. Ibid., 132.

10. Ibid., 133.

11. Kelhoffer writes: "We must . . . acknowledge the likelihood that the super-apostles and their supporters in Corinth (cf. 1 Cor 1:11–13) would have rejected Paul's valuation of his suffering as a confirmation of the very authority they had denied him. The possibility must also be recognized that super-apostles may have had their own assessment of the value of Paul's . . . suffering" (Kelhoffer, *Persecution*, 61).

12. Of particular interest here is Paul's belief that those with faith in Christ—both Jews and non-Jews—belong to a new inclusive community that must patiently endure the hostility of those—both Jews and non-Jews—who oppose Christ and hence remain alienated from God. Inasmuch as this belief is visualized and confirmed by Luke's diverse depictions of persecution—involving both Jewish and non-Jewish persecutors—it is fair to say that Luke's narrative takes a very Pauline stance towards the problem of persecution.

13. By placing Paul's persecutions within the same frame as the persecutions inflicted upon the pillars in Jerusalem, Luke is doing something very Pauline. He is depicting Paul as a bona fide apostle whose tireless efforts on behalf of the *one true gospel*, carried out despite many obstacles and tremendous opposition, have earned him a place of honor and authority beside Jesus' earthly disciples and even beside Jesus' earthly

So then, in view of Schnabel's point concerning the non-stereotypical nature of the persecution recounted in Acts, it is implausible to suppose that Acts is *emphasizing* the illegitimacy of non-Christian Judaism. What the persecution stories in Acts show is that the Pauline mission is so frequently embroiled in trouble not because it is ineffective or anti-Jewish, but because both non-Christian Jews and non-Christian Gentiles are alienated from God and hence liable to oppose the preaching of the gospel. And this serves both to vindicate Paul and to disseminate Paul's teaching that the church must not become too much at home in the world in which it finds itself—even if that world happens to be culturally Jewish—because alienation from the world is inherent in the gospel itself.

CONCLUSION

In conclusion, I wish to thank both scholars for the privilege of engaging with their work. Porter has done us a service by reminding us where the true focus of Paul's thinking lies as regards exile, dispersion, and alienation—namely, with the conviction that all of humanity is alienated from God in such a way that no earthly people or kingdom will ever fully embody the promise of the Promised Land until that day when Christ returns and sets up his kingdom. And for his part, Schnabel has reminded us that Christian characters in Acts experience widespread persecution in a wide range of ways for a wide range of reasons—so that Acts ends up illustrating Paul's thinking.

BIBLIOGRAPHY

Barrett, C. K. "Paul: Councils and Controversies." In *Conflicts and Challenges in Early Christianity*, edited by D. A. Hagner, 42–74. Harrisburg, PA: Trinity, 1999.

Baur, F. C. "Die Christuspartei in der korinthischen Gemeinde, der Gegensatz des petrinischen und paulinischen Christenthums in der ältesten Kirche, der Apostel Petrus in Rom." *Tübinger Zeitschrift für Theologie* 4 (1831) 61–206.

———. *Paulus, der Apostel Jesu Christi: Sein Leben und Wirken, seine Briefe und seine Lehre*. Stuttgart: Becher & Müller, 1845.

Goulder, M. D. *St. Paul versus St. Peter: A Tale of Two Missions*. Louisville, KY: Westminster John Knox, 1994.

———. *Paul and the Competing Mission in Corinth*. Library of Pauline Studies. Peabody, MA: Hendrickson, 2002.

---

brother—despite various controversies that might seem to call into question this unity of status and purpose (1 Cor 15:1–11; 2 Cor 11:1–6; 12:11–13; Gal 2:1–10, 14; cf. Eph 2:19—3:13; Phil 1:12–18; Col 1:21—2:5).

Kelhoffer, J. A. *Persecution, Persuasion and Power: Readiness to Withstand Hardship as a Corroboration of Legitimacy in the New Testament*. WUNT 270. Tübingen: Mohr Siebeck, 2010.

———. "Suffering as Defense of Paul's Apostolic Authority in Galatians and 2 Corinthians 11." *Svensk Exegetisk Årsbok* 74 (2009) 127–43.

Land, C. D. "The Integrity of 2 Corinthians from a Linguistic Perspective: Is There a Text in These Meanings?" Unpublished PhD diss., McMaster Divinity College, 2013.

Miller, J. C. "The Jewish Context of Paul's Gentile Mission." *TynBul* 58 (2007) 101–15.

Sanders, J. T. *The Jews in Luke-Acts*. Philadelphia: Fortress, 1987.

Zahn, T. *Die Apostelgeschichte des Lucas: Erste Hälfte Kap. 1–12*. Kommentar zum Neuen Testament 5. Leipzig: Deichertsche, 1919.

10

"Diaspora Missions"
Contemporary Missiological Significance of People on the Move

NARRY F. SANTOS

THE UNPRECEDENTED MOVEMENTS OF people in huge numbers and high frequency have marked a global trend in the twenty-first century. Such a global and unprecedented trend of mobility and migration has led Castles and Miller to call this present period the Age of Migration.[1] According to the United Nations Development Program, there are now 214 million international migrants, who make up 3 percent of the world's population.[2] If this number of international migrants represented a single country's population, it would be the fifth largest nation in the world. In other words, one out of every 33 persons in the world today is a migrant.

Undoubtedly, all nations have been affected by international mass migration. Experts across disciplines are paying close attention to migration patterns and their implications for politics, economics, law, anthropology, sociology, geography, religion, and other fields.[3] In particular, missiologists and church planters are monitoring and analyzing the recent mass movements of people. Winter and Koch note, "As history unfolds and global migration increases, more and more people groups are being dispersed

---

1. Castles and Miller, *Age of Migration*. The term "age of migration" affirms that we are living in an unprecedented age of mobility and migration.
2. United Nations High Commission for Refugees, "Refugees."
3. Massey, "Theories of International Migration," 432.

throughout the entire globe . . . Not many agencies take note of the strategic value of reaching the more accessible fragments of these "global peoples."[4]

This essay seeks to spell out the strategic value of understanding this global phenomenon of people on the move and to explore the contemporary significance of diaspora in the light of global Christian missions. It seeks to investigate what the implications of this global phenomenon are missiologically, and how such unprecedented movements of people can be used towards "diaspora missions." As a concrete missiological application of this phenomenon, this essay concludes with an example of "diaspora missions" church-planting to and through the Filipino diaspora in Canada.

DEFINITION OF TERMS

Before further describing the realities and value of the "global peoples" and before understanding their significant role missiologically, we need to define the important terms used in this essay regarding migration and diaspora.

1. *Migration*: Migration refers to the "movement of a people from one location of residence to another location of residence."[5]

2. *Migrants*: Migrants generally refer to a broad range of people on the move. They can be categorized as long-term or short-term workers, students, refugees, stateless peoples, asylum seekers, and people in the process of immigrating, as well as those who have immigrated to another country.[6]

3. *Immigration:* Immigration is defined as the movement of people into a different country to settle.

4. *Refugee*: The refugee is a person who has been forced to leave his or her home and to seek refuge elsewhere. Specifically, the United Nations High Commissioner for Refugees considers a refugee to be a person who "owing to a well-founded fear of being persecuted for reasons of race, religion, nationality, membership of a particular social group or political opinion, is outside the country of his nationality, and is unable to, or owing to such fear, is unwilling to avail himself

---

4. Winter and Koch, "Finishing the Task," 537.
5. Payne, *Strangers Next Door*, 27.
6. Ibid., 28.

of the protection of that country."⁷ The definition of refugee is later expanded to include a person who has fled war or other violence in the home country.⁸

5. *Diaspora*: The term "diaspora," which is a Greek verbal substantive commonly translated as "scattering," originally refers to the Jewish dispersion (i.e., the scattering of Jews outside Palestine).⁹ The Jewish dispersion began with the deportations by the Assyrians (722 BCE) and the Babylonians (597 BCE), and included the spreading of Jews throughout the Roman Empire to Egypt, Asia Minor, Greece, and Italy. Thus, "the Diaspora" generally refers to Jews living outside of Palestine. It is also the technical name for all the nations outside of Palestine where Jewish people have come to live.¹⁰ However, the applicability of the term "diaspora" has been widened to refer to any religious or racial minority living within the territory of another religious or political society. For this study, *diaspora* refers to the unprecedented movements of people, or the scattering or dispersion of people from their homeland.¹¹

6. *Diaspora Missiology*: Diaspora Missiology, an emerging new field in missiology, refers to the "missiological framework for understanding and participating in God's redemptive mission among people living outside their place of origin."¹²

---

7. United Nations High Commission for Refugees, "Refugees."

8. The concept of refugee was expanded by the United Nations Convention Relating to the Status of Refugees in its 1967 Protocol and by the regional conventions in Africa and Latin America to include persons who have fled war and other violence in their home country. Cf. United Nations High Commissioner for Refugees Information Bulletin (2003).

9. Santos, "Survey of the Diaspora," 53. Cf. Santos, "Diaspora in the New Testament"; Santos, "Exploring the Major Dispersion Terms."

10. Moo, *James*, 50.

11. Tira and Santos, "Diaspora Church Planting," 63. Casiño considers diaspora and migration as complementary, but not identical or interchangeable. See Casiño, "Why People Move," 30. For him, diaspora refers to the global phenomenon of the dispersion of people to various parts of the world, while migration facilitates geographical or demographic mobility that eventually results in diasporic conditions. He also differentiates the two terms this way: "Therefore, diaspora refers to the overarching structure under which all forms of mobility take place, while migration serves a tool to account for a diasporic process or condition."

12. LDLT, *Scattered to Gather*, 12. This definition is part of the Seoul Declaration on Diaspora Missiology at the Lausanne Diaspora Educators Consultation on November

7. *Diaspora Missions*: Diaspora Missions refers to "the ways and means of fulfilling the Great Commission by ministering to and through the diaspora groups."[13] It involves the practice of Christian missions in the twenty-first century with consideration of the current socio-cultural shifts of globalization, urbanization, and demography.[14]

WHY PEOPLE ARE ON THE MOVE

There are many reasons why people migrate. As Enoch Wan writes, "People move on voluntary basis (for education, freedom, economic betterment, etc.), and are being moved for involuntary reasons (e.g., refugee, human trafficking, etc.). They move because of personal and/or non-personal reasons."[15] In table form below, Wan shows why there is an international migration wave:

Table 1: The Pull and Push Forces Moving People[16]

Push	Pull
World poverty growth and attractiveness of wealth in countries of desirable destination	Media exposure of "greener pasture" elsewhere
Political persecution and abuse of power, e.g., exploitation of women and children	Political freedom and human equality, e.g., gender equality and great opportunity

---

11–14, 2009, in Seoul, Korea. Two other helpful definitions for diaspora missiology are as follows: (1) "a missiological study of the phenomena of diaspora groups being scattered geographically and the strategy of gathering for the kingdom" (Wan, "Diaspora Missiology," 3); and (2) "the science of mission that studies the phenomenon of diaspora or people scattered or in transition" (Zaretsky, "Missiological Study of Jewish Diaspora," 3). For more information on this emerging field of missiology, see Wan, *Diaspora Missiology*; Wan and Tira, *Missions Practice in the 21st Century*; Wan and Pocock, *Missions from the Majority World*; and Prill, *Global Mission on Our Doorstep*. For diaspora missiology focused on Filipinos, Africans, and Koreans, see Pantoja, Tira, and Wan, *Scattered*; Hanciles, *Beyond Christendom*; and Kim and Ma, *Korean Diaspora*.

13. Tira and Wan, "Filipino Experience in Diaspora Missions."
14. LDLT, *Scattered to Gather*, 25.
15. Wan, "Diaspora Missiology," 3.
16. LDLT, *Scattered to Gather*, 23.

Push	Pull
Natural disaster	Quality of life
Man-made disasters: accident, pollution, social isolation, psychological stress, etc.	Relief, opportunity, the "American dream"
Obligation to improve the state of left-behind group, e.g., family or community	Success story of or invitation from loved ones (family or friends abroad)

Ernest George Ravenstein, an English geographer, developed the pioneering theory of geographical mobility as an academic discipline. Using an economic framework, Ravenstein's theory evolved later into what is now commonly known as the "push" and "pull" factors in migration flows. With the 1871–81 census of England and Wales in hand, Ravenstein observed that migration was governed by two conditions. These two conditions are as follows: (1) the unfavorable conditions in one place (e.g., oppressive laws; heavy taxation; lack of jobs; lack of accessible health care) and (2) the favorable conditions outside and beyond one's original location.[17]

These two conditions can coincide with Ravenstein's earlier concepts of "absorption" and "dispersion." Dispersion refers to native inhabitants who moved from their original place of abode because of the unfavorable conditions in that place (thus, the direction of "push" out of that place), while "absorption" refers to the nation that receives more non-natives because of the favorable conditions in that place (thus, the direction of "pull" into that place).[18]

In light of these "push" and "pull" factors and "dispersion" and "absorption" concepts, it is possible to ascertain some conditions and processes that the diaspora groups usually experience. Robin Cohen presents the following descriptions of what they can possibly go through: (1) they are traumatically dispersed from their homeland; (2) they leave their homeland in search of work, trade, or a better life; (3) they share a collective memory and myth about the homeland; (4) they possess an idealization of the supposed

17. Casiño, "Why People Move," 20–21.
18. Corbett, "Ravenstein." Cf. Ravenstein, "Laws of Migration."

REJECTION

ancestral home; (5) there is a return movement or at least a continuing connection observed among them; (6) they tend to have a strong ethnic group consciousness sustained over a long time and a troubled relationship with host countries; and (7) they share a sense of responsibility with co-ethnic members in other countries and possess the possibility of a distinctive, creative, and enriching life in a tolerant host nation.[19]

GLOBAL MIGRATION TRENDS AND SIGNIFICANCE OF CONTEMPORARY DIASPORA

So far, we have seen that the "push" and "pull" factors in migration have led people to be on the move, whether voluntarily (e.g., for education or financial advancement) or involuntarily (e.g., due to natural disasters, war, or by human trafficking), whether permanently or temporarily. Such movements of people can be further observed in the following statistics of global migration trends listed by J. D. Payne:[20]

1. The total estimated number of international migrants in 2010 was expected to reach 214 million, about 3 percent of the world's population.

2. Europe was expected to host almost 70 million international migrants by 2010, one-third of the global total; Asia 61 million; North America 50 million.

3. Between 2000 and 2010 nine countries gained over a million international migrants each: (a) the United States of America (8 million); (2) Spain (4.6 million); (3) Italy (2.3 million); (4) Saudi Arabia (2.2 million); (5) the United Kingdom (1.7 million); (6) Canada (1.6 million); (7) the Syrian Arab Republic (1.3 million); (8) Jordan (1 million); and (9) the United Arab Emirates (1 million).

4. In 2010 Asia was expected to host 10.9 million refugees, making up 66 percent of the global number of refugees. Africa was expected to host 2.6 million (16 percent of global refugees), Europe 1.6 million refugees (10 percent); North America 730,000, and Latin America and the Caribbean 530,000.[21]

19. Cohen, *Global Diasporas*, 17–18.

20. Payne, *Strangers Next Door*, 39–40, updated by United Nations Department of Economic and Social Affairs, Population Division, *International Migration Report 2009*, xix.

21. United Nations Department of Economic and Social Affairs, *Trends in International Migrant Stock: The 2008 Revision*.

5. In 2009, countries with at least 20 million inhabitants where international migrants constituted high proportions of the population included: Saudi Arabia (27.8) Canada (21.3), Spain (14.1), United States (13.5 percent), Germany (13.1), Ukraine (11.16), France (10.7), UK (10.4), Russian Federation (8.7 percent).[22]

6. From 2000 to 2007 the number of international students more than doubled to over two million. The main destination countries were the United States, the United Kingdom, Germany, France, and Australia. The greatest percentage increases occurred in New Zealand, South Korea, the Netherlands, Greece, Spain, Italy, and Ireland.[23]

7. Statistics Canada's 2011 National Household Survey has found that about 19 percent of the country's total population is now "visible minority"—an almost three-point increase from 2006. The percentage of foreign-born people in Canada is also up from 2006, surpassing 20 percent for the first time ever in 2011. Among the immigrants who came to Canada before 1971, 12.4 percent were members of visible minorities. Among the new immigrants who arrived between 2006 and 2011, 78 percent were part of the visible minorities. The census points to Asia as the largest source of immigrants to Canada, with newcomers from the Philippines, China, and India making up the lion's share of that group.[24]

These global migration trends show that the size and significance of diaspora have increased in the twenty-first century.[25] Additionally, these geographic and demographic realities directly and indirectly affect the nations of the world, especially when we realize that people are moving "from south to north, and from east to west."[26]

---

22. United Nations Department of Economic and Social Affairs, Population Division, *International Migration Report 2009*, xix.

23. Organisation for Economic Co-operation and Development (OECD), *International Migration Outlook: SOPEMI 2010 Edition*, 21.

24. Statistics Canada, 2001 Census, *The Canadian Population in 2011*, 1–2. Belanger and Malenfant's 2005 projection for 2017 that one Canadian in five could be a visible minority person has occurred much sooner. See Belanger and Malenfant, "Ethnocultural Diversity in Canada," 19.

25. For more information on researches and data on diaspora studies, see Ember, Ember, and Skoggard, *Encyclopedia of Diasporas*.

26. Marsella and Ring, "Human Migration and Immigration," 16.

In *The Next Christendom: The Coming of Global Christianity*, Philip Jenkins notes that the center of gravity of the Christian world has shifted from Europe and the United States to the Southern Hemisphere. This demographic shift is evident in the nearly 50 million Protestant believers and over 400 million Catholics in South America.[27]

MISSIOLOGICAL IMPLICATIONS OF THE DIASPORA PHENOMENON

From a Christian missions point of view, the study of migration and diaspora goes beyond mere numbers, ethnicity, and shifts in demographics. While the natural, social, economic, educational, and political factors of mobility need to be understood, the missiological aspects of the unprecedented movements of people must also be considered. After all, these movements do not simply happen naturally; they occur under God's providential direction.

As Tom Houston and others affirm regarding such people movements, "God controls these movements. The Bible is full of examples, from Genesis to Revelation of God using them for his purposes."[28] God uses people's mobility to advance the gospel. Wherever the diaspora peoples move, God also makes the gospel move, and opens up opportunities to advance his Kingdom. Thus, the dispersion or scattering of people can play a strategic missiological role in fulfilling the Great Commission.[29]

There are three missiological implications of the diaspora phenomenon. First, mission is now at our doorstep. While it remains important that missionaries must continue to be sent throughout the world, the current global migration flows now allow for more Great Commission opportunities in the West (which is the most common destination of migrants from the South and East). Payne writes, "Something is missiologically malignant when we are willing to send people across the oceans, risking life and limb and spending enormous amounts of money, but we are not willing to walk next door and minister to the strangers living there."[30] In other words, as we go to the nations, we must remember that the nations have come to us.

Second, some of the world's unreached and least reached groups can now be reached because of their diaspora. According to the Global Research

27. Jenkins, *Next Christendom*, 57.
28. Houston et al., *New People Next Door*, 10.
29. Casiño, "Why People Move," 34.
30. Payne, *Strangers Next Door*, 33.

Department of the International Mission Board (Southern Baptist), an unreached people group (UPG) is a people group that has less than 2 percent evangelical Christians in its population.[31] The Joshua Project upholds the same definition but adds this other condition: a group with less than 5 percent Christian adherence (i.e., those who call themselves Christians).[32]

Missionaries have difficulties reaching the UPGs because these groups are usually part of a country that has governmental opposition to missionary work. Missionaries can get into visa problems and can incur a lot of travel costs in seeking entry into those UPG areas. However, with some members of those UPGs already in the West, missionaries can avoid the government opposition, visa problems, and travel costs that hinder the sharing of the good news with the least reached groups.

Consider below the table prepared by Payne regarding the number of UPGs in Canada and the United States, using the statistics from the Joshua Project and Global Research:

Table 2: Unreached Peoples in Canada and the United States (Joshua Project and Global Research)[33]

Country	UPGs, Joshua Project	UPGs, Joshua Project (with Adherent % Removed)	UPGs, Gloval Research
Canada	41	132	180
United States	73	242	361
Total	114	374	541

Whether the actual number of UPGs in Canada and the United States is 114, 374, or 541 (or somewhere close), this is a sizable number of unreached groups that can be creatively reached by the Christians in these two countries—with no need for a visa or international travel.

31. Global Research Department, "Understand."
32. Joshua Project, "Why Include Adherents."
33. Payne, *Strangers Next Door*, 62.

Third, the new demographic trends make it imperative that we seize the moment and be intentional in ministering to the diaspora in new, strategic, and creative ways. Seizing the moment is critical because, as Wan and Tira say,

> diaspora people as people in transition (e.g., migrants and immigrants taken away from the comfort and security of their homeland) are more receptive to changes, including conversion to Christian faith. Some of them are in dire need, especially the displaced people and victims of human trafficking. Carrying out the Great Commission by including hospitality and charity in evangelism will be highly effective with these people groups.[34]

DIASPORA MISSIONS: MISSIOLOGICAL RESPONSE TO THE DIASPORA PHENOMENON

A new, strategic, and creative way to intentionally minister to the diaspora is through diaspora missions. Diaspora missions is defined as the ways and means of fulfilling the Great Commission by ministering to and through the diaspora groups. It can be described this way: "The integration of migration research and missiological study has resulted in practical 'diaspora missiology'—a new strategy for missions. Diaspora missions is a providential and strategic way to minister to 'the nations' by the diaspora and through the diaspora."[35]

Diaspora missions is born out of diaspora missiology, which is meant to complement, not substitute for, the traditional approach of sending missionaries to other lands. In diaspora missiology, "the traditional missiological distinction between 'foreign missions' and 'local missions' is to be replaced by a 'multi-directional approach' to Christian missions."[36]

Wan differentiates between traditional missions and diaspora missions in the table below:

---

34. Wan and Tira, "Diaspora Missiology," 55.
35. LDLT, *Scattered to Gather*, 27.
36. Wan, "Phenomenon of Diaspora," online, 9.

Table 3: "Traditional Missions" Compared to "Diaspora Missions"[37]

Area	Traditional	Diaspora
Perspective	Geographically divided: foreign missions vs. local mission; urban vs. rural; Geo-political boundary: state/nation to state/nation; Disciplinary compartmentalization (e.g., theology of missions/ strategy of missions)	Non-spatial; "Borderless," no boundary to worry about, transnational and global; New approach: integrated and interdisciplinary
Paradigm	Old Testament: missions = Gentile-proselyte—coming; New Testament: missions = the Great Commission—going; Modern missions: E1, E2, E3, or M1, M2, M3, etc.	New reality in the 21st century viewing and following God's way of providentially moving people spatially and spiritually; Moving targets and move with the targets

37. Wan, "Diaspora Missiology," 6.

Rejection

Area	Traditional	Diaspora
Ministry Pattern	Old Testament: calling of Gentiles to Jehovah (coming); New Testament: sending out disciples by Jesus in the 4 Gospels and by the Holy Spirit in Acts (going); Modern missions: sending missionary and money; self-sufficiency of mission entity	New way of doing Christian missions: "missions at the doorstep"; "Ministry without borders"; "Networking and partnership" for the Kingdom; "Borderless church"; "liquid church"; "church on the oceans"
Ministry Style	Cultural-linguistic barrier: E1, E2, etc. Thus various types M1, M2, etc. "People group" identity; Evangelistic scale: reached to unreached; "Competitive spirit"; "self-sufficiency"	No barrier to worry about; Mobile and fluid; Hyphenated identity and ethnicity; No unreached people; "Partnership," "networking" and synergy

Because of the versatility of diaspora missions (as seen in the third column of Table 3), it has the potential of conducting missions in three ways; namely: (1) missions to the diaspora peoples; (2) missions through the diaspora peoples; and (3) missions beyond the diaspora peoples.

Missions to the Diasporas

Missions to the diasporas refers to the first aspect of diaspora missions that seeks to reach and minister to the diasporas that have geographically moved to a host nation. Many presumed "unreached" people (the UPGs) are now accessible due to the global trend of migrant populations. Missions to the diasporas seeks to reach the newcomers in the neighborhood without crossing borders geographically, linguistically, and culturally.[38]

Missions through the Diasporas

Missions through the diasporas refers to the second aspect of diaspora missions being done by the diaspora that seeks to reach and minister to their kinsmen at home or elsewhere. This second aspect can maximize the potential of expatriates from their homeland to return as "self-supporting diaspora missionaries" or "reverse missionaries." "The reality is that Christians living in the diaspora context represent the largest self-supporting missionary force which has been located within many of the so-called 'unreached peoples' and [is] accessible to practically all people-groups of the world today."[39]

Missions beyond the Diasporas

Missions beyond the diasporas refers to the third aspect of diaspora missions being done by the diaspora people cross-culturally to reach and minister to the members of the host society and other ethnic groups in their context. "After acquiring the language and making cultural adjustment, diaspora Christians are the best bridges for cross-cultural evangelism. Their spiritual vitality can contribute positively to existing local congregations of the host society and in the planting of new ones."[40]

Thus, the church can respond missiologically to the diaspora phenomenon through diaspora missions, with the intent of accomplishing its three aspects of missions to the diasporas, missions through the diasporas, and missions beyond the diasporas. One of the effective ways to conduct diaspora missions is to engage in diaspora church-planting in a multicultural context.

---

38. LDLT, *Scattered to Gather*, 27.
39. Ibid., 28.
40. Ibid., 29.

Rejection

EXAMPLE OF "DIASPORA MISSIONS" CHURCH-PLANTING IN CANADA[41]

After doing church-planting in the Philippines for 10 years (which produced three other church plants), our church in Manila (Greenhills Christian Fellowship [GCF]) sent my family and me in April 2007 to do church planting in Canada. In our first planning retreat with the leaders of GCF-Toronto, I told them three things: (1) We are in Canada for a purpose; we are not here by accident; (2) it does not make sense to be a church reaching only Filipinos in Toronto, one of the most multicultural cities in the world; and (3) we need to be a church-planting church.

These initial statements later gave birth to GCF-Toronto's 3M philosophy of ministry: (1) missional (i.e., we will be on mission with God by planting churches and adding value to the community where we belong by serving the people there); (2) metropolitan (i.e., we will go where the people are flocking—the cities or urban centers); and (3) multicultural (i.e., we will reach out to the diasporas by beginning with the Filipinos, then continuing with other ethnic groups and Canada-born citizens).

Based on the Acts 1:8 principle of progress, we developed our Triple Vision (i.e., planting a church commencing with our Jerusalem, continuing with our Judea and Samaria, and culminating with our ends of the earth). Each new church plant would adopt its own Triple Vision.

For the first seven-year cycle (2007–2014), we trusted God for this GCF-Canada Strategic Vision: seven GCF satellites in seven years in four provinces of Canada (Ontario, British Columbia, Alberta, and Manitoba). This was the proposed breakdown of the triple vision per satellite:

Initial GFC Triple Vision:

The vision to launch GCF-Toronto (our Jerusalem)
The vision to birth GCF-Peel (our Judea and Samaria)
The vision to birth GCF-Vancouver (our Ends of the Earth)

GCF-Peel Triple Vision:
The vision to launch GCF-Peel (our Jerusalem)
The vision to birth GCF-York (our Judea and Samaria)

---

41. For details on this diaspora missions church-planting in Canada, see Tira and Santos, "Diaspora Church-Planting"; Santos, "What's a Missionary Doing in Canada?"; Santos and Irwin, "Filipino Congregation."

The vision to birth GCF-Winnipeg (our Ends of the Earth)

GCF-Vancouver Triple Vision:
The vision to launch GCF-Vancouver (our Jerusalem)
The vision to birth GCF-Surrey (our Judea and Samaria)
The vision to birth GCF-Calgary (our Ends of the Earth).

Our plan is that once the GCF-Toronto Triple Vision (first cycle) is fulfilled, GCF-Toronto will pause, pray, and plan for the second cycle of its triple vision. God willing, the next GCF-Toronto Triple Vision will be by countries: (1) GCF-Canada as GCF-Canada's Jerusalem; (2) GCF-USA as GCF-Canada's Judea and Samaria; and (3) GCF-Australia as GCF-Canada's ends of the earth.

In the first four years of GCF, we saw six church plants launched and birthed: (1) GCF-Toronto (May 2007); (2) GCF-Peel (March 2008); (3) GCF-Vancouver (May 2010); (4) GCF-Calgary (May 2010); (5) GCF-York (June 2011); and (6) GCF-Winnipeg (October 2011). Currently, GCF-Surrey is being developed by GCF-Vancouver, and GCF-Toronto is experimenting with an intentionally intercultural church-plant in the eastern part of Toronto (Ajax, Durham).

GCF-Toronto has also started reaching other ethnic groups that reside at Tuxedo Court, a high-need area in Scarborough or East Toronto (with approximately 5,500 people housed in five buildings, one of which is part of Toronto Community Housing). In Tuxedo Court, 81 percent are considered visible minorities, the majority of whom are South Asians, and in the 2006 census, the unemployment rate there was 14.8 percent (compared to the 6.7 percent average for the rest of Toronto). By developing relationships of trust and conducting community events and Canada holiday celebrations, we are now able to hold weekly Bible studies with the residents and monthly worship services with them.

GCF-Toronto has also started reaching international students at the Centennial College Residence and Conference Centre through weekly "Chips and Chow" get-togethers at the residence, weekly Bible studies at the campus library, and summer events at the park.

Our GCF-Canada diaspora missions experience through church-planting reinforces in us the value of doing missions to the diaspora (beginning with the Filipino diaspora in Canada), missions through the diaspora (GCF-Canada), and missions beyond the diaspora (residents of Tuxedo Court and the Centennial College international students).

CONCLUSION

The global and unprecedented movements of people have opened opportunities for twenty-first-century Christians to do new and strategic missions in the diaspora. This diaspora missions serves as a pathway of creatively engaging missions to the diasporas, missions through the diasporas, and missions beyond the diasporas. May we discern to seize the moment in partnering with one another to do missions at our doorstep.

BIBLIOGRAPHY

Belanger, Alain, and Eric Caron Malenfant. "Ethnocultural Diversity in Canada: Prospects for 2017." *Canadian Social Trends* (Winter 2005) 18–21.

Casiño, Tereso C. "Why People Move: A Prolegomenon to Diaspora Missiology." *Torch Trinity Journal* 13, no. 1 (2010) 19–44.

Castles, Stephen, and Mark J. Miller. *The Age of Migration: International Population Movements in the Modern World*. 4th ed. New York: Guilford, 2009.

Cohen, Robin. *Global Diasporas: An Introduction*. London: University College London Press, 2008.

Corbett, John. "Ernest George Ravenstein: The Laws of Migration, 1885." UC Santa Barbara: Center for Spatially Integrated Social Science. No pages. Online: http://www.csiss.org/classics/content/90.

Ember, Melvin, Carol R. Ember, and Ian Skoggard, eds. *Encyclopedia of Diasporas: Immigrant and Refugee Cultures around the World*. New York: Springer, 2005.

Global Research Department. "Understand." On *People Groups*, the website of the Global Research Department, International Missions Board (Southern Baptist Church). Online: http://www.peoplegroups.org/understand/294.aspx#309.

Hanciles, Jehu J. *Beyond Christendom: Globalization, African Migration, and the Transformation of the West*. Maryknoll, NY: Orbis, 2008.

Houston, Tom, et al. *The New People Next Door: A Call to Seize the Opportunities*. Occasional Papers no. 55. New Delhi: South Asian Concern/Lausanne Committee for World Evangelization, 2005.

Jenkins, Philip. *The Next Christendom: The Coming Global Christianity*. Oxford: Oxford University Press, 2002.

Joshua Project. "Why Include Adherents When Defining Unreached?" Online: http://www.joshuaproject.net/why-include-christian-adherent.php.

Kim, S. Hun, and Wonsuk Ma, eds. *Korean Diaspora and Christian Mission*. Eugene, OR: Wipf & Stock, 2011.

LDLT. (Lausanne Diasporas Leadership Team). *Scattered to Gather: Embracing the Global Trend of Diaspora*. Manila: LifeChange, 2010.

Marsella, Anthony J., and Erin Ring. "Human Migration and Immigration: An Overview." In *Migration, Immigration and Emigration in International Perspective*, edited by Leonore Loeb Adler and Uwe P. Gielen, 3–22. Westport, CT: Praeger, 2003.

Massey, Douglas, et al. "Theories of International Migration: A Review and Appraisal." *Population and Development Review* 19, no. 3 (September 1993) 431–66.

Moo, Douglas J. *The Letter of James*. Grand Rapids: Eerdmans, 2000.

OECD (Organisation for Economic Co-operation and Development). *International Migration Outlook: SOPEMI 2010 Edition*. 21. Online: http://www.nbbmuseum.be/doc/seminar2010/nl/bibliografie/kansengroepen/sopemi2010.pdf.

Pantoja, Luis, Jr., Sadiri Joy Tira, and Enoch Wan. *Scattered: The Filipino Global Presence*. Manila: LifeChange, 2004.

Payne, J. D. *Strangers Next Door: Immigration, Migration, and Mission*. Downers Grove, IL: InterVarsity, 2012.

Prill, Thorsten. *Global Mission on Our Doorstep: Forced Migration and the Future of the Church*. Munster, Germany: MV Wissenschaft, 2008.

Ravenstein, E. G. "The Laws of Migration." *Journal of the Statistical Society of London* 48, no. 2 (June 1885) 167–235.

Santos, Narry F. "Diaspora in the New Testament and Its Impact on Christian Mission." *Torch Trinity Journal* 13, no. 1 (2010) 3–18.

———. "Exploring the Major Dispersion Terms and Realities in the Bible." In *Diaspora Missiology: Theory, Methodology, and Practice*, edited by Enock Wan, 21–38. Portland, OR: Institute of Diaspora Studies Western Seminary, 2011.

———. "Survey of the Diaspora Occurrences in the Bible and of Their Contexts in Christian Missions." In *Scattered: The Filipino Global Presence*, edited by Luis Pantoja, Jr., Sadiri Joy Tira, and Enoch Wan, 53–66. Manila: LifeChange, 2004.

———. "What's a Missionary Doing in Canada?" In *Green Shoots out of Dry Ground: Growing a New Future for the Church in Canada*, edited by John Bowen, 95–108. Eugene, OR: Wipf & Stock, 2013.

Santos, Narry F., and Eunice L. Irwin. "A Filipino Congregation in Diaspora as Church-Planting Revitalization Movement." In *Revitalization amid Diaspora (Consultation Three: Explorations in World Christian Revitalization Movements)*, edited by J. Steven O'Malley, 37–57. Lexington, KY: Emeth, 2013.

Statistics Canada, 2001 Census. *The Canadian Population in 2011: Population Counts and Growth*. "Highlights and Part 1: National Portrait." Online: http://www12.statcan.gc.ca/census-recensement/2011/as-sa/98-310-x/98-310-x2011001-eng.cfm.

Tira, Sadiri Joy, and Enoch Wan. "Filipino Experience in Diaspora Missions: A Case Study of Christian Communities in Contemporary Contexts." Paper presented at Edinburgh 2010 Missionary Conference, Commission 7: Christian Communities in Contemporary Contexts, Edinburgh, June 12–13, 2009.

Tira, Sadiri Joy, and Narry F. Santos. "Diaspora Church-Planting in a Multi-Cultural City: A Case Study of Greenhills Christian Fellowship." In *Reflecting God's Glory Together: Diversity in Evangelical Mission*, edited by Scott Moreau and Beth Snodderly, 63–90. Evangelical Missiological Society Series 19. Pasadena, CA: William Carey Library, 2011.

United Nations High Commissioner for Refugees Information Bulletin. Ottawa: United Nations Refugee Agency, 2003.

United Nations High Commissioner for Refugees, "Refugees." Online: http://www.unhcr.org/pages/49c3646c125.html.

United Nations Department of Economic and Social Affairs. *Trends in International Migrant Stock: The 2008 Revision*. Online: http://www.un.org/esa/population/migration/UN_MigStock_2008.pdf.

United Nations Department of Economic and Social Affairs, Population Division. *International Migration Report 2009*. Online: http://www.un.org/esa/population/publications/migration/WorldMigrationReport2009.pdf

Wan, Enoch. "Diaspora Missiology." *Occasional Bulletin* 20, no. 2 (2007) 3–7.

———. *Diaspora Missiology: Theory, Methodology, and Practice.* Portland, OR: Institute of Diaspora Studies Western Seminary, 2011.

———. "The Phenomenon of Diaspora: Missiological Implications for Christian Missions." *Global Missiology* (2012) vol. [issue] 4, article 9. Online: http://ojs.globalmissiology.org/index.php/english/article/viewFile/1036/2415. A paper originally presented at the Filipino Diaspora Missions Consultation, Seoul, South Korea, April 12–15, 2004. Also published in *Asian American Christianity: A Reader*, edited by Viji Nakka-Cammauf and Timothy Tseng, 153–63. N.p.: Institute for the Study of Asian American Christianity (ISAAC), 2009.

Wan, Enoch, and Michael Pocock, eds. *Missions from the Majority World: Progress, Challenges, and Case Studies.* Pasadena, CA: William Carey Library, 2009.

Wan, Enoch, and Sadiri Joy Tira. "Diaspora Missiology and Missions in the Context of the Twenty-First Century." *Torch Trinity Journal* 13, no. 1 (2010) 45–56.

———. *Missions Practice in the 21st Century.* Pasadena, CA: William Carey International University Press, 2009.

Winter, Ralph D., and Bruce A. Koch. "Finishing the Task: The Unreached Peoples Challenge." In *Perspectives on the World Christian Movement: A Reader*, edited by Ralph D. Winter and Steven C. Hawthorne, 531–46. Pasadena, CA: William Carey Library, 2009.

Zaretsky, Tuvya. "A Missiological Study of Jewish Diaspora." Paper presented at the Global Diaspora Consultation. Taylor University College, Edmonton, Alberta, Canada, November 15–18, 2006.

Modern Authors Index

Ahn, John J., 32n20, 34, 34n24–27n29, 35, 36, 37, 38, 40, 41, 44, 53, 55
Albertz, R., 29
Anderson, Francis I., 51n7
Angel, Joseph, 63n11
Arnaoutoglou, Ilias N., 166n65
Aune, David E., 114n1

Balsdon, J. P., 166n68
Baltzer, Klaus, 54n22
Bamberger, B. J., 91n19
Barclay, John M. G., 57n1, 122
Barrett, C. K., 100n44, 101n45, 106n58, 147n14, 151n26, 154n29, 156n36, 157n37, 158n41, 166n69, 169n77, 187n6
Barstad, Hans M., 30n13
Barth, Markus, 102n49
Barton, John, 6n16, 14n37
Bauckham, Richard, 99n42
Baur, F. C., 91, 186n6
Beach, Lee, 1n1
Bechtel, Carol M., 16n45
Becker, Adam H., 85n2, 117n7
Bedford, Peter R., 7n20, 9n25
Belanger, Alain, 197n24
Berg, Sandra Beth, 10n28, 22n59
Berlin, Adele, 5n13, 9n26, 10n27–28, 13n34
Bibby, Reginald W., 55
Bird, Michael F., 118n8n9, 120n15, 121n17, 123
Blanke, Helmut, 102n49
Blass, Friedrich, 167n70
Blenkinsopp, Joseph, 44n58, 54n22
Block, Daniel I., 51n9
Blumenthal, Fred, 20n53, 21n54, 23n62
Boccaccini, Gabriele, 91n19

Bock, Darrell L., 100n43–44, 106n58, 156n36, 157n37, 158n39
Boda, Mark J., 6n15, 7n19, 11n31, 23n61, 48–50, 52, 90
Boffo, Laura, 159n46
Bömer, Franz, 167n72
Bond, H. K., 147n16, 149n23
Bornkamm, Günther, 151n26
Botermann, Helga, 162n53
Bottomley, Gillian, 3n7, 4n8
Boyarin, Daniel, 21n55, 95n32, 96n32, 117n7
Boyarin, Jonathan, 21n55
Braude, W. E., 91n19
Braund, D. C., 149n23
Broadhead, Edwin K., 86n5, 87n6, 97n34, 98n37
Brubaker, Rogers, 3n6
Bruce, F. F., 151n26, 164n58, 168n76
Brueggemann, Walter, 22n56, 29n10, 30, 31, 32–33, 37, 39, 42, 43n55, 45

Cadbury, Henry J., 155
Campbell, Constantine R., 129n8
Carroll, Robert P., 28n4, 30n13, 32–33
Casiño, Tereso C., 193n11, 195n17, 198n29
Castles, Stephen, 191
Charles, R. H., 69n21
Cirafesi, Wally V., 131n11
Clifford, James, 2n4, 3n7, 4n9
Cohen, Robin, 1, 2n4, 3, 19–21, 44n60, 48–50, 195, 196n19
Cohen, Shaye, 97n34–35, 98n37
Collins, Adela Yabro, 114n1
Collins, John J., 5n13, 6n16, 22n59, 48n1, 51n13, 52n14
Corbett, John, 195n18

Modern Authors Index

Costas, Orlando, 16n45
Cross, Frank Moore, 52n17
Cunningham, Scott, 141

Davies, P. R., 6n16, 16n42, 17n47, 59n3
Davies, W. D., 127n5
Dempster, Stephen, 6n15
Dimant, Devorah, 58n2
Dix, George, 84n1
Dommershausen, W., 168n74
Donaldson, Terence L., 88n8, 89, 90, 92n21, 93, 94n26n28, 118, 119-20, 121
Donfried, Karl Paul, 167n72
Dufoix, Stéphane, 1n2
Dunn, James D. G., 85n3, 103n52, 107n59, 156n36, 159n44, 164n58

Eck, Werner, 166n68
Elliott, Matthew A., 172n82
Ember, Carol R., 197n25
Ember, Melvin, 197n25
Enderlein, Steven E., 131n11
Evans, Paul S., 48, 53-55

Feldman, Louis H., 91n19, 165n61
Fewster, Gregory P., 139n24
Fitzmyer, Joseph A., 64n13, 65n14n17, 166n69
Fox, Michael V., 8n21, 9n24
Frankfurter, David, 87
Frederiksen, Paula, 86n4

Gafni, Isaiah, 57n1
Gamauf, Richard, 163n55
Georgi, Dieter, 91n19
Gerdmar, Anders, 91n17
Gerleman, Gilles, 13n36
Giri, Bed Prasad, 1n3, 4n11
Gizewski, Christian, 155n33
Goldingay, John, 13n33, 14n37
Goodman, Martin, 84n1, 92n19, 146n11
Goulder, M. D., 186n6
Gruen, Erich, 57n1
Gussmann, Oliver, 146n8, 147n16

Hacham, Noah, 58n2

Hanciles, Jehu J., 194n12
Hanson, Paul D., 69n21
Haran, Menahem, 44n58
Hardin, Justin K., 166n65, 167n70n72
Harnack, Adolf von, 91n19
Hauerwas, Stanley, 29n10
Heaton, Eric William, 23n61
Hellholm, David, 114n1
Hengel, Martin, 121, 148n21, 149n23
Herrmann, Peter, 167n72
Himmelfarb, Martha, 63, 115n3
Hogan, Karina, 74n28
Horsley, Greg H. R., 151n25
Houston, Tom, 198
Humphrey, Edith McEwan, 77n30
Humphreys, W. Lee, 5n13, 9n24, 11n30, 12n32, 13n34, 21n54, 22n57-58
Hurtado, Larry W., 169n78
Husbands, Mark, 132n13
Hvalvik, Reidar, 86n5, 99n41

Ilan, Tal, 147n15
Irwin, Eunice L., 204n41

Jackson-McCabe, Matt, 86n5, 117n7
Jenkins, Philip, 198
Jeremias, Joachim, 146n9, 147n14n18
Jervell, Jacob, 158n41, 165n60, 169n78
Jewett, Robert, 103n52
Johnson, Luke Timothy, 166n69, 169n78
Judge, Edwin A., 167n70-71

Kasher, Aryeh, 165n61
Kee, Howard C., 147n18
Kelhoffer, James A., 141, 142n4-5, 172n83, 174n86-87, 184-88
Kiefer, Jörn., 41n51
Kierdorf, Wilhelm, 161n52
Kim, S. Hun, 194n12
King, Philip J., 50n6, 51n12
Kittel, G., 104n54
Klein, Ralph W., 29n10, 34n28, 35n30
Knoppers, Gary N., 52n15
Koch, Bruce A., 191, 192n4
Kokkinos, Nikos, 149n23
Köstenberger, Andreas, 92n23
Kraabel, A. Thomas, 92n19

Modern Authors Index

Lake, Kirsopp, 155n31
Land, C. D., 187n7
Laniak, Timothy S., 9n26, 13n36, 14n38, 15n40, 19n52
Lavatori, Renzo, 141
Lemke, J. L., 101n47
Levick, B. M., 166n68
Levine, Baruch A., 51n13
Levinson, Jon D., 48n1
Lohse, Eduard, 147n18
Lombardi, Guido, 167n73
Longenecker, Bruce W., 76n29, 102n48
Longman, Tremper, III, 48n1
Lösch, Stephan, 165n60
Lucas, Ernest, 5n14, 16n43, 48n1
Lundblom, Jack, 54n21

Ma, Wonsuk, 194n12
Malenfant, Eric Caron, 197n24
Malherbe, Abraham J., 156n36
Marsella, Anthony J., 197n26
Marshall, I. Howard, 158n42
Mason, Steve, 147n18
Massey, Douglas, 191n3
Matt, Susan J., 27n2, 28n3, 39, 40n41
McDonald, Lee Martin, 126n3, 130n9, 137n22–23
McKelvey, R. Jack, 169n79
McKnight, Scot, 92n19, 134n15
Mernissi, Fatima, 104n54
Metzger, Bruce M., 74n27
Metzner, Rainer, 146n12, 147n16, 149n23
Meyer, Reinhold, 165n61
Meyer-Ortmanns, Hildegard, 91n18
Milik, Józef T., 59n3
Miller, J. C., 185n4
Miller, Mark J., 191
Mitford, Terence B., 167n72
Modica, Joseph B., 134n15
Moo, Douglas J., 193n10
Moore, Carey A., 65n14
Moore, George Foot, 91n19
Moule, C. F. D., 157n37
Munck, Johannes, 92n19

Neyrey, Jerome H., 167n73

Nickelsburg, George W. E., 60, 64n13, 116n5
Nodet, Étienne, 146n11

O'Brien, Peter T., 92n23, 102n49
Oded, Bustenay, 21n55, 22n57
Omerzu, Heike, 162n54, 163n55, 165n60–61n63, 167n70n73, 168n76
Oster, R., 161n50

Padilla, Osvaldo, 167n73
Paget, James Carleton, 117n7
Pantoja, Luis, Jr., 194n12
Parsons, Mikeal C., 167n73
Payne, J. D., 192n5n6, 196, 198, 199
Pervo, Richard I., 167n73
Pesch, Rudolf, 155n35, 158n40
Peterson, David G., 169n80
Pilhofer, Peter, 161n51
Pitts, Andrew W., 127n3n4
Pocock, Michael, 194n12
Porteous, Norman W., 6n16
Porter, Stanley E., 126n3, 129n8, 130n9, 131n10n11, 132n14, 135n17–19, 137n21–23, 181–84, 189
Portier-Young, Anathea E., 60n5, 114n2, 116, 117n6
Prill, Thorsten, 194n12
Pucci Ben Zeev, Miriam, 158n43

Radl, W., 153n28
Radner, Ephraim, 29n10
Ramsay, William M., 151n26
Rapske, Brian M., 155n31–32, 167n73
Ravenstein, E. G., 195
Reed, Annette Yoshiko, 85n2, 86n4, 117n7
Reeves, John C., 59n3
Reimer, David J., 41n49n52, 42, 43, 44n57
Riesner, Rainer, 162n53
Ring, Erin, 197n26
Rohde, J., 147n17
Rose, Jacqueline, 1n3
Rowley, H. H., 69n21
Rubesh, Ted, 44n60

Modern Authors Index

Safran, William, 2n4, 3n7, 4n8
Sanders, E. P., 85n3, 147n18
Sanders, J. A., 23n63, 29
Sanders, J. T., 186n5
Santos, Narry F., 193n9n11, 204n41
Schnabel, E. J., 103n50, 104n53,105n57, 147n18, 158n43, 159n44–45, 165n61, 181, 182, 184–86, 189
Schürer, Emil, 91n19, 146n9, 147n18, 149n23
Schwartz, Baruch J., 53n20
Schwartz, Daniel R., 149n23
Schwemer, Anna Maria, 148n21, 149n23
Scobie, Charles H. H., 6n15
Segal, Alan F., 158n39
Seifrid, Mark A., 132n12
Seow, C. L., 5n13, 6n15–16
Sheffer, Gabriel, 3n7
Sherwin-White, Adrian Nicolas, 156n36, 165n62
Skarsaune, Oskar, 86, 117n7
Skoggard, Ian, 197n25
Smith-Christopher, Daniel, 5n13, 7n17, 17n46
Soards, Marion L., 167n73
Sole, Luciano, 141
Spicq, Ceslaus, 155n32
Stager, Lawrence E., 50n6, 51n12
Stählin, Gustav, 155n31
Stegemann, Wolfgang, 163n55
Stemberger, Günter, 146n11
Stern, Elsie R., 5n14, 8n23, 9n26, 13n35–36, 15n41, 16n44, 19n52, 49n2
Stone, Michael E., 79n34, 115n4
Stuckenbruck, Loren T., 59n3, 68n20, 69n22, 70n23, 72n25, 74n26, 77n31, 113–17, 123
Suleiman, Susan Rubin, 29n10
Suter, David W., 60n6, 63n9
Sweeney, Marvin A., 6n15

Tajra, Harry W., 167n70
Tannehill, Robert C., 169n78

Thiselton, Anthony C., 103n51
Thomas, Christine M., 160n49
Thompson, Michael B., 85n3
Tira, Sadiri Joy, 193n11–13, 194n12, 200, 204n41
Tölölyan, Khachig, 4n9
Towner, Philip H., 104n54
Towner, W. Sibley, 6n16, 48n1
Treier, Daniel J., 132n13
Tuval, Michael, 57n1

Valeta, David M., 7n17
Van Unnik, Willem C., 161n51–52
Vanderhooft, David S., 51n9
VanderKam, James C., 146n12, 147n16
Végh, Zoltán, 163n55
von Rad, Gerhard, 44n58
Von Ungern-Sternberg, Jürgen, 163n55

Wan, Enoch, 194, 200, 201n37
Weinberg, Joel P., 52n14
Westerholm, Stephen, 132n12
Westermann, Claus, 44n58
Westfall, Cynthia Long, 92n23, 105n55–56, 113, 117–23, 187n6
White, Sidnie Ann, 9n24
Williamson, H. G. M., 48n1, 52n15, 53n19
Willimon, William H., 29n10
Wilson, Robert R., 55
Winter, Bruce W., 162n54, 167n73
Winter, Ralph D., 191, 192n4
Witherington, Ben, 158n41, 167n73, 168n75
Wolfe, Thomas, 27n1, 128
Wright, Archie T., 60n6
Wright, N. T., 29, 29n8n9, 85n3, 134n16

Zahn, T., 183n1
Zaretsky, Tuvya, 194n12
Zmijewski, Josef, 155n31, 157n37, 158n40

Ancient Sources Index

OLD TESTAMENT

Genesis

1:11–13	60
1:20–22	60
1:24–30	60
3	28
4	28
6–9	59n3
6:1–4	59n3
6:5—8:22	62
9:4–6	94n27
9:21	40n44
10:3	62
10:16–22	62
10:16	62
11:1–9	28
11:30—12:9	28
12:10–20	28
28–32	28
31:42	18n50
31:53	18n50
33	18
35:7	40n44
37	18
46	18

Exodus

1:8–14	28
3	79
12:43–45	95n31
17:14	10n27, 52
20:9–10	95n30
20:26	40n44
21:12–13	119

Leviticus

18:6–19	40n44
20:11	40n44
20:17–21	40n44
25	18
25:44–46	95n31
26:33	29n5

Numbers

22:31	40n44
24:4	40n44
24:16	40n44
35:9–15	119

Deuteronomy

2:25	18n50
4:19	41n45
4:27	41
4:41–43	119
5:13–14	95n30
11:25	18n50
13:6	41n45
13:11	41n45
13:14	41n45
14:20–29	95n30
16:10–14	95n30
19:5–6	119
21:22–23	155
22:1	41n45
22:5	72
23:1	40n44
23:2	63
24:13–14	95n30
25:17–19	10n27, 52

Deuteronomy (continued)

26:11–12	95n30
27:20	40n44
28–30	70
28	70, 71
28:7	71
28:13	71
28:29	71
28:33	71
28:36	71
28:44	71
28:48	71
28:62	71
28:64	29n5, 41
28:65	71
28:66	71
28:68	29n5
29:28	40n44
30:1	41n45
30:3	41
30:4	41n45
30:17	41n 45
31:11–12	95n30

Joshua

2:1–24	95n32
20:1–6	119

Judges

18:30	40n44

Ruth

3:4	40n44
3:7	40n44
4:4	40n44

1 Samuel

2:27	40n44
3:7	40n44
3:21	40n44
4:21–22	40n44
9:15	40n44
11:7	18n50
14:8	40n44
14:11	40n44
15	9, 52
15:22–23	169n77
15:28	9n26
20:2	40n44
20:12–13	n4440
21:10–15	28
22:8	40n44
22:17	40n44
27:2–7	28

2 Samuel

6:20	40n44
7:27	40n44
15:19	40n44
22:16	40n44

1 Kings

8:46	29n5
8:62–65	168n74

2 Kings

15:29	40n44, 41
16:9	40n44, 41n46
17:6	40n44, 41n46
17:11	40n44, 41n46
17:23	40n44, 41n46
17:26–28	40n44, 41n46
17:33	40n44, 41n46
18:9–12	28
18:11	40n44, 41n46
24–25	28
24	36n32
24:3–4	35
24:14–15	40n44
24:14	36n32
24:15	41n46
24:16	36n32
24:18—25:30	34
25:11	40n44, 41n36
25:12	34
25:21	40n44, 41n46
25:26	28

1 Chronicles

5:6	40n44

Ancient Sources Index

5:26	40n44	7:10	29, 52n16
5:41	40n44	7:11	52n16
8:6–7	40n44	7:27–28	8
9:1	40n44	7:28	52n16
14:17	18n50	8:15–20	53n19
17:25	40n44	8:21–23	8
		8:22	49

2 Chronicles

		8:23	49
14:13	18n50	8:25	52n16
17:10	18n50	8:29	52n16
20:29	18n50	8:35	52
36:20	40n44	9–10	8
36:21	54	9	12
36:22–23	54	9:1	52n16
		9:22	49n3
		10:2	52n16
		10:5	52n16

Ezra

1–10	11
1–6	7, 8, 12
1	10, 16, 17, 18, 22
1:7	11
1:8	29
1:11	29
2	10
2:1	40n44
2:2	14, 51n10, 52n16
2:59	52
3:1–6	12
3:2	14, 29
3:8	29
3:11	52n16
4:1–5	8
4:1–3	15
4:3	52n16
4:6	7n19
4:7–23	7n19
4:12–16	49n3
6:1	11n29
6:16–18	168n74
6:16	51n11, 52n16
6:17	52
6:19–22	12
6:21	51n11
7–10	12
7–8	16
7	7, 8, 10, 17, 22
7:6	29

Nehemiah

1–13	8, 11
1–2	5n13
1	11, 12, 22
1:2–3	11
1:2	52n18
1:4–11	8
1:6	51n11, 52n16
1:8–9	54
1:8	11
1:9	11
2	17
2:2	17
2:4	8
2:9	49
2:16	52n18
2:19	49n3
4:12	52n18
4:21–23	49n3
5:1–13	54n22
5:1	52n18
5:8	52n18
5:17	52n18
6:5–9	49n3
7–13	12
7:1–5	11
7:6	40n44
7:7	51n10, 52n16
7:67	52n16

215

Ancient Sources Index

Nehemiah (continued)

8:9	29
8:14	51n11
8:17	51n11
9:1	51n11
9:36	29n9
10:33	52n16
10:39	52n16
10:40	51n11
12:47	52n16
13	7, 8, 15
13:2	51n11
13:3	52n16
13:6–7	18n51
13:18	52n16
13:26	52n16

Esther

1:19	9n26
2:5–7	8
2:5	8, 9n24, 15
2:6	8, 12, 19, 40n44, 51n12
2:7	8, 9
2:15	8n22
3:1	9
3:6	50
3:8	16n44
3:13	50
3:14	40n44
4:13	10
4:14	52
4:16	10
6:28	50
8:11	18, 50
8:13	40n44, 50
8:17	16n44, 18n50
9:1–2	18
9:1	50
9:2	18n50
9:5	50
9:16	50
9:20	50
9:22	50
9:24	50
9:27–28	52
10:2–3	9n24
10:3	50

Job

12:22	40n44
20:27–28	40n44
33:16	40n44
36:10	40n44
36:15	40n44
38–40	114
38:17	40n44
41:5	40n44

Psalms

18:16	40n44
98:2	40n44
105:38	18n50
118:22	169
119:18	40n44
137	37
146:6	60

Proverbs

11:13	40n44
18:2	40n44
20:19	40n44
25:9	40n44
26:26	40n44
27:5	40n44
27:25	40n44

Isaiah

2:2–4	94n28
5:13	40n44
9:9–10	94n28
16:3	40n44
22:8	40n44
22:14	40n44
23:1	40n44
24:11	40n44
25:6	94n28
26:21	40n44
38:12	40n44
40–48	44
40:1–5	54
40:5	40n44

Ancient Sources Index

40:27–31	34	30:10–11	54
43:4–7	54	30:17	41n48
43:18–19	35	32:11	40n44
47:2–3	40n44	32:14	40n44
49	54	32:37	41n48
49:8–12	54n22	33:6	40n44
49:8	54	39:9	40n44, 41n47
49:9	40n44	39:10	34
49:11	54n22	40:1	40n44, 41n47
49:21	40n44	40:4–6	34
51:9–11	44	40:7	40n44, 41n47
53:1	40n44	40:12	34, 41n48
56:1	40n44	43:3	40n44, 41n47
57:8	40n44	43:5	41n48
66:19	94n28	46:27–28	54
		46:28	41n48
JEREMIAH		49:5	41n48
1:3	40n44, 41n47	49:10	40n44
7:22–23	169n77	49:36	41n48
8:3	41n48	50:17	41n48
9:16	41n52	50:18–20	54
11:20	40n44	52	34, 36
13:19	40n44, 41n47	52:15	40n44, 41n47
13:22	40n44	52:16	34
16:15	41n48	52:27–28	40n44, 41n47
17:11	72	52:30	40n44, 41n47
20:4	40n44, 41n47		
20:12	40n44	**LAMENTATIONS**	
22:12	40n44, 41n47	1:3	40n44
22:13	72	2:14	40n44
23:2–3	41n48	4:22	40n44
23:8	41n48		
24:1	40n44, 41n47	**EZEKIEL**	
24:9	41n48	4:13	41n52
25:11–12	54	6:8	41n52
27:10	41n48	6:9	41n52
27:15	41n48	11:16–17	41n50
27:20	40n44, 41n47	11:16	41n52
29	38, 54	11:17	53
29:1	40n44, 41n47	12:1–15	53
29:4	40n44, 41n47	12:3	40n44
29:5–6	38	12:15	41n50n52
29:7	40n44, 41n47, 43	13:14	40n44, 41n49
29:10–14	54	16:36–37	40n44, 41n49
29:11	35	16:51–63	53
29:14	40n44, 41n47–48	16:57	40n44, 41n49
29:18	41n48		

217

Ezekiel (continued)

20:23	41n50n52
20:30–44	53
20:34	41n50
20:41	41n50
21:24	41n49
21:29	40n44
22:10	40n44, 41n49
22:15	41n50n52
23:10	40n44, 41n49
23:18	40n44, 41n49
23:29	40n44, 41n49
28:25	41n50
29:12–13	41n50
29:12	41n52
30:23	41n50n52
30:26	41n50n52
32:9	41n52
34:5–6	41n50
34:12	41n50
36:19	41n50n52
36:24–28	53
39:23	40n44, 41
39:28	40n44, 41

Daniel

1–6	5n13, 6n17, 48n1, 115
1	16
1:1	51n8n12
1:2	13, 51n12
1:3–7	51
1:3	51
1:4	6
1:5	6
1:6–7	6
1:6	14, 51
1:7	14
1:8—2:48	14
1:8	6, 12, 49n4
1:9	6
1:10	17n48
1:12–19	50
1:19–20	6, 49n4
2:14	51n8
2:18–23	12
2:19–23	7
2:20–30	16n43
2:20–23	50
2:25	51
2:26	15
2:47	7, 50
2:48	49n4
2:49—3:30	14
2:49	15
3:8	52n18
3:12–18	12
3:12	7, 52n18
3:14–18	50
3:26	7
3:28–29	7, 50
3:30	49n4
4:1–37	7
4:8	15
4:9	15
4:18	15
4:19	15
4:34b–35	50
5:1	51n8
5:2	7, 51n8
5:3	7
5:11	51n8
5:12	15
5:13	51
5:18	51n8
5:29	49n4
5:31	51n8
6	20n53
6:2	49n4
6:3	49
6:6	51n8
6:10–11	7
6:10	7, 12, 50, 54n23
6:12–13	7
6:13	7n18, 51
6:25–27	7
6:25	51n8
6:26–27	50
6:28	49, 50n4, 51n8
7–12	48n1, 54n23
7:1	51n8
8:1	51n8
8:16	51n8
9	7, 13, 14n37, 18, 20

Ancient Sources Index

9:1–21	7	**Amos**	
9:1	51n8	1:5–6	40n44
9:2	13, 51n8, 54	3:7	40n44
9:4	51	5:5	40n44
9:7	51	5:11	72
9:8	13	5:27	40n44
9:9	13	6:6	72
9:10	13	6:7	40n44
9:11	51	7:11	40n44
9:13	13	7:17	40n44
9:14	13		
9:15	13	**Micah**	
9:16	13	1:6	40n44
9:17	13	1:16	40n44
9:19	13	4:1–3	94n28
9:20	13, 51		
9:21	51n8	**Nahum**	
10:1	40n44, 51n8	2:8	40n44
10:13	51n8	3:5	40n44
10:21	51n8		
11:1	51n8	**Haggai**	
11:31	54n23	1:12	29
12:11	54n23	2:21–22	94n28
Hosea		**Zechariah**	
2:12	40n44	1:12	54
7:1	40n44	7:5	54
10:5	40n44	8:20–23	94n28
		9:6	63

NEW TESTAMENT

Matthew		**Luke**	
27:25	107	5:21	148n20
28:19–20	99	5:30	148n20
		6:7	148n20
Mark		6:22–23	172
6:3	103n51	6:40	175
6:15–28	149	8:1	172
13:10	99	9:22	148n19
		11:53	148n20
		12:11	176

Ancient Sources Index

Luke (continued)

12:12	176
13:52	172
15:2	148n20
19:47	148n19
20:1	148n19
20:19	148n19
21:15	176
22:2	148n19
22:4	146n7–8
22:52	146n7–8
22:66	148n19
23:1	166n67
23:10	148n19
23:19	163n55
23:25	163n55
23:38	166n67
24:47	99

John

17:11	23
17:14	23
17:15–16	44
19:19	166n67

Acts of the Apostles

1:8	23, 204
2	23, 57n1
2:5	99
2:11	99
2:23	153
4–5	175
4	xix
4:1	146n8, 153n27
4:1–22	142, 152
4:2	157
4:5	146, 147
4:6	146n7
4:8–12	168
4:10–12	169
4:11	168
4:18	168, 171
4:19	169, 176
4:20	170
4:24–31	170
4:31	170
5:12	142
5:16	173n84
5:17	146, 148
5:17–41	142
5:21	171
5:24	146n7–8
5:25	171
5:26	146n7–8
5:41	172n83, 185n2
6:8–10	91n18
6:9—7:60	143, 152
6:9–11	148
6:9	98n40
6:12	147, 148
7:1	143, 148
7:1–53	169
7:52	169
7:54–60	143
7:54	147
7:55–56	157
7:57–60	147
7:57	157
8:1	23, 143, 148
8:3	143, 148
8:4	171
9:1–19	129
9:1–14	143
9:1–2	148
9:1	148
9:4	128 n6
9:13–14	172
9:23–25	173
9:23–24	143
9:24	148n22
9:29–30	143, 148, 173
9:29	148
9:32–43	171
10:1–48	171
10:1–47	99
10:2	95
11:3	99
11:5	99
11:19–21	99
11:19	118, 143
12:1–19	143, 149
12:5	170
12:18	163n55

Ancient Sources Index

13:5	122	17:10	173
13:14	122	17:13–14	144
13:28	158	17:14	173
13:45	155, 158, 159	17:15–17	172
13:46	171	18:4	122
13:47	171	18:12–17	151
13:50–51	144, 152	18:12–16	144
13:50	149, 150	18:12	151
13:51	170	18:13	162
14:1	122	18:18	172
14:5–6	144	19:9	145n6
14:5	150	19:23–41	145
14:6–7	171	19:23	163n55
14:6	173	19:24	151
14:19	144, 149, 150	19:25	151, 160
14:21	171	19:26	162
14:25	152	19:27	160
15	122	19:30–31	145
15:1	100	19:37	160n47
15:19	101	19:40	163n55
15:21	100	20:1	163n55
15:24	163n55	20:3	145, 148n22, 151, 173
16:1–3	97n35, 106	20:6	173
16:3	97n35, 101n46	20:10	163n55
16:13	122	20:19	148n22
16:16–40	144	21	122
16:16	150	21:20–26	122
16:17	161n51	21:20–25	101
16:18	160, 161	21:20	86, 87
16:19	150, 160	21:21	90, 148
16:20–21	163n55	21:24	106
16:20	150, 163	21:27–36	145
16:21	161	21:27–30	167
16:25	170	21:27	148
16:30–34	171	21:28–29	98n40
16:35–39	170	21:28	90, 164, 168
17:1–4	172	21:34	163n55
17:1–2	122	21:38	163n55–56
17:2	122	22	129
17:3	166	22:3–21	173
17:5–10	144	22:3	127
17:5	150, 159, 163n55	23:12–33	145
17:6	151, 163n55, 166	23:16	127
17:7	166n69	23:29	164
17:8	151, 163n55	23:30	148n22
17:9	156	24–25	xix
17:10–12	172	24:1—25:12	145

221

Ancient Sources Index

24:1	145, 148
24:5–6	145

Acts of the Apostles (continued)

24:5	163n55, 164
24:6	167
24:10–21	173
24:11	173
24:12–13	173
24:14–15	174
24:16–18	174
24:18	163n55
24:19–21	174
25:2–3	145
26	129

Romans

1–8	xix, 131, 133
1	122n20
1:18–32	95n29
1:18	131
1:28–31	131
2:14–15	95n29
3:3–4	131
3:6	138
3:19	138
3:22	132
3:23	131
5:12	138
6:4	132
8:18–25	138
11	122
11:13–14	187n7
13:1–7	137
13:1	134
14:1—15:13	187n7
15:19–20	103n52
15:19	103n52
15:20–24	86
15:20	86, 103, 108
15:23	103

1 Corinthians

1:11–13	188n11
1:20	138
1:27	138
3:19	138
5:10	138
6:2	138
9:5	86, 103
9:19–23	187n7
9:20–23	101
9:20–21	97n35
12:3	155n35
12:12–30	136
15	133
15:1–11	189n13
15:42	133
15:57	133

2 Corinthians

4:4	138
5:18–21	132
11:1–6	189n13
11:32	149, 152
12:11–13	189n13

Galatians

1–2	118
1:4	138
1:17	152
2:1–10	189n13
2:7–9	86
2:8–9	86
2:9	86, 87
2:14	189n13
3:13	155n35
4:3	138
5:4	102
6:14	138

Ephesians

2:16	132
2:19—3:13	189n13
5:23–32	136
6:12	138

Philippians

1:12–18	189n13
1:13	137

Ancient Sources Index

1:27–29	138
1:27	138
2:15	138
3:4–6	127
3:5–6	128, 129
3:19–21	138
3:20	137
4:22	137

Colossians

1:21—2:5	189n13
1:22	132
1:24	136
2:8	138
2:16	102
2:20	138

1 Thessalonians

2:17	156n36
2:18	156n36
4:3–8	133
4:13–18	133
4:16	167n71
5:2–3	167n71

2 Thessalonians

2:3–12	167n71

1 Timothy

1:4	104
6:7	138

Titus

3:9	104

Hebrews

4:1	146
10:32–34	172n82
11:13	45
11:15–16	45

James

1:2–4	172n82

1 Peter

1:6–7	172n82
2:4–10	104
4:13–14	172n82

Revelation

21:3	45

OLD TESTAMENT APOCRYPHA AND PSEUDEPIGRAPHA

1 Enoch

1–36	58, 59
1–5	59, 63
6–16	63, 68
6–11	59, 60, 62, 63, 64, 72
6:1—8:3	72
6:6	63
7:1	59
7:3–4	60
7:5	61
8:3	59
8:4	61
9:1	61
9:2–3	61
9:4–11	59, 61, 64, 69
10:1—11:2	62
10:1–3	59
10:9	63
10:16—11:2	80
12–16	59, 63
12:2–3	63n12
13:4	63n12
13:7–9	63
14	63
15:1	63n12
15:2—16:4	64n12
17–36	68

1 Enoch (continued)

17–19	59, 63
20–36	63
21–36	59
91–105	68n19
91:1–10	68n19
91:1	68n19
91:11–17	68n19
91:11–12	117
91:18–19	68n19
92	58
92:1–5	68n19
92:1	68
92:2–5	68
93:1–10	68n19
93:11—105:2	58, 68
93:11–15	68
94:1–4	68
94:5—104:8	68
94:6—95:2	69
94:7	72
95:4–7	69
95:5–6	72
96:4–8	69
97:6	68n19
97:7–10	69
97:8	72
98:2	72
98:4–6	72
98:9—99:2	69, 70
99:11–16	69
100:7–9	69
103:2	68
103:5–8	69
103:9–15	69, 70
105:1–2	80
106–107	68n19

4 Ezra

3:1–3	73
3:3–35	73
5:23–30	73
6:55–59	73
7:26	78
9:17–22	75
9:23–27	77
9:25—10:59	74
9:26–37	73
10:3	77
10:5–17	74
10:7	74
10:10	74, 75
10:11	74
10:12–14	75
10:16	75
10:18–19	74
10:18	74, 77
10:19–24	74, 75
10:20	76n29
10:21–23	75
10:24	76
10:25	76
10:27	76, 78
10:29–54	75
10:33–54	77
10:38–54	75
10:38	78
10:39	78
10:42	78
10:44	75, 76, 77
10:48	77
10:50	78
10:53	77
10:54	78
10:55–56	78
10:55	79
10:56–57	79
11:1—12:51	79
12:3–5	79n33
12:7	78
12:10	78
13:1–58	79
13:13	79n33
13:14	78
13:21	78
13:51–52	78
14:1–48	79
14:2–3	78
14:19–20	78
14:23	78

Ancient Sources Index

Tobit

1:1–7	64
1:2–3	65
1:2	66
1:3	66
1:4–8	65
1:4	65
1:6–8	66
1:10—12:22	65
1:10	65
3:2–6	66
3:3–4	65
3:4	80
3:12	65n16
7–15	66
7:10—11:19	65
8:5–8	66
11:14–15	66
13	66, 67
13:1–18	64
13:1–2	66
13:1	66
13:6	66
13:9–18	66
13:16–17	66
13:16	65, 66
13:18	66
14	67
14:4	65
14:5–7	29n9, 64, 66
14:5	67, 68
14:6–7	67
14:14	65

1 Maccabees

1:60–61	98
1:60	97n35
2:46	98n38
4:36–59	168n74
10:61	164n59
15:21	164n59

2 Maccabees

1:27–29	29n9
2:21	98n39
4:13	98n39
5:7	148n22
6:10	98n38
7:2	169n77
10:1–8	168n74

3 Maccabees

1:2	148n22
1:6	148n22

4 Maccabees

4:25	98n38
5:16–21	169n77

Baruch

3:7–8	29n9

Wisdom of Solomon

1:1–2	93n25

Jubilees

7:20–28	94n27

Bel and the Dragon

1:28–29	96n33

Sibylline Oracles

4:24–39	94n25

Testament of Abraham

10:12–14	93–94n25
12:12–13	93–94n25

Dead Sea Scrolls

4Q201	59
4Q202 1 ii 22	68

Ancient Sources Index

RABBINIC LITERATURE

Babylonian Talmud

Šebiʿit

7b	100n43

m. Tamid

7:3	146n10

m. Yoma

3:9	146n10
4:1	146n10

y. Yoma

3.41a (5)	147n14
41a	146n9

Philo

Spec. leg.

1.5–7	97n36
1.51–52	119n11
1.52	89n12
2.42	94
2.47	94

Virt.

219	93

Emb.

245	94

Josephus

J. War

2:240–243	146n13
2.243	146n8
2:256	146n13
2:409	146n8
2.454	92n20
3.444	95
5.519	95
6:294	146n8

Ant.

2.34	96
11.3–5	95
11.285	92n20
12.22	94
13.257–258	92n20
13.318–319	92n20
15.254–255	92n20
16.225	92n20
17.159	169n77
18.26	146n12
18.35	147n15
18.95	146n13
18.123	146n13
18.235	154n29
18.268	169n77
19.292–316	149n23
19.313	146n13
20.34–48	92n22, 96, 122n21, 123n23
20.131	146n8
20.163	146n13
20.208	146n8

Ag. Ap.

2.282	93

EARLY CHRISTIAN LITERATURE

Eusebius

Hist. eccl.

2.1.10–17	103n51
3.11	103n51

Jerome

Corr.

55.381–382	107n60

GRECO-ROMAN LITERATURE

Aelius Aristides

Or.

23.24	160n48

Ancient Sources Index

DEMOSTHENES			STRABO	
Or.			*Geo.*	
25.80	164n59	14.5		126n3

EPICTETUS			SUETONIUS	
1.30.1	169n77		*Claud.*	
		25:3–4		162n53

LIVY			THUCYDIDES	
39.37	169n77	7.86.1		154n29

PLUTARCH			XENOPHON	
Sept. sap. conv.			*Eph.*	
152c(7)	169n77	1.11:5		160n47

PAPYRI AND INSCRIPTIONS

BGU			P.OSLO	
iii 7	154n29	II 31		154n30

OGIS			P.OXY	
419	159n46	VI 918		154n30

P.KÖLN			SB I	
VII 322	154n30	4661		154n30
		5168		154n30
P.LOND		5320		154n30
VI 1912	165n61			

www.ingramcontent.com/pod-product-compliance
Lightning Source LLC
Chambersburg PA
CBHW050440240426
43661CB00055B/2461